Caring Leadership in Turbulent Times

Tackling Neoliberal Education Reform

A volume in
Educational Leadership for Social Justice
Jeffrey S. Brooks, *Series Editor*

Advance Praise for

Caring Leadership in Turbulent Times

"Mary Green has lived the ethical minefield of educational reform as a leader. As a researcher she brings an unflinching principled scrutiny to the impacts of neoliberal reforms on the lives of those who are charged with their implementation and those whose work and lives have been deeply affected. Educational research in the critical tradition is too rarely infused with hope. Mary Green does not stop at critique but confronts the most difficult question of how education leaders can act justly and sustainably in turbulent times."

—**Sue Nichols,** University of South Australia

"Mary Green's candid and reflexive writing models an ethic of care as she accesses both theory and praxis through the prism of story to investigate the relevance of critical incidents toward more effective, balanced leadership in education specifically, and in organizations generally. Emotion and reason, in equal measure, in personal narrative contexts contribute legitimate insights to illuminate what is problematic and what is possible in turbulent workplace climates, validating the merits of a culture of care for us all."

—**Paula Sarson,** Editor, Halifax, NS

"Mary Green uses her voice of experience and her knowledge of theory to inform readers of the importance of the ethic of caring in organizations that are constantly dealing with change. She advises that our relationships with people need to be valued as we strive to create more caring and effective organizations. Her recommendations on achieving a caring environment are significant and thought-provoking. As a senior district administrator who has lived through similar turbulent education reform, I recommend this book as a beneficial resource for leaders in school boards."

—**Deborah Armstrong,** former School District Director and CEO, NL

"Mary Green's book is a welcome reminder that school systems are more than a collection of structural elements that can be rearranged like playing pieces on a game board. For educators and administrators, whose work is normally about building educational communities, education reform is a profoundly personal, often uncertain, and sometimes dissonant life event. *Caring Leadership in Turbulent Times: Tackling Neoliberal Education Reform* is a careful exploration of the need to reintroduce care and compassion as fundamental criteria for education policy-making.

This book should be on the desk of every public administrator striving towards more humanistic and ethical decision-making."
—**Gerald Galway,** Associate Dean, Faculty of Education
Memorial University, NL

"Green takes the nuanced and complicated dynamics of neoliberalism in education and translates them to an easy to understand paradigm that will inspire readers to action. Her experiences as a teacher, leader, and scholar give her voice a credibility that resonates. Furthermore, she offers legitimate insights in terms of action focused on disrupting neoliberal structures. In sum, I found her voice, and her book, inspiring."
—**Dr. Autumn Tooms Cyprès,** Professor and Chair
Department of Educational Leadership
Virginia Commonwealth University

"In a time of many educational challenges and woes, this book takes a courageous look at the clandestine and malignant neoliberal agenda. It challenges a transactional model of leadership and calls for something more transformative, nay, revolutionary in the form of care and social justice. A must-read for any leader."
—**Dr. Azadeh F. Osanloo,** Stan Fulton Endowed Chair for Education
New Mexico State University

"Green's volume serves as a window into one school district's struggle with education reform situated in historical and global contexts that gives voice to the actors of neoliberal policy implementation with particular attention to care and respect for human dignity for all stakeholders involved. Green offers a unique perspective that challenges readers to think through and beyond the intricacies of education reform to include the emotional aspects of leadership in a school district and its surrounding community."
—**Dr. Whitney Sherman Newcomb,** Professor
Department of Educational Leadership
Virginia Commonwealth University

"In a time when democratic education is under assault by a neoliberal agenda, Mary Green has written a timely addition to the global concerns of educational administration. Green exposes how ideologies promote privatization and pseudo-reform and exposes the corporate culture that shapes policies and controls public education."
—**Dr. Noelle Witherspoon Arnold**
President of the University Council for Educational Administration
and Associate Professor of Educational Leadership & Policy Analysis
University of Missouri–Columbia

"*Caring Leadership in Turbulent Times*... is at once sweeping and focused. Green examines women and gender in education and furnishes new insights about the commonalities of people in educational institutions to dramatically transform education. The net effect is inspirational but also insightful about the issues of equity, power, and politics."
                    —**Dr. Anthony H. Normore,** Professor of Educational Leadership
                                California State University Dominguez Hills

"*Caring Leadership in Turbulent Times* is an interesting read for any educator concerned with the ways educational leaders struggle to negotiate competing political agendas with their ethical commitments to social justice. Mary Green's work is apropos to audiences worldwide, as she highlights the scholarship of researchers across the world as well as traces the historical trajectories of education politics globally. The book is a welcome juxtaposition of feminist and other critical perspectives against the neoliberal philosophy that has dominated education policy and practices the past 30 years."

                    —**Dr. Katherine Cumings Mansfield,** Assistant Professor
                                        Virginia Commonwealth University

Caring Leadership in Turbulent Times

Tackling Neoliberal Education Reform

Mary G. Green

Acadia University

INFORMATION AGE PUBLISHING, INC.
Charlotte, NC • www.infoagepub.com

Library of Congress Cataloging-in-Publication Data

A CIP record for this book is available from the Library of Congress
http://www.loc.gov

ISBN: 978-1-62396-729-1 (Paperback)
       978-1-62396-730-7 (Hardcover)
       978-1-62396-731-4 (ebook)

With hope for improved work relationships
and more effective organizations,
this book is dedicated to
professionals who care . . . despite the challenges.

Contents

Foreword

Educational authorities across the globe are engaged in remarkably similar improvement agendas. Governments—public servants and policy makers alike—anxiously await the latest release of international data to see whether their jurisdiction has moved up—or down—the league tables. Any movement up is seen as a vindication of policy, and movement down a reason to engage in additional effort. The improvement strategy now takes a very similar approach right around the world, regardless of local histories, strengths, and needs.

Pasi Sahlberg (2012) has coined the notion of GERM—the Global Educational Reform Movement—to describe the particular combination of school devolution and the introduction of privatized forms of public education, the introduction of choice, a national curriculum, and national testing that constitute this general reform approach. GERM is inevitably accompanied, or even heralded, by a rash of reorganization, downsizing, and contracting out of services previously run by governments. While not all of GERM is evident in the Canadian context, some of its workings are plain to see. While Canadian students do comparatively well in international tests, they are not at the very top. This less-than-number-one-ness allows politicians who are so-minded to argue that things can always be better, and they must. As Lauren La Rose in the Canadian Huffington Post puts it:

> A new international study ranks Canadian students among the top of the class in key subject areas, but there has been a noticeable decline over the years in math and science scores among the country's pupils. (2012,

Caring Leadership in Turbulent Times, pages xiii–xvi
Copyright © 2014 by Information Age Publishing
All rights of reproduction in any form reserved.

http://www.huffingtonpost.ca/2013/12/03/pisa-results-canada-student-rankings_n_4376190.html)

Not as good as Finland, Shanghai, Korea, and Singapore is apparently all it takes for some to suggest that Canadian educators must do much more. Atlantic Canadian provinces in particular have been continually castigated for their test scores, which have been consistently shy of the national average. If only they could do better in the tests, then all of Canada could. As Mike Corbett, writing in 2004 in the middle of the changes described by Mary Green in this book, put it:

> The recent release of results by the Project International Student Assessment (PISA) is always a subject for hand-wringing and apologetics on the part of Atlantic Canadian educators and bluster and recriminations from groups like the Atlantic Institute for Market Studies. As usual, Atlantic Canada's performance is mediocre by Canadian national standards and somewhere in the middle of the pack internationally along with countries like Germany, Denmark and Sweden. Canada as a whole and particularly Alberta (and to a lesser extent, Ontario and British Columbia) leads most of the world on these assessments causing us all to wonder what they are doing right and what we are doing wrong. (https://www.policyalternatives.ca/publications/commentary/ learning-tower-pisa#sthash.Zb939iWj.dpuf)

Alberta was the first Canadian province to take up the GERM agenda, indeed arguably inventing some of it (Barlow & Robertson, 1994). Its trademark educational policies—charter schools, contracts, and competition—have spread unevenly across the nation, colliding with local particularities.

As Green outlines in this book, Newfoundland was facing specific local challenges of its own: a history of under-spending on education; a difficult geography with many highly isolated schools and school districts; a system in which schools were organized around religions as well as territories. When the fishing industry collapsed and population decline began in earnest, the Newfoundland provincial government faced an unenviable task. They had little option but to try to save money as well as to improve the quality of public provision at the same time. This was a big ask, and one which is rarely acknowledged in national discussions of educational performance. Restructuring the whole provincial system was thus inevitable. However, the way in which this was to be achieved was not.

GERM has been accompanied, my colleagues and I argue (Thomson, Gunter, & Blackmore, 2013), by the TLP, the Transnational Leadership Package. The TLP has been spread across the world by a select group of highly paid educational consultants and researchers who promote a particular kind of administrative regime. The TLP holds that it is important for leaders to have a vision, to share leadership among staff, and to implement an appraisal and development approach which focuses on "core business" (e.g., Fullan, 2011; Leithwood & Day, 2007). This process is usually expressed via strategic plans which highlight overall performance on academic test results and exams as the key performance indicators to be applied to schools, district offices, and systems alike. What happens in classrooms thus matters to everyone in the system. The TLP also advocates recognizing the importance of values, but does not offer any in particular. Rather the TLP asserts that leaders must develop and spread their version of values throughout their organization. The TLP lauds leadership but diminishes the importance of management. It focuses primarily on compliance systems and almost never discusses governance. Because of this, critics (and I am one) argue that key TLP ideas such as "distributed leadership" are actually about the delegation of responsibility, rather than a genuine sharing of ideas, actions, and power (Gunter, 2011; Hatcher, 2005).

Mary Green's book is a personal and professional examination of the advent of GERM, and of the workings of the TLP. While there is a great deal of research and writing about the workings of both GERM and the TLP, there is very little which actually documents what it is like to be part of their implementation. We hear about the deskilling of teachers, the increasingly instrumental focus on curriculum, the difficulties for school principals (e.g., Ball, 2008; Gerwitz, Mahony, Hextall, & Cribb, 2009; Thomson, 2009), but much less often about what it means to work in a restructuring school system in a leadership role, as someone to whom the responsibility for restructuring has been distributed. This book opens up the fraught practices of systemic change from a manager's perspective. We read about the difficulties that are caused for long-term relationships, both in families and with professional colleagues. We read about the pressures of meeting externally set deadlines that create no-win situations for all concerned. We read about mistakes and sleepless nights and the contradictory events that emerge as individuals and groups attempt to hang onto practices and values that they hold to be essential.

As an actor in this set of events, Mary Green struggled to find a place where she could reconcile her overarching commitment to "care" with the way that educational restructuring was undertaken in her school district. She offers, through analysis of what happened, a potential alternative way that things might have been done—a detailed counter account of "care" and its implications for management in difficult circumstances. This, she proposes, is a value that might make inevitable but difficult processes "work" more smoothly and with less long-term damage. Green was unable to ensure that care was always the modus operandi in her school district. However it did exist, and she benefitted from its sporadic exercise through the gift of study leave. This example shows, of course, that restructuring school systems are never simply one thing, never simply managerial, impersonal, and callous, but also at the same time, humane and—yes—even caring.

I commend this book to you as a rare account of life in the eye of the educational storm. While it is written from the Canadian margins I can attest, as one who has had not dissimilar experiences on the other side of the world, that there is a "truth" in the telling of this story that has global resonance.

—**Pat Thomson**
Professor of Education, School of Education
The University of Nottingham

References

Ball, S. (2008). *The education debate*. Bristol: The Policy Press.

Barlow, M., & Robertson, H. (1994). *Class Warfare. The Assault on Canada's Schools*. Toronto, Canada: Key Porter Books.

Fullan, M. (2011). *Change leader: Learning to do what matters most*. San Francisco: Jossey Bass.

Gerwitz, S., Mahony, P., Hextall, I., & Cribb, A. (Eds.). (2009). *Changing teacher professionalism. International trends, challenges, and ways forward*. London: Routledge.

Gunter, H. (2011). *Leadership and the reform of education*. Bristol: Policy Press.

Hatcher, R. (2005). The distribution of leadership and power in schools. *British Journal of Sociology of Education*, 26(2), 253–267.

Leithwood, K., & Day, C. (Eds.). (2007). *Successful principalship. International perspectives*. Dordrecht: Springer.

Sahlberg, P. (2012). *Finnish lessons: What can the world learn from educational change in Finland?* London: Routledge.

Thomson, P. (2009). *School leadership—heads on the block?* London: Routledge.

Thomson, P., Gunter, H., & Blackmore, J. (2013). *Series foreword Critical Leadership Series*. London: Routledge.

Series Editor's Preface

I am pleased to serve as series editor for this book series, *Educational Leadership for Social Justice*, with Information Age Publishing. The idea for this series grew out of the work of a committed group of leadership for scholars associated with the American Educational Research Association's (AERA) Leadership for Social Justice Special Interest Group (LSJ SIG). This group existed for many years before being officially affiliated with AERA, and has benefitted greatly from the ongoing leadership, support, and counsel of Dr. Catherine Marshall (University of North Carolina-Chapel Hill). It is also important to acknowledge the contributions of the LSJ SIG's first Chair, Dr. Ernestine Enomoto (University of Hawaii at Manoa), whose wisdom, stewardship, and guidance helped ease a transition into AERA's more formal organizational structures. This organizational change was at times difficult to reconcile with scholars who largely identified as nontraditional thinkers and push toward innovation rather than accept the status quo. As the second Chair of the LSJ SIG, I appreciate all of Ernestine's hard work and friendship. Moreover, I also thank Drs. Gaetane Jean-Marie and Whitney Sherman Newcomb, the third and fourth Chairs of the LSJ SIG for their visionary leadership, steadfast commitment to high standards, and collaborative scholarship and friendship.

I am particularly indebted to my colleagues on the LSJ SIG's first Publications Committee, which I chaired from 2005 to 2007: Dr. Denise Armstrong, Brock University; Dr. Ira Bogotch, Florida Atlantic University; Dr. Sandra Harris, Lamar University; Dr. Whitney Sherman, Virginia Commonwealth University; and Dr. George Theoharis, Syracuse University. This

Caring Leadership in Turbulent Times, pages xvii–xviii
Copyright © 2014 by Information Age Publishing
All rights of reproduction in any form reserved.

committee was a joy to work with and I am pleased we have found many more ways to collaborate—now as my fellow Series Editors of this book series—as we seek to provide publication opportunities for scholarship in the area of leadership for social justice.

This book, *Caring Leadership in Turbulent Times: Tackling Neoliberal Education Reform* by Mary G. Green, is the fifteenth in the series. It makes an important contribution by critiquing neoliberalism during a time when its influence on education is largely accepted as normal and acceptable.

Again, welcome to this fifteenth book in this Information Age Publishing series, *Educational Leadership for Social Justice.* You can learn more about the series at our website: http://www.infoagepub.com/series/Educational-Leadership-for-Social-Justice. I invite you to contribute your own work on equity and influence to the series. We look forward to you joining the conversation.

—**Dr. Jeffrey S. Brooks**
University of Idaho

Preface

We need each other more than ever before. We need everybody's creativity
and caring and open hearts to find our way through.

—Margaret Wheatley

I have been moved by my experiences as a teacher, curriculum consultant, and district administrator to ponder ways of working as a leader within education, specifically the impact of the reform policies I have had a hand in developing and implementing. Often in my work, I found myself in untenable positions where my personal values were questioned. I have seen many people hurt, discouraged, disheartened, and disillusioned through the course of mandated school reform processes. I have used my research on education to interrogate the policies and practices inherent in the reform mandate to highlight the necessity for educational leaders to apply humanistic approaches in policy production and implementation.

The last quarter century in education has been turbulent for educators. Since the 1990s, work has been defined by increasing personal risks through downsizing or employer restructuring, rising workloads, and growing family tensions. Job actions have been interrupting life and learning. There are demands to do more with less, blame for the underachievement of students, fiscal restraint, and greater scrutiny and accountability with abundant testing and evaluation processes. During these challenging times, there are communication breakdowns, more unilateral decision making, mistrust, skepticism, and a lack of care. All of this is negative

Caring Leadership in Turbulent Times, pages xix–xxv
Copyright © 2014 by Information Age Publishing

for individuals and groups, as well as for organizations as a whole. Work in education is indeed stressful and often contradicts the commonly held perspective and dominant discourse that it is a nurturing and caring environment.

While some organizations claim to value caring work relationships and recognize the need for more care, there is limited evidence of this in the policies and practices of our workplaces, and the value of care for others is rarely evident in the hierarchical and managerial contexts in which we work. I have found an absence of humanistic approaches in the direction education policy and practice are taking. This book explores the concept of caring within the context of neoliberal education policy direction and seeks possibilities for intervention and new leadership approaches. I examine some dominant themes influencing education as well as the discourses of care reflected in policy and practice.

This volume also examines the impact of neoliberal reform on the people leading its implementation in a particular school district and explores alternative approaches. Reflection on and analysis of a local reform movement illuminates a past burdened with the financial responsibility of a publicly funded religious-based education system in a shrinking population base and in the midst of an economic crisis. While the book focuses on education reform in one Canadian province, reform challenges reverberate throughout global education contexts. A hopeful beacon for future reforms, this book discusses the historical, cultural, economic, and global influences in education reform during the last decade of the twentieth century and first decade of the twenty-first with attention to personal assessments and narratives from educators who lived through and contributed to the reform policies and processes. I offer helpful and hopeful recommendations for future reforms that relate to the importance of relationships and the need for greater attention to the humanistic elements so critical in any change process.

In an effort to quiet turbulence and foster more care, I propose a new path of

- ideas (caring in education administration and organizational learning contexts);
- conceptual moments (workplace relations);
- public memories (strikes, consultation sessions, school and district consolidations);
- altering away from frustrations (exclusion, binaries, hierarchy, patriarchy, bureaucracy);

- collaborations (shared decisions, team meetings, feedback sessions); and
- desires (social equity, respect for diversity, inclusive democratic organizations, caring relationships, greater productivity, accomplishment, and reward).

This book draws from my doctoral research completed through the University of South Australia in 2008 that examined the contradictory ways in which educators, including myself, in the Atlantic School District (ASD) managed competing agendas. My research examined various conceptions and theories of care, relevant policies and practices, and I explored how care and its potential were experienced by leaders implementing neoliberal reform mandates. I utilized qualitative research methods that combined data collection approaches such as in-depth interviews and focus group discussions, as well as document analysis of professional journals. I also examined provincial- and district-generated policy documents that guided educators' everyday practices. The interviews provided participants with an opportunity to reflect on their conceptions and experiences of care while giving meaning to the complexities and contradictions in their work environments. Some of the participants shared their personal and professional experiences with others through a group interview.

Additionally, I use aspects of my own life and work in order to open up dialogue about themes that have been difficult to discuss in many educational work contexts—gender equity, the need for more care, and how people are treated during demanding and chaotic times. I tell stories to illuminate the cultural, organizational, historical, patriarchal, and contradictory narratives that are sometimes invisible or considered inappropriate to talk about on a daily basis. When we pursue our missions, we do not pause to think about how people, including ourselves, are treated. We do not think about how we create, perpetuate, or challenge with our words and deeds the culture in which we live and work through our daily encounters. This is not to negate the necessity of change and reform but rather to highlight and reflect on the ways we as leaders carry out reform mandates, and reconsider alternate, more humanistic ways of working. I hope to inspire both thought and feeling through this book.

In order for us to become all that we are capable of, we need to reflect on who we are, where we have come from, and critique that in honest ways through various lenses if we hope to make our world of work and education more socially just. My goal is not to make others think like me, but instead to present examples of my experiences and perspectives, as well as those of my colleagues, as valid "other" stories. I hope that readers will relate to, consider, and adjust some of their own attitudes and practices to be more caring and respectful of people with whom they work.

The stories I tell are an attempt to reveal the subtle workings of educational organizations. By paying attention to the everyday experiences of educators in a local context, we begin to understand the bigger picture. We have to be able to relate to one another before we can understand our interdependence and the complexity of our work. Some important questions I found helpful to consider include:

- Who has privilege?
- Who is marginalized?
- Whose opinions count?
- How should people be treated?
- What must change?

My interpretations and stories are not adequate to convey the full range of experiences in our workplaces. We need more stories. Other stories have been louder, more powerful, more dominant than mine; however, mine are equally valid and have the potential to motivate change toward a better balanced understanding of how we should be working with each other. My aim in some respects is to challenge current systems of oppression, exploitation, power, and privilege—the dominant bureaucratic ways of working. I believe we must hear more of such stories in order to create new and different ones.

While the research literature reports on various conceptions and processes of care (see Chapter 1), there is little attention given to the potential and practice of caring educators working in bureaucratic and hierarchical organizations during times of "severe turbulence" (Shapiro & Gross, 2008). There is an absence of literature about the contexts in which caring educators carry out their work, how individuals are positioned in contradictory ways, and how they manage multiple and competing agendas. I attempt to address that gap through sharing the findings of the ethnographic case study I conducted as part of my doctoral studies (Green, 2008). I profile the everyday reality and turbulence experienced by individuals involved in the process of education reform and address some practical questions and dilemmas. I explore how a particular educational work environment and the relationships between and among colleagues provide learning opportunities for future organizations and examine some of the contradictions and paradoxes that shape the lives of members of the organization. My examination of educational policies, interview and focus group transcripts, personal journal entries, and critical incidents highlight the impact on people as we struggled to deliver on neoliberal reform mandates imposed upon us and our efforts to settle the turbulence we experienced as a consequence. Having worked as a colleague (in the position of district administrator) alongside my participants, I included myself as a participant and describe our theories and practices of care and caring by telling the experiences of our work in education and offer it as personal practical knowledge (Clandinin & Connelly, 2000).

My research pertained specifically to ASD, a learning institution undergoing external and internal pressure, where people believed caring could be beneficial, but in practice caring was complicated and difficult to achieve. The challenge to implement managerialist agendas with a caring perspective and to create change in the lives of disenfranchised employees was not a straightforward process. Turbulent times give cause for reflection on the future, about how we treat people, and the potential of caring practices to improve the quality of employees' work relationships, which can positively affect organizational productivity and accomplishment. Certainly, good intent and significant action were exerted to establish a collaborative and caring work environment with various structures and policies put in place, as well as many individuals doing their best to work in caring and collaborative ways. Much can be learned from the ASD experience that can benefit other educational organizations attempting to practice care within hierarchical and bureaucratic environments.

In developing the book, I have taken care to maintain a balance between theory and practice, although the contents tend more toward practice. Consequently, the book gives educational practitioners a repertoire of examples, stories, and reflections in accessible language to facilitate the process of practising more care for individuals and groups throughout all aspects of the education system.

The book is organized in three parts. Part I, A Quest for Social Justice and Humanism in Turbulent Times, situates the author as a social researcher and active participant who worked in the middle of a provincially mandated education reform process. Chapter 1 provides information as to the theoretical perspectives and guiding principles that inform the book. Positioning myself as a researcher practitioner and taking a social justice perspective, I draw on theories of care and turbulence and discuss their application to education reform. Proposing a nontraditional approach to educational leadership, I make connections with major writers in the field and propose a more humanistic and democratic approach to work in education. Chapter 2 reveals my subjectivities as a critical feminist researcher and provides insight into my personal and professional narrative. Chapter 3 addresses the influences of global neoliberal policies on national and provincial education systems that provide the context of the legislated education reform process in Newfoundland and Labrador, Canada. The chapter provides a description of the province's education system, including information about the historical, cultural, economic, political, legal, and social conditions of the time.

Part II, One Canadian School District's Turbulent Reform Experience, reports on an ethnographic case study I conducted within the school district at the time of the reform (Green, 2008). I profile the everyday reality and turbulence experienced by "insiders," employees positioned at various levels within the organization and implementers involved in the process of education reform, and address various practical questions and dilemmas. (Pseudonyms are used and some contextual details have been changed to protect confidentiality.) Having worked alongside the participants as a colleague, I include myself as a participant and describe our theories and practices of care and caring by recounting the experiences of our work in education. We all felt the impact of education reform on our personal as well as professional lives. I explore how a particular work environment and the relationships between and among colleagues provide learning opportunities for future organizations and examine numerous contradictions and paradoxes that defined our lives in the school district. Using methods of critical discourse analysis, Chapter 4 interrogates three district policies in terms of their neoliberal emphasis and contradictory attention to and provision of care to/for the district's education community. Chapter 5 chronicles everyday experiences that became "critical incidents" representative and illustrative of what the reform embodied. Descriptions are highlighted of how people were thrown into turbulence and chaos and expected to work in some uncaring, as well as caring, ways. Chapter 6 emphasizes "insider" voices that were often silenced, describes the human costs, opportunities, and challenges of education reform, as well as the potential of more caring policies and practices.

The research focused on a small number of professionals working in a particular educational context so the findings are limited in terms of our ability to generalize from them. However, they are useful to educational policy makers as well as practitioners who wish to improve relationships within organizational settings. The findings contribute to the broader body of knowledge derived from research into the processes of change and work relationships within educational contexts and organizations generally. The research identified factors unique to one school district in one Canadian province that strived to overcome organizational barriers, enable individuals to work together, and support caring processes. A better understanding of these factors will provide insight into the potential barriers and supports for future caring practices in organizations and assist others in responding to some of the dilemmas that any education reform process is likely to involve.

Finally, Part III, Calming the Turbulence, offers insights gained for future reform initiatives and concludes with calls to action. Chapter 7 in particular theorizes the lessons learned and proposes a refreshing, positive alternative to patriarchal neoliberal policy agendas in education. In conclusion, Chapter 8 argues for more socially just policy and practice and discusses the implications of what has been learned for future education reform, leadership development programs, organizational management, the treatment of people in workplaces, and for further research.

Examining learning from the shortcomings of the past provides a critical element that can help determine the success or failure of future efforts by shedding light on obstacles to avoid, problems to correct, and methods to embrace. With these insights, we may strive to overcome hurt and disappointment and foster more caring and effective educational organizations.

Acknowledgements

The only people to get even with are those who have helped you.
—Anonymous

Joan Tronto articulates the essence of my gratitude. "One comes to appreciate care best by being involved in relationships of care" (1993, p. xii). Accordingly, I would like to thank and acknowledge my family, many colleagues and friends who introduced me to invaluable caring values, perspectives, opinions, and practices. Years of caring demonstrated toward me have led me to, or affirmed my place in, the absorbing and fascinating field of education.

I owe more than I can express to my parents, children, siblings, and husband for our caring relationships. I could not have put my heart and soul into my work as I have without the wonderful support I received. If it were not for caring family who encouraged me, I would not have been able to write about caring. Most important in this regard are my children, Heather and Josh, my parents, Eileen and Calvin Green, and my husband, Greg. They deserve special thanks for loving me and giving me the freedom and energy to write. They have been caring role models and their belief and confidence in me have been inspiring.

My research has arisen from a basic interest in people and the importance of our relationships with each other at work. I recall with affection and respect many colleagues who were instrumental to my success and sustenance. I have profited greatly from the exchange of ideas with my research

Caring Leadership in Turbulent Times, pages xxvii–xxix
Copyright © 2014 by Information Age Publishing
xxvii

participants, all colleagues in the school district, and over the years, I have been blessed to work with several faithful administrative assistants. They were caring as well as competent people. Thank you.

Parts of this book came together between steps backward and forward, in the care of family, and generally the ebb and flow of everyday life. The genesis of the book came after a productive working session with friend and colleague Janice Tucker, when we developed an American Educational Research Association paper proposal. We brainstormed ideas for book chapters and whenever we got together we would think back over our careers in public education administration. We marvelled at what we lived through, accomplished, and survived during that time in our lives and often wondered what gems we might be able to publish had we kept a journal of our life experiences. We discussed some of the stories that are fond memories now and some that were career-defining moments.

I am grateful for my learning through the people and programs at the University of South Australia. I feel proud that, despite experiencing many life changes from my start of the Doctor of Education program, every day I reap personal as well as professional rewards. I am especially thankful to my university supervisors and professors Pat Thomson, Marie Brennan, Suzanne Franzway, and Sue Nichols who helped "trouble" my perspectives, inspired me to think more analytically and critically about my experiences, and who, in their own and different ways helped me to see my doctoral thesis to its happy end.

Acadia University has given me the opportunity and academic forum to share my theory, research, and practice with students and colleagues. Through collaborative research projects with colleagues Ann Vibert and Michael Corbett in the School of Education, I continue to feel engaged and excited to learn.

Any work like this becomes personal and Barbara Case, a long-time friend, provided ongoing support, critical questions, dinner and wine on occasion, as well as some insightful commentary on several chapters of this volume. Words I discovered by William Penn do justice in describing my friend Barbara: "A true friend embosoms freely, advises justly, assists readily, adventures boldly, takes all patiently, defends courageously, and continues a friend unchangeably."

Paula Sarson, a first-class professional editor, relentlessly and passionately attended to the minute details of my writing and offered intelligent and thoughtful suggestions that have been invaluable. Working with Paula has been personally as well as professionally rewarding. Jeff Brooks,

IAP series editor, also offered helpful guidance and provided insight that helped me sharpen and "raise my voice."

Thank you to all the women and men in my life who assisted in shaping my thinking, expectations, and actions. Your forthright and courageous voices have helped me to speak and afforded me many rich personal experiences that combine leadership, gender, and care.

PART I

*A Quest for Social Justice
and Humanism in Turbulent Times*

1

Framing the Issues

Theoretical Dispositions and Guiding Principles

> *I've found that I can only change how I act if I stay aware of my beliefs*
> *and assumptions. Thoughts always reveal themselves in behavior. As humans,*
> *we often contradict ourselves—we say one thing and do another. We state who we are,*
> *but then act contrary to that. We say we're open-minded, but then judge someone*
> *for their appearance. We say we're a team, but then gossip about a colleague.*
> *If we want to change behavior, we need to notice our actions, and see if we can*
> *uncover the belief that led to that response.*
>
> —Margaret Wheatley

Arguably the greatest task for education organizations is caring for their people—energizing, motivating, and encouraging them so that they feel valued, continue to learn, and contribute to the success and achievement of personal, professional, and organizational goals. However, today most institutions are subscribing to a corporate managerial agenda that has negative impacts on the people working within them. Many crises are experienced and people feel marginalized and undervalued. In too many workplaces people are busy cutting, counting, measuring, comparing, striving, and surviving and seem not to care enough about each other to make a difference. We spend a lot of time hoping things will change as we hurry to respond to

Caring Leadership in Turbulent Times, pages 3–32

the next initiative imposed from above, the latest "way to go" to solve our problems and make things better.

I have discovered an absence of research literature about the contexts in which caring educators carry out their work, how individuals are positioned in contradictory ways, and how they manage multiple and competing agendas. Placed in an organizational structure that advertises itself as caring, the lack of research and aligned resources become an even more glaring gap. Using a feminist lens, this book provides a discussion on the value of an ethic of care and how it might operate in the changing globalized world of work, offering care as a way to reconstruct work in current times to be more respectful of relations, more democratic, more just, and in the end more effective. I examine conceptions and theories of care and caring and the potential and challenges of caring work in organizations generally and education specifically. The practice of more care among employees within organizations can boost morale, enhance employee satisfaction and well-being, and also positively affect the bottom-line goals of organizations.

My interest in the concept of care derives from the perspective of a woman practitioner working in professional relationships in the field of public education. This book is a response to my turbulent experience implementing government-mandated education reform. The text explores the possibilities as well as the difficulties of practicing caring relationships to improve the quality of employees' lives and also contributes to reform and improvement within educational organizations. My research is undertaken from the position of a white middle-class feminist leader in education. As a participant and observer in the education reform of schools and districts in Newfoundland and Labrador, Canada, I am in an advantaged position to reflect upon and be reflexive about the impacts and effects of the change processes on the people involved.

I have worked for more than 30 years in education and experienced first-hand many contradictions and challenges that are not unique to me, but I believe these need to be explored and examined. Writing this book provided me with a unique opportunity to develop a critical sense of myself and understand how, throughout my early life and schooling, my gender identity was shaped and reshaped (Chapter 2). Patriarchy was an inherent construction of my identity as a woman, and rich experiences enabled me to contest dominant perceptions of gender discourse both in my personal life and in my work. I realize how privileged I am to have been born into my family and our community, with encouragement and support to educate myself and work in whatever environments I chose. Understanding my life experiences helps me to examine and reflect on the social contexts that influence my journey of becoming who I am today.

"The proposition of rethinking women's lives as legitimate sources of intellectual thought is likely to signal a fundamental rethinking in the field itself.... Education represents an occupational field that has, historically, consisted of women; yet, its intellectual foundations were authored by men writing in the contexts of men's lives" (Neumann & Peterson, 1997, pp. 2, 6). As educators we are encouraged to think of our work as a mission, to be able to articulate insightful visions, and to put the needs of others before our own. If education is considered a caring profession, then particular questions must be explored.

- What are employees' understandings and expectations of care and caring in their workplaces?
- Where does caring for self and others fit in our work environments and relationships?
- How can educators, administrators, and women care and yet not be consumed by it?
- How can we influence change to bring about desired results and improved conditions for all?

These are the questions subsequent chapters of this book address.

Up to now, research in education administration about caring has failed to meaningfully identify or address the different problems of a lack of care. This is because until only recently male-dominated approaches, attitudes, and methods were used and much still is unknown about organizational theory—particularly caring in that context. Although my intention is to use my results to enhance caring practices, I also draw attention to the problems of a lack of care.

Broad changes in society and specifically reform in education have led to the emergence of new challenges for practitioners. I interpret my version of the story to implement a provincially legislated education reform process in Newfoundland and Labrador, Canada, through analysis of key policy texts and stories told by colleagues of our day-to-day work (Chapters 4, 5, and 6). I grounded my research in history to help illuminate how things came to be the way they were (Chapter 3) and how this limited our possibilities for caring action. My study showed how certain groups and individuals throughout the education system had the right to act and speak whereas others were silenced, and I address how the different groups attempted to draw on various discourses (for example, of care, shared decision making, leadership, and power). I am interested in how and why the social world comes to have the meanings that it does and how I am implicated in that process. Certainly, there are multiple interpretations and meanings; I hope to encourage debate, as I believe we need different points of reference to interrogate our work.

A Humanities Perspective

My early university education was in English, social studies, and education so I am essentially a humanities person. After teaching high school students for 10 years, I completed a Master of Education and began to study and work in public administration. My impression growing up was that public administration was a boring technical field of study, and its practice was fraught with politics that I did not find at all appealing. As a district administrator and later provincial consultant I discovered that only in certain respects were my initial impressions accurate. Although public administration work is a technical enterprise and a professional discipline that is primarily managerial, its central focus is people and humanities. I learned first-hand the inside workings of district administration. Later, through my role as consultant to a Provincial Royal Commission Implementation Secretariat, my initial impressions of administrative work were reinforced.

I worked with teams of senior technocrats to redesign K–12 curricula, rationalize and downsize the number of schools, and evaluate educational programs and services. In my district work I felt at times, as we sketched out various options and scenarios for the amalgamation and/or reorganization of schooling, that we were moving groups of people around as one would pieces on a chessboard. We calculated the distances students would travel, personnel requirements, where money could be saved and jobs eliminated. I discovered that the drafting of policy to bring new schools and districts into being meant that even minor changes in wording affected large numbers of employees, the structure of their work lives, and the quality of their social interactions. How I saw myself, my colleagues, as well as whole communities of people being treated during that rapid change process became a huge concern to me.

In our day-to-day work we encounter struggle, hardship, hurt, and disappointment, but through hard work and concern for how we treat each other, I believe we can appreciate our vulnerabilities and discover things we each can do to help ourselves and others. We can start by being more caring and involving people in making the decisions that affect them. Some of us are capable of literally changing the world; others can do smaller things to impact personally on a single life. Everyone has potential, and our contributions are important, giving us all hope that real change will happen.

This book does not lay out a concrete path to follow; it is not my interest to prescribe fixed methods and programs. Instead I offer a framework of values, thoughts, and experienced behaviors as a mirror to reflect on our educational community's values (Chapters 7 and 8). If we could look to the future and know what it holds, would we feel better, sleep better? Reflecting on and learning from the past as well as looking to the future might inform us about where our education system is headed.

> By all accounts, humankind itself finds itself at a life and death turning point in the twenty-first century. We are on a course of unprecedented environmental destruction in terms of species extinction, global warming, and natural depletion.... Humanity is at war with itself in escalating numbers of regional, ethnic and religious conflicts. Moreover the global economy and institutions of modernism—like education—have fallen prey to short-sightedness and a mostly economic agenda. These problems equate to turbulence for us.... Regrettably, human suffering will likely increase in the coming centuries as we struggle toward a more equitable, sustainable way of life for all living beings. (Seymour, 2004a, pp. 1, 2)

How might education bridge the troubled waters of today's deeply turbulent world to a future that will be calmer, more caring, and more socially just? In times of disaster people put aside their differences (religious, political, racial, and cultural) and work together. We see beyond the borders and differences that separate us and feel connection with those less fortunate. We donate our time, talent, and resources to help provide safe water, medication, shelter, and food. Children and teachers in schools are phenomenal examples of selfless people in times of need and display charity and good will toward others; however, some in education get distracted by the busyness of our lives, and unfortunately it takes a tsunami or tragic shooting for our selflessness to surface. In times of great need, teachers and students become admirable role models for the rest of us. They demonstrate real sensitivity for the hardship of others and respond with caring action. As we go "up the line" in bureaucratic and hierarchical organizations, much of that sensitivity and caring get lost.

What was missing in public administration during our education reform process was a humanities perspective. Care and caring—considered "soft," impractical—were thought not to fit within our bureaucratic management agenda and were consequently discarded. Investigations into or even concern for the relationship among human values, ideals, and social relations, as well as any critique of the bureaucracy in values terms or the ethics applicable to administration were absent. To provide the conceptual basis for analyzing the discussions that follow in the rest of the book, I outline in this chapter some of the theories and assumptions that dominate my discussions. I explore pertinent views of critical theory, care and caring, education reform, and other interconnected themes and practices. I address how taken-for-granted practices in education contribute to the marginalization and exclusion of different groups and how government and educational organizations reproduce the existing social order, contributing to further alienating and disenfranchising these groups. Paradoxically, education holds the key to changing the status quo through policies and practices that are caring, socially just, and validating to the identities of all.

Critical Theory

Critical theorists propose an alternative view of society that offers possibility for changing social institutions. With a focus on two issues—how schools help dominant groups maintain power and control, and how challenge and interrogation can interrupt the dominance—critical theory offers direction for change (Apple, 2004; Kincheloe, 2005; McLaren, 2007).

Rejecting the view that educational organizations are sites where all interaction ongoing within them can be reduced to economics and the transmission of values and practices of corporate managerialism (Blackmore, 2007), critical theorists see education as a site of power struggles between dominant and nondominant groups. They believe in the potential of education to transform how we work, and these theorists hold the key to change through just and inclusive practices. While perpetuating domination through patriarchal, bureaucratic hierarchies, there are possibilities for transformation and emancipatory practice. This critical theory offers a framework that is pertinent to the discussion of care and caring in education.

Adherents of critical theory concerned about the role of educational institutions in perpetuating social injustice (Freire, 1970; Kincheloe, 2005; McLaren, 2007) advocate critical pedagogy that analyzes the relationship between power and knowledge in education. They critique, interrogate, and challenge practices that privilege and reward certain kinds of knowledge and devalue others. Critical pedagogists see education reform as a politically and socially charged activity that has the potential to disempower people and perpetuate unequal power relations. Critical theorists argue for transformative knowledge and practice that would allow educators to interrogate dominant assumptions about the social world, realign their perspectives, and gain understanding of the structures and practices that impact on their lives.

Hegemony

Hegemony relates to the "invisible" process of maintaining power and social control by dominant groups through government and social institutions. "Through the process of normalization, oppressed groups internalize and accept their subordinate condition while they are oblivious to the colonizing process that is actually at work" (Egbo, 2009, p. 8). As a concept, it offers insights into the study of power and the ways in which domination becomes reproduced as common sense thinking (Kincheloe, 2005). "In simple terms, hegemony is unobtrusive power and its potency lies in its invisibility and subsequent acceptance by those who are oppressed" (Egbo, 2009, p. 8). When hegemony is at work, dominant groups are able to eliminate resistance and opposition by representing imposed ideology as normal. It is insidious in that it appears harmless and "normal," making it difficult to discern deception.

This concept relates to the analysis of care and caring in a Canadian school district because many of the oppressive structures and practices in the district are inadvertently reinforced by those who are on the receiving end. For example, members of certain social groups can internalize and reinforce the dominant group's perceptions, a kind of self-fulfilling prophecy. Some groups accept oppressive and exclusionary practices as "normal" and they unwittingly concede to those in power. However, when people become conscious of disempowering social structures (as in the case of the public consultation sessions in Chapter 5), they develop resistance and challenge the status quo, including unfair practices, ideologies, and subtle attitudes that are transmitted through explicit policy and practice.

Theories of Care and Caring

Caring is a term with which everyone is familiar. "Without having care at the center of our lives, life becomes superficial, hectic, a continual pursuit of an elusive something in which people's lives lose meaning" (Seymour, 2004b, p. 90). Caring permeates our ordinary accounts of everyday life and is central to how we think about our family, friends, lovers, and colleagues but it cannot be neatly defined. There are so many different understandings of what care and caring are that it is important to clarify what they mean, and for the purposes of this book, how these apply in an organizational context. I offer care as a way to energize, motivate, and encourage employees so they feel valued and believe their work is worth their effort. I explore the potential of caring relationships to improve the quality of employees' lives, as well as the possible contributions of care to reform and improve life in organizations.

There is an extensive body of research on caring, particularly within families, personal relationships, health care professions of social work and nursing (Abel, Nelson, & Nelson, 1990; J. Acker, 1990; S. Acker, 1999; Beck, 1994; Bubeck, 1995; Daly, 2002; Enomoto, 1997; Fisher & Tronto, 1990; Green, 2008; Hankivsky, 2004; Hatch & Wisniewski, 1995; Henry & Henry, 2006; Imre, 1982; Noddings, 1984, 1992, 2001; Tronto, 1993). The studies related to caring in education focus primarily on care for students and the variety of ways student needs are met, or attempted to be met. The emphasis of my research has been more narrowly focused on caring relations between and among employees in large organizations, specifically within educational institutions. I prefer a definition of caring that involves both "disposition and practice" (Tronto, 1993, p. 104). Caring is an attitude on the part of the one(s) caring—concern for the well-being of those cared for—and it requires response, demonstrating connection, and responsibility.

To a considerable extent education has been viewed as a caring profession, with caring for students and others a goal that is written into policies and factored into change efforts (Williams & Sparkes, 2000; Williams, Warren, & Pound-Curtis, 1992). Some educational and organizational philosophies are complementary with theories of care, but their implementation has been hampered by the realities of global influences (Blackmore, 2000; Burbules & Torres, 2000; Franzway, 2005; Levin & Riffel, 1997; Ungerleider, 1996), neoliberal politics (Buzzanell, 2000; McLaren & Farahmandpur, 2005), and the imposition of corporate agendas (Barlow & Robertson, 1994; Boyd, 1997; Du Gay, 1996; Folbre, 2001; Hochschild, 1983). I draw mainly from the theoretical work on care of Nel Noddings (1984, 1992, 2002) and Joan Tronto (1989, 1993) as well as their core ideas, concepts, and methodologies to synthesize an approach that offers a vision for the reconstruction of work.

In essence, a philosophy of caring asserts that people should have opportunities to speak, be heard, be valued and respected, and be successful and productive within an organization (Brunner, 1998; Delong, 2002; Evans, 1996; Grogan & VanDeman Blackmon, 1999; Noddings, 1992). The ways people in organizations can be cared about are specific. People treat others the way they would like to be treated. People feel cared about when their input is sought and welcomed. People are given equal input as a part of caring about all individuals. The aim is to have each person feeling powerful so that they feel motivated and bring positive energy and change to the organization (Sernak, 1998). In caring workplaces people have opportunities to collaborate with colleagues as well as work independently, and accomplishments are acknowledged and rewarded (Grogan, 2003; Grogan & VanDeman Blackmon, 2001; Sernak, 1998). Employees are encouraged, given opportunity to learn, and provided constructive and supportive guidance when they experience challenge or difficulty (District, 2003a, 2003b). They feel free to take risks and share their views. Caring workplaces are concerned with personal as well as professional well-being, encourage a balanced life, care about employees' health, and there is respect for family time and life beyond work (Lowe, 2000). Essentially, work relationships are not focused from a contractual or legalistic standpoint, but rather from a standpoint of absolute regard (Starratt, 1991) and each person's dignity and worth are honored. Instead of formal and controlled communication, top-down decision making, neutral application of policy, and impersonal, detached administrative practice, caring and the building and nurturing of relationships emerge as dominant themes (Lowe, 2000; Lucas, 1999; Sernak, 1998).

One of the most striking changes to the meaning of care is that it is no longer assumed to be situated exclusively in the private domain or limited along the lines of gender, as a feminine ethic (Tronto, 1989, 1993). Organizational workplaces have been thought to be characterized by qualitatively different relations or demonstrations of care than those at home. Home relations are thought of as closer, more personal and emotive, whereas work relations are thought of as rational, businesslike, impersonal, and detached.

Breaking free of these hegemonic and limiting assumptions about care and caring is a difficult task because the framework has been historically established and is widely used throughout the social sciences. Although care originates in the private world of love, intimacy, families, and friendships, much of it is now carried out in the public world of work, organizations, markets, and government (Stone, 2000). Definitions and discourses of care in the research literature have implications for how we understand and support healthier relationships among people in workplaces. I use them to support the argument that the practice of more care has the potential and possibility to enhance employee well-being and also contribute to the accomplishment of organizational goals.

Influential research undertaken by Nel Noddings, a leading educational philosopher, explains the moral value, virtues, and dilemmas arising from caring. Her work provides a starting point for the "deconstruction" of theories of care within the context of contemporary educational reform and attempts to offer alternatives to hierarchical models of leadership based on top-down decision making. She writes that one cares for something or someone if one has regard for or inclination toward that something or someone. She says we care for people if we have regard for their views and interests. Noddings elaborates that the essential elements of caring are located in the relation between the one caring and the cared for, and that to care requires action on behalf of the cared for (1984). The emotional state of "engrossment" (1984) in another person's reality is basic to care. To act as one caring then is to act with special regard for particular people in a concrete situation and they act in a nonrule-bound fashion. Noddings also refers to caring as an activity (caretaking and caregiving) but has been criticized for her lack of consideration for the institutional and structural settings of her ideal of caring; she has not explained how we might cope with conflict within caring relations (Tronto, 1993).

Fisher and Tronto define caring as a species activity that includes everything we do to maintain, continue, and repair our "world" so that we can live in it as well as possible (Fisher & Tronto, 1990; Tronto, 1993). "World" includes our bodies, ourselves, and our environment, all of which seek to interweave in a complex, life-sustaining web. In this definition, caring is extremely inclusive and broadly defined. Tronto does not seem to define care as the meeting of needs in others as does Noddings. What is central is the perspective of taking the other's needs as the starting point for what must be done. Care involves some kind of ongoing connection. Tronto outlines four phases of caring: caring about, taking care of, caregiving, and care receiving. This broad and comprehensive definition, like Noddings's, includes public and private domains and integrates both males and females into the process. It does not assume that women rather than men have a special ability. However, Fisher and Tronto address the ways caring often entails and perpetuates oppression of women.

> Although the central institutions of modern life claim to promote caring, both marketplace and bureaucracy seriously distort and fragment caring activities. . . . In all of these institutions, too, women still assume the burden of caring, a burden made oppressive by inequalities in responsibility for caregiving and by the distortions of the caring process that result from these institutions. . . . As feminists, we need to discover directions for change that facilitate caring itself and embody equality, justice and trust. (1990, p. 50)

Nancy Folbre (2001) argues that economists have not taken seriously the role of care in social well-being. There is a paradigm that achievement guides the market, and Folbre declares that "the invisible heart" of care has been ignored. There is a "predominant culture that maintains a professional silence on matters of emotion" (Beatty, 2009, p. 150), but in her book *The Schoolhome,* Jane Roland Martin (1992) espouses three Cs—care, concern, and connection—as a way to approach the world through education. It is not a stretch to recognize that people and schools are profoundly social and that learning rests upon the depth and strength of the connections we make with others.

This is true of relationships within the school, between the school and its communities, and between ourselves and people in other countries—as we go beyond nationalism and affirm kinship with all the people of the world. In this light, a spirit of multiculturalism must become a priority in our own thinking and made a reality in our schools by honoring social justice, addressing issues of racial and gender bias in our systems, and affirming the need for culturally sensitive curriculum and instruction (Seymour, 2004a, p. 9).

The Rational/Irrational Gender Divide

A number of feminist scholars are sympathetic to the idea that an ethic of care is more characteristic of women or is more apt to be explicit in the experience and ideas of women and that an ethic of justice or rights is more explicit in the experience of men (Gilligan, 1995; Noddings, 1984); others take issue with that perspective. Claudia Card (1990) argues that as gendered beings in a society with a history of patriarchy, women and men inherit different pasts and consequently different social expectations, lines of communication, opportunities, and barriers. "Emotions, care, and responsibility have been discursively related to female attributes" (Blackmore & Sachs, 2007, p. 206) and rationality is more related to masculine ethics. Men dominated the "public," the world of rationality, competitiveness, positivism, and linear thinking, and women occupied the "private," the world of mothering, emotion, expressiveness, and imagination (Chodorow, 1978). For centuries women were socialized and conditioned to be obedient and quiet; it was considered feminine to ask permission, while men were expected to take charge, make decisions, and be directive (Brunner, 1999, 2000b; Grogan, 2003).

We sometimes discuss emotion in terms of the rational/irrational divide, so it can also be characterized in terms of a gender divide. Gender stereotypes would have us believe that men are rational and cool, therefore superior, and women are irrational, emotional, too personal, and thus inferior. Social values and gender stereotypes can serve to make the rational approach seem superior (Sachs & Blackmore, 1998). When women display what might be viewed as unprofessional, nonrational negative emotions, for example anger, they can be viewed as uncaring. If they cry, they are seen as weak. Women can be trapped into the positive aspects of emotion such as warmth, care, and patience, and (at the same time) have to manage the negative emotions of others. They must be both "vulnerable and strong" (Blackmore, 1999, p. 165). These and other cultural traditions and practices are imposed, justified, and carried on. They prevail due to the hegemony of male power, so it is important that women seize their "power and authority to bring equitable social order within their communities as well as

Canadian society, where they can discuss issues of all inequality"(Hamdan, 2009, p. 69). Tronto (1993) emphasizes the ongoing responsibility and commitment implied in caring. For her, caring is necessarily relational and she makes the point simply that traditional gender roles in our society imply that men care *about* but women care *for*.

The interplay between emotional and rational is subtle (Richardson, 1973). "The leader's understanding of the emotional aspect of the school can be central not only to planning, but also to managing difficult interpersonal situations" (Crawford, 2009, p. 81). This is a crucial part of the emotional context in schools. "Leaders can realize that although there may be a cognitive rationale for actions, there is an underlying and probably stronger affective rationale, even though emotion may not be apparent on the surface" (Crawford, 2009, p. 104).

The ways societal and cultural norms and practices construct and reproduce gender discourses in particular (Hamdan, 2009) provide a framework for discussion in this book. Traditional ways of viewing women and girls, sexist traditions, have alarming significance. Tradition is the culprit behind patriarchal oppression, tradition that benefits men only. "Men throughout the world continue to control politics and the economy while girls and women are disadvantaged and exploited in a variety of ways" (Weiler, 2001, p. 11). Women's position in the family has traditionally been that of caregiver, nurturer, supporter, and we developed our gender identity through our socialization in those roles. This happened first by our parents and later through school teachers, religious leaders, and employers.

The perception that women are naturally suited to certain tasks over others gives men more control (Hamdan, 2009). It is frustrating that the private sphere is culturally constructed to be women's realm and the public sphere is relegated to men. Still today people question a woman's ability to perform a task just because it is normalized as "a male task" (Hamdan, 2009), even though both men and women are capable. Consequently, women's role in being treated inequitably needs to be examined to discern how through passivity we actually perpetuate suppression. If women have equal rights, roles, and responsibilities, and if we are highly valued and given positions of respect, why are there so few women in senior administrative positions in education? Why are these positions still "dominated" by men? Competition between the sexes disrupts relations and prevents co-operation and collaboration. "Many women who are raised in male-dominated cultures have to struggle against the impulse to maintain complementarity without dependency" (Bateson, 1990, p. 240).

Educational restructuring has facilitated a re-masculinization of executive power consistent with the new mode of control (Collard & Reynolds, 2005). Although women have tended to make inroads in educational
achievement in recent years, gender is often absent from the literature on
educational reform and restructuring (Blackmore, 2000). Despite inroads
made in social policy in previous years, women are being disadvantaged
in the new regime. It is from that perspective this study examines issues of
gender, power, and position which shape the views and perspectives applied
in this book.

Because some careers and workplaces are still considered predominantly male and others predominantly female, frustration with cultural
tradition became an aspect of my study. Gender discourses persistently reinforce patriarchy within various contexts. "Many women are subjected to
these gender discourses in a variety of ways and in a variety of contexts,
sometimes even indirectly" (Hamdan, 2009, p. 64) and require education
in order to break free and see other possibilities. "Women's education and
economic stability would lead to women's independence, which would
also result in their ability to control and maintain power" (Hamdan, 2009,
p. 65). Self-concept is important to understand because it changes with experience. "Peoples' theories about themselves as individuals are important
to leadership ... and it is argued that there is a strong emotional component to this perception of self" (Crawford, 2009, p. 45).

Fineman (2003) proposes that the idea of the rational organization
as a place where emotion can be controlled out of existence is a naïve assumption by those who manage. "Decision-making is most often conceptualized as a rational process in educational leadership texts" (Crawford,
2009, p. 30). Work carried out in neurology provides evidence that suggests
feelings are necessary to make good decisions (George, 2000). Although
very intense emotions may make decision making more difficult, an intense
reduction in emotion may also lead to irrational behavior. Emotional management does not mean suppression of feelings, as this may lead to greater
emotional dissonance and stress.

"Decision making is portrayed as rational in retrospect but is often an
unfolding conflictual process" (Fineman, 2000, p. 96). There is a Western
tendency to rationalize our emotions and make them look reasoned, as
emotion is not seen as a legitimate way of either presenting ideas or suggest-
ing how we can reach conclusions (Fineman, 2000). In his influential book
Emotional Intelligence, Goleman (1995) argues that the emotionally intelligent have abilities in five main domains: they know their emotions, manage their emotions, motivate themselves, recognize emotions in others, and
handle relationships. The affective side of leadership—no matter whether

male or female, experienced or inexperienced, in large or small organizations—is complex, challenging, and vitally important but is not addressed or acknowledged in the day-to-day environment of education.

Turbulence

At no time has the work of educators been more important than today as the social, economic, and ecological patterns of the world become more chaotic and certainty is an illusion. Global devastation abounds from natural disasters, tsunamis, oil spills, floods, fires, nuclear spills, civil unrest and wars, dictatorships, and the persecution of women. Turbulent global themes in education include reform, downsizing, and improving achievement on standardized tests. Throughout local education systems, turbulence is manifested through school board consolidations, school closures, strikes, and authority over versus shared decision-making processes. Educators at all levels and in all localities are dealing with a multitude of paradoxes and complexities. During challenging times, more and more is expected of people and there is more and more stress among employees, communication breakdowns, unilateral decision making, cutbacks, mistrust, and a general lack of care for individuals and groups of employees, as well as for the effectiveness of organizations as a whole. People are acting in ways that conflict with their values, and there is considerable burnout with significant numbers of educators exiting the system.

Turbulence theory provides a helpful way to analyze and assess any reform process, its accompanying issues and dilemmas, and helps us to devise solutions or at least strategies to diminish the level of turmoil and conflict. I use the definition of turbulence developed by Shapiro and Gross (2008), who studied 10 schools and districts and discovered that turbulence could be divided into four levels. *Light turbulence* refers to the ongoing normal issues of the school, for example, dealing with a disjointed community. Light turbulence is part of the institutional environment and can be easily handled. *Moderate turbulence* is related to specific and important issues that need to be solved, such as the loss of a support structure or rapid growth or decline in student population. Moderate turbulence is not part of normal operations but gets everyone's attention and can be dealt with in a concerted and focused way. *Severe turbulence* is evident when an entire enterprise seems threatened, as when there is a conflict of community values and members are divided in their reaction to specific reforms. The demise of the denominational education system in Newfoundland and Labrador required a constitutional amendment and was used as a political lever or strategy necessary to accomplish the reform. Severe turbulence, such as that reform, is so serious that "normal administrative actions seem inadequate" (Shapiro & Gross, 2008, p. 9). A coordinated set of strategies is needed and normal operations are suspended. *Extreme Turbulence* means "there is serious danger of the destruction of the institution...the institution becomes unraveled" (Shapiro & Gross, 2008, p.9). There is a cascading series of pressures on the entire reform process.

Neoliberalism

Broad social, economic, cultural, and political changes are taking place around the globe (M. Apple, Kenway, & Singh, 2005; M. Apple, 2000; Taylor, Rizvi, Lingard, & Henry, 1997) aimed at preparing people and nations to be more globally competitive, causing turbulence within education systems. "All institutions are under intense pressure to operate as if they were a business. The corporate model, based on head-to-head competition and survival of the fittest, is the prototype for all government and, more recently, educational institutions" (Barlow & Robertson, 1994, p. 94).

Changing bureaucracies are emphasizing strategic plans, outcomes and efficiency, the devolution of financial responsibility, a focus on entrepreneurialism, industry relevance, and quality measurement. As well, they are focusing on the development of human capital. "Government decision making has been captured by and reflects the interests of the world's powerful elites, who are not directly accountable for these decisions, and yet they have real effects on people's everyday lives" (Reid, 2005, p. 286). As a result we are all trying to come to terms with new technologies, new social movements, and a changing global economy.

> The industrial society is rapidly being replaced with a knowledge society and advances in technology are making the world a smaller place. Dramatic shifts in the job market due to the expansion of multinational corporations and the outsourcing of jobs place new demands on schools to prepare graduates for a future that can no longer be predicted with any certainty by inferring from our industrial past. (Brien & Williams, 2009, p. 7)

The contemporary context for education is responsible for many challenges for administrators. Agendas of high-stakes accountability, national and international competitiveness, standardized curriculum, the centralization of power (Gidney, 1999; Hargreaves, 1994; Lingard & Douglas, 1999; Pollock, 2008), rising levels of diversity (Ryan, 2006), technological advances (Haughney, 2006), and the changing nature of labor relations have changed the nature of administrators' work over the past number of years (Ball, 2003, 2008; Blackmore & Sachs, 2007; Court & O'Neill, 2011).

The rational organization of the mid- to late twentieth century brought structures and codes, organizational charts, process charts, career paths, job descriptions, policy manuals, and finely tuned procedures. Strategic planning and the learning organization are the capstones of this rational direction, but because progress has not been nearly as neat as the rational model would suggest, there have also been abuses. Many educational institutions are "greedy institutions" (Coser, 1974; Franzway, 2001) that expect voluntary compliance from loyal and committed members, and demand increased workloads and unbounded time from their employees. The power of the state, public bureaucracies, governance, citizens, and education have all been subjected to structural adjustments that limit and oppress rather than liberate (Franzway, 2005). Employees in these organizations are struggling to respond to all the constraints imposed by the organizations within which they work, and either give more or less of themselves, experience stress, withdraw, or detach themselves.

Global trends of neoliberalism, the erosion of local input and control, resulting in a loss of autonomy and corporate managerialism, are evidenced through a marketplace mentality (Burbules & Torres, 2000). Workplaces emphasize economic utility and focus on efficiency with downsizing, accountability and cost-cutting, job losses, hierarchical and bureaucratic structures, and impersonal and stressful work environments (Lowe, 2000). Top-down decisions are imposed at the local levels and are rational, output- and plan-based (Lowe, 2000). Workplaces are management led and competitive. Workers are expected to do more with less and to make personal sacrifices, to spend more hours at work and less with family (Hochschild, 1997).

National competitiveness depends on creating flexible workplaces, "learning organizations," and effective education and training systems (Lowe, 2000). However, statements like this mean nothing unless accompanied by sweeping changes within workplaces that challenge conventional views of how work should be organized and rewarded. For too long workers have been treated as costs that have to be trimmed and controlled (Lowe, 2000), and the imperative to downsize has dominated government and business mandates.

Because Newfoundland and Labrador must compete in a global marketplace, just as other regions do, politicians forecasted dire consequences that underperforming schools would have on the economic stability of our nation. Governments in Ontario, Alberta, New Brunswick, and Newfoundland and Labrador embarked on centralized strategies to make schools the engines for economic success (Brien & Williams, 2009). As a consequence, leadership focused on the improvement of student outcomes and the achievement of high standards.

Education Reform

Schools are modeling their reforms on those that have succeeded in business. "The challenge for education reformers today is to adapt the corporate model of learning organizations to make schools places where continuous learning by teachers supports the improved learning of students" (Brien & Williams, 2009, p. 8). As in business, traditional educational management emphasizes control, authority, and decision making—requiring attributes traditionally perceived as masculine, including analytical ability, rationality, and toughness (Brady & Hammett, 1999). The tendency of Western cultures to overvalue individualism, autonomy, and competition has deeply defined the character of our nation's higher education and professional programs (Brody & Witherall, 1991). "School has been expected to perform such miracles as single-handedly putting an end to a nation's social ills or making it a leader in the global economy" (Martin, 2011, p. 183).

The prime reason given for education reform is the need for increased educational skill requirements of labor force change (Levin & Riffel, 1997; Williams & Sparkes, 2000). The argument for more education as the key to economic growth is widely accepted (Williams et al., 1992). The OECD (Organization for Economic Co-operation and Development) provided a good example in this excerpt from a report on education.

> Only a well-trained and highly adaptable labour force can provide the capacity to adjust to structural change and seize new employment opportunities created by technological progress. Achieving this will in many cases entail a re-examination, perhaps radical, of the economic treatment of human resources and education. (OECD, 1993, p. 3)

The knowledge society and global community for which we hope to educate our children and ourselves exist because advances in information and communication technology have removed barriers previously imposed by location (Sheppard, 2000b). "The goal of school reform is to produce measurable improvement in student achievement within the term of office of the party in power. Long-term leadership, although important, often gives way to demands for short-term results. In a system as complex as education, this often translates into well-intentioned but poorly executed reform initiatives" (Brien & Williams, 2009, p. 16).

"In an era of accountability and global competitiveness, school leaders and administrators face immense pressures to ensure that students in their schools are meeting standards of success as demonstrated mainly through tests and other measurable indices" (Daniel, 2009, p. 45). Yet, "the fear and resentment associated with labeling and blaming entire schools, has done a tremendous amount of damage" (Beatty, 2009, p. 151). In the current context, as accountability measures continue to mount, the appeal of a career in education—especially in school leadership—continues to dwindle.

Noddings pronounced in her interview with Seymour:

> The current school reform movement that concentrates on standards and standardized testing is really destroying our schools.... [T]he curriculum reform is a poor technical solution ... to lay a standards movement on all the schools, thereby destroying the creativity in some of the best of them, is just awful. (Seymour, 2004b, p. 91)

Often change seems to mean more work piled on teachers who are already stressed and on the verge of burnout. Yet they are being asked to shift from comfortably private solo work to vulnerable, relatively public, collaborative, data-driven practices, from teacher-centered to student-centered learning processes and back again, with the resurgence in popularity of *direct instruction.* "For teachers to learn new practices, and rework old ones for new applications, they need support from each other that can come from collaborative learning leaders who can model a different way" (Beatty, 2009, p. 153).

"Negative publicity has been used to shift schools from complacency to compliance with new accountability measures" (Tschannen-Moran, 2004, p. 11). Educators are resisting and resenting these measures because they do not foster a productive school culture. Governments have been

> impatient with the slow pace of change and try to force rapid change upon their reluctant faculty, generating resistance and resentment instead of improved outcomes.... [I]t takes wisdom ... to patiently apply both support and challenge to lead a school toward fruitful change. (Tschannen-Moran, 2004, p. 11)

Michael Fullan, Canada's school change expert, cautions that politically motivated reforms produce overload, unrealistic timelines, uncoordinated demands, simplistic solutions, misdirected efforts, inconsistencies, and underestimation of what it takes to bring about reform (Fullan, 2005; Fullan & Steigelbauer, 1991). The emotional demands of developing respectful, caring, connected, and socially responsible relationships are real; when fear surfaces, anger, shame, and blame are often right around the corner. "Left unexamined, emotional pressures can lead to betrayal and damaged relationships that quickly become a liability to learning" (Beatty, 2009, p. 152), and I argue, a liability to the success of any reform initiative. In moving toward a corporate model of education, the end can become the end in itself, rather than a means to accomplishing something worthwhile. Budget and personnel cuts are made for efficiency rather than improvement, measures are taken to reduce costs rather than improve education programs and services, and downsizing is emphasized over better serving people's needs.

The dismal record of restructuring efforts during the 1990s pointed to the fact that there were no great leaders who understood the educational system.

> The restructuring reforms of the 1990s—with its expansion centralized authority and decentralized responsibility—brought back a directive leadership style at the highest provincial levels. Expectations that standards would be achieved by edict and that hierarchical control could produce the professional collaboration necessary for school improvement characterized the new leadership mentality. In the provinces that adopted this directive leadership mentality the changes in structure worked counter to the development of an innovative school culture.... Now after a decade of centralized authority's failure to achieve significant improvements in student results, many provinces are embarking on a different leadership approach—a transformational approach that underlies a learning community. (Brien & Williams, 2009, p. 15)

Also, many of the failures were the result of attempting to mandate rather than facilitate educational change (Hargreaves, 2003; Schlechty, 1990, 1997). A moral use of power and a proactive ethical stance are required to support student success (Ryan, 2009; Sergiovanni, 1992).

The restructuring efforts by government held the potential to raise standards, but politicians who embraced a directive leadership approach seemed to doubt the professionals' motivation and capacity. At a time when the professional bureaucracy should have been ascendant, the politicians' will in some provinces undermined teachers' potential to lead. Educational change in these provinces during the 1990s in many ways reflected the antithesis of what research supported as effective practice (Brien & Williams, 2009, p. 13).

Mandate-based reform failed to consider the complexity of schools and the reality of classrooms—a failure that Senge (2000) argued has prevented school reform for decades. The failure of reform stemmed not from a lack of passion or positive intentions, but from a failure to examine our mental models, those underlying beliefs that define our culture and color our perspectives of reality. Political leaders who rely primarily on plans and policies to promote educational excellence would do well to heed Wheatley (1999) when she argues for the use of goals rather than "intricate directions, timelines, plans, and organizational charts" (p. 6), stating that leaders who honor and trust the people who work with them, "have unleashed startlingly high levels of productivity and creativity" (p. 4).

> As we enter a new century, a third wave of large-scale school reform is emerging, one that will demand far greater changes in the leadership approach

that currently exists at each level of the education system. As we move forward with the development of professional learning communities for our
educational model, we must use our knowledge of leadership theory and
practice and do a better job at redefining educational leadership in Canada.
(Brien & Williams, 2009, p. 19)

Trust among adults in schools is proven to be predictive of student
performance (Tschannen-Moran, 2004), and wisely we are beginning to
acknowledge that constructive engagement with the emotional complexities of schools, schooling, and school leadership can help promote the relational connectedness that is necessary for schools to succeed (Noddings,
2007). "With a firm footing in resilient relationships people can afford to
make themselves vulnerable to bold self-critique and get on with the important business of improving their practices together, especially in such trying
times" (Beatty, 2009, p. 158).

Competition Versus Social Responsibility

Human resources and career experts have been advising corporations that
maintaining a reputation for caring for employees and stakeholders is important to the best and brightest future job hunters who prefer positions
in organizations that demonstrate a set of socially responsible values in the
way they do business. An attitude of working well together and treating
people well is important, for clients and employees (Launt, 2006). "Despite
that, the competition for jobs is becoming fiercer. We are becoming a harder people, less compassionate about the unemployed, less responsible to
one another" (Barlow & Robertson, 1994, p. 97). The nature of education
in Canada is becoming more privatized, operating on a more commercial
basis. The birth of large, bureaucratic, and highly organized school institutions, using economic models (Bingham & Sidorkin, 2004), has created
a growing problem of alienation. Students, teachers, and parents increasingly find themselves in situations void of meaningful human contact, rife
with frustration and anonymity.

Work in education is stressful and actually contradicts the commonly
held perspective and dominant discourse that it is a nurturing and caring
environment. The last decade in education has been very difficult for educators. With demands to do more with less, blame for the underachievement of students, fiscal restraint, and greater scrutiny and accountability
with testing and evaluation processes in abundance, the value of care for
others is not always evident. "This pressure to be seen to be performing will
lead many leaders to lean on and alienate teachers and manipulate student

performance results to satisfy their communities' hunger for evidence of their school's success" (Beatty, 2009, p. 153).

Educational leaders are emulating corporate bottom-line philosophies and neglecting their impacts on people. "Pressure from the data-driven accountability movement has caused some educators to overlook the equation that supports team-oriented problem-solving in favor of a win-at-all-costs attitude" (Zimbalist, 2005, pp. 27–28). If the Western formula for corporate leadership is dominated by a bottom-line philosophy of competition, power, speed, and profit, where do individuals fit in? Has education in adopting the corporate bottom-line philosophy moved too far in objective analysis of data, without regard for the values of building stable relationships?

As much as parents and the public want improved academic performance, they also expect schools to develop happy, socially well-adjusted, moral human beings. Simply put, students and educators cannot and will not do a good job within discouraging and alienating environments. Educational organizations must focus on human relations and address the core of the problem. Perhaps the greatest challenge in educational accountability is keeping the focus on improvement without forgetting the rest of the agenda (Sergiovanni, 2000).

Caring relationships can be difficult to sustain in work environments where individuals and groups are under the pressure of competing interests and demands. "There is a long standing tradition in educational leadership of doing anything but trusting others" (Beatty, 2009, p. 153). There are options emerging from the collaboration of groups and communities and the caring approaches and policies of leaders. An encouraging trend in current school reform efforts focuses on building partnerships that require a balance of authority, control, and power through shared decision making and management. Decisions are to be shared among educators, administrators, students, parents, and various other government and community groups, which fits the model of empowering leadership (Grogan & VanDeman Blackmon, 1999). The aim is to develop more people-oriented, relational, and collaborative ways of working, where people care about one another (Sernak, 1998). Despite the current pressures of imposed agendas from above, hurried time frames, and insecurities related to employment that complicate efforts to care, organizations of education hold out the promise of care; there is an argument that in spite of deteriorating conditions, it is possible to work with others in compassionate, generous, and nurturing ways. "The success and wellbeing of school leaders are enhanced by the explicit integration of emotional meaning making as part of a reconceptualization of leader professionalism" (Beatty, 2009, p. 149).

Education is about human beings who are in relation with one another, who need to meet together, as a group of people, if learning is to take place (Bingham & Sidorkin, 2004). Educators must focus on human relations and move from struggling against something to struggling toward something. "Arguments are being made for a pedagogy of relations based on the notion of democratic relations" (Bingham & Sidorkin, 2004, p. 6). To improve schools, one must invest in people, support people, and develop people.

> In our daily life, we encounter people who are angry, deceitful, intent only on satisfying their own needs. There is also so much anger, distrust, greed, and pettiness that we are losing our capacity to work well together. Many of us are more withdrawn and distrustful than ever. Yet this incessant display of the worst in us makes it essential that we rely on human goodness. Without that belief in each other, there really is no hope. (Wheatley, 2002, p. 72)

Programs, policies, and test scores are not the driving forces behind many successful change agents. We need to recognize the human factor as the essential element of the change process and people's need for care as an important aspect of it. "Employees are the greatest asset of any educational organization" (Dufour & Eaker, 1992, p. 10). What I am arguing here is that relationships, emotion, connection are all as relevant and important at work as they are in our personal lives, and there is greater potential for logic and emotion to work together to result in more productive workplaces and happier employees.

Educational Leadership

"The organizational model for schools for much of their existence has been a bureaucratic one" (Brien & Williams, 2009, p. 11). There has been a misapplication of positivistic business models of leadership within the education system (Ryan, 2009). Consequently, Canadian educational leadership is situated within a framework of redefinition, transformation, improvement, moral literacy, multiculturalism, emotions, and evolution (Ryan, 2009). Crawford (2009) stresses the interplay among leadership, emotion, and the organization and how "growing understandings of emotion can enhance and even challenge some prevailing orthodoxies in regard to educational leadership" (p. 2).

Research into leadership of educational organizations started with successful schools and their need for strong leaders (Brien & Williams, 2009; Fullan, 2005; Leithwood & Jantzi, 2000) and with the principal being seen as key in effecting school reform (Fullan & Steigelbauer, 1991). Significant focus was given to why certain individuals are more effective leaders than others. A prominent theme in the corporate and educational leadership literature has been the evolution from an emphasis on trait and situational considerations towards transactional and transformational theories of leadership.

Merriam-Webster Dictionary defines a leader as "a person who leads" and to lead is to "to guide on a way especially by going in advance."

> Leadership, therefore, was seen to be about articulating and sharing ideas; taking the initiative at particular moments and responsibility for planning and action; working outside/against/within the dominant way of thinking; nurturing, mentoring, and caring for others; communicating often about decisions; and developing collaborative and collegial relations based on trust, ethics, reciprocity, and mutual recognition. (Day, 2004, p. 561)

This aligns with what the literature says about the transformational leader who leads by example rather than control, builds leadership capacity (Lambert, 1998), and is a leader of leaders (Barth, 2001)—promotes leadership among students, teachers, parents, and with the larger community.

School leader has traditionally meant someone particularly proficient in command-and-control tactics, the all-powerful, all-knowing, larger than life, heroic commander-in-chief. These qualities have all been well respected and rewarded in days gone by. Yet "what is needed is openness and humility in leaders, leaders who understand that they are learning, too, and are given space by those they lead to make mistake [sic] as they learn . . . there is a tendency to lose sensitivity to self and others' needs" (Beatty, 2009, p. 153).

Leaders are constantly asked to provide "once-and-for-all answers" to big problems that are "complex, rife with paradoxes and dilemmas" (Fullen, 2001, p. 2). In this complex and challenging era, more and more is being expected of leaders. For the purposes of this book, educational leadership is defined to encompass not only administrators but anyone who takes on decision-making roles through shared leadership (Brunner, 2000a; Grogan, 1996, 2003; Shapiro & Gross, 2008; Wheatley, 2005). Educational leaders include a long list of positions and titles, such as teachers, program coordinators, curriculum specialists, department heads, school board members, special educators, department and school board personnel, union leaders, and special interest groups. All are facing problems and difficult issues in education because there are clashes and value conflicts.

Goleman (1995) discussed the "two minds," the rational and the emotional. This book argues for an amalgamation of the two and the need for balance between these two ways of knowing (Gilligan, 1982). To deal with paradoxes and ethical dilemmas in educational leadership, using both the head and the heart is important (Crawford, 2009). Leadership is about emotional as well as intellectual toughness (Blackmore & Sachs, 2007, p. 209).

> Leadership is undeniably about exercising multiple modes of power and influence through networks, rules, regulations, and systemic authority, as well as individual capacity to develop, synthesize, communicate, and enact ideas, and to motivate, persuade and nurture others to adopt particular practices. Power is exercised variously: through systems and by individuals through influence and persuasion, consent and coercion, consciously and unconsciously, through the exertion of authority and relationships of trust, without a source. (Blackmore & Sachs, 2007, p. 164)

Transformational leadership taps into employees' pride in their work. Rather than describe a process by which principals transformed teachers, transformational leadership became a term to describe how the sharing of leadership between administration and the teaching staff transformed schools into better learning environments (Brien & Williams, 2009; Fullan, 2005; Leithwood & Jantzi, 2000).

The purpose of school leadership entered a new phase as the 1990s closed. The standards-based approach with its focus on top-down control had failed to produce the expected results and there was a general recognition that educational leadership had to change. As the leadership focus shifted from telling teachers how to teach to consulting with them about how to improve learning, the role of teachers in shared leadership expanded. "At present the primary purpose of school leadership is to mobilize staffs to work together to create a synergistic culture of co-learning and to build leadership as a school-wide capacity" (Brien & Williams, 2009, p. 14).

Leadership after 2000 has shifted to a transformational approach. Recognizing the complexity of not only the structure of schools but also the professional culture that defined teaching made it clear that, as Wheatley (1999) argued, "you can't direct people into perfection, you can only engage them enough so that they want to do perfect work" (p. 25). Wheatley (1999) went on to say that in times of complex change, we need self-organizing systems built upon trust rather than control and that leadership must focus on "helping everyone stay clear on what we want to accomplish and who we want to be" (p. 25). Yet, "collaborative cultures are far easier to put into policy than into practice" (Beatty, 2009, p. 152). Further study is required to determine why it is so difficult for educators to communicate openly and freely with each other and to share decision making. Transformative leadership focuses on the ethical and moral dimensions and acknowledges the centrality of relationships (Shields, 2004). To respond to the call for moral leadership, leaders need to "address the pressures for performativity, without losing their integrity" (Beatty, 2009, p. 153).

From Learning Organizations to Communities of Learners

Organizational learning is a perspective frequently used to better understand nonschool organizations, but it is beginning to be applied to schools and other educational organizations. At first glance, the emphasis of organizational learning theory on structures and systems seems inconsistent and incompatible with that of caring or commitment to others. I explore whether there are spaces within an organizational learning context (Senge, 1990, 2000, 2006) to provide more care. My aim is to determine if a learning organization can be redesigned so that caring has a chance to be initiated and completed.

Although there is no single generally accepted definition of a learning organization, it has been described as a group of people pursuing common purposes (individual purposes as well) with a collective commitment to regularly weighing the value of those purposes, modifying them when that makes sense, and continuously developing more effective and efficient ways of accomplishing those purposes (Leithwood & Aiken, 1995). Organizational learning recognizes that change is implemented through the people within an organization.

The concept of a learning organization originated in systems thinking (Silins, Zarins, & Mulford, 2002) and is typified by Peter Senge's model of the five disciplines of a learning organization (1990): systems thinking, personal mastery, mental models, team learning, and shared vision. Senge explains that learning organizations are characterized by valuing and developing these five disciplines. He refers to organizational learning as a group of people collectively enhancing their capacities to produce the outcome they really want to produce (Senge, 2006; Senge et al., 2004). Organizational learning emphasizes capacity building: the capacities to constantly learn, adapt, and respond as new situations arise. Intentionality and deliberateness are essential elements in successful learning. Learning is associated with deliberate representation, deliberate inclusion, and through these vehicles, deliberate knowledge acquisition. According to Senge,

> learning organizations are settings where people continually expand their capacity to create the results they truly desire, where new and expansive patterns of thinking are nurtured, where collective aspiration is set free, and where people are continually learning to see the whole together. (Senge 1990, p. 14)

Organizational learning (Senge, 1990, 2000) is about people, individual personalities as professional identities. It is about creating one's own personal and professional knowledge and contributing that knowledge for the betterment of the organization. Learning occurs at the individual level, and that is where knowledge acquisition for the organization first occurs. When individuals share their knowledge, they do so with a collection of individuals. Team learning (Senge, 1990) occurs when all of those individuals work together to bring to the organization all that they know—their strengths, needs, ideas, observations, and assessments. When all knowledge is brought together and shared, it can then be utilized for the betterment of the overall organization.

Organizational learning concepts come from business literatures and are argued to benefit individual participants through attention to the development of personal mastery, which in turn benefits the organization. Leaders become accountable for the learning needs of each individual, as well as the school community as a whole. Despite these admirable goals and efforts, organizations are questioned about the extent to which they care about the personal and professional development of individuals. Some researchers as well as practitioners argue that personal mastery is more about an organization's attempt to get more out of people where the organization learns and benefits for itself (Du Gay, 1996; Lucas, 1999; Sennett, 1998). Some research publications challenge the underlying motivation of the organizational learning literatures as being self-serving, a means to get more for less. Others describe some organizations as all-consuming and greedy (Coser, 1974; Franzway, 2001; Sennett, 1998, 2004) and pushing always to be competitive and innovative with long stressful work hours as well as commitment to the organization and its values. These "greedy" organizations evoke personal sacrifice and loyalty and require a wide range of skills.

Organizational learning is a metaphor implying that organizations learn through the learning activities of their members. Workplace innovation leading toward high-quality work is only on the margins of the public policy agenda in Canada today, and the changes being proposed have yet to get to the heart of the human problems in workplaces (Lowe, 2000). While workplaces since the 1990s have changed dramatically, they often have not moved in the direction of "people development" (Lowe, 2000). The latest cost-cutting or restructuring tactics are adopted, usually with negative effects on employee morale, confidence, and productivity. Restoring a human dimension to corporate and government management agendas may well be a critical step towards ensuring future national economic prosperity in Canada (Lowe, 2000).

Educational organizations have been facing uncertain, changing, and ambiguous conditions with continuing demands for restructuring, greater efficiency and effectiveness, and improved student achievement. We measure the level of success of learning organizations by answering questions about what the people are trying to accomplish (Senge, 2006):

- Are they much more effective at doing it?
- Are they having a better time at doing it?
- Are they enjoying learning together?

Organizational learning is about establishing sustainable processes of continual growth and capacity. Senge (1990, 2000) suggests that after a performance peak, there's a price to pay if people are worn out, do not stick around, or become ineffective because they are overtaxed. The most fundamental assessment is long-term sustainable improvement in people accomplishing what they really want to accomplish. In learning organizations, people feel excited about their work, are passionate, and have networks of others with whom they work. Most people enjoy their work and find meetings to be productive and helpful. They examine what has been happening and see real progress. Those people do not have to talk about systems thinking, mental models, or the other disciplines that are aspects of a learning organization. They understand the concepts, but that is not where their attention is.

The Challenge to Create Caring Transformative Communities

I argue that care for others, not the dispensing of knowledge, must be the starting point if real learning is to occur. Research literature provides few personal accounts of the experience of developing caring practices within the context of a learning organization. Despite growing awareness among senior management of the importance of workers' knowledge, skills, and involvement in decision making, the fact remains that traditional work structures, control systems, and an overriding focus on costs and achievement make it difficult to nurture these human qualities and behaviors that foster socially just workplaces. On the one hand, organizational learning theory claims to emphasize teamwork, collaboration, and personal mastery, and on the other, it sets up structures and systems thinking that seem to reinforce old models and outdated thought.

Successful organizations of the twenty-first century will move beyond the rational planning model that underpins strategic planning and learning organization thinking to the nonrational core passion and emotion that drives what, how much, and how well we learn, respond, and innovate (Lucas, 1999). Critics of the dominant management and leadership research literatures argue that incentives and recognitions are merely ways to control employees and entice them to give more of themselves for the "greedy organization" (Franzway, 2001; Hochschild, 1983). It is also argued that organizations cannot be ethical because they demand loyalty, insist upon the affirmation of certain beliefs, separate members from nonmembers on principle, and frequently insist on obedience to rules and adherence to ritual, which contribute to the erosion of genuine caring (Noddings, 1984).

From an institutional/organizational perspective, caring involves leaders responding not only to the particular needs of individuals, but also to the needs of the entire system. Leaders must make sense of all the talk and action in terms of what would benefit the entire organization. They have to factor in the expectations of superiors and make decisions that sometimes anger, frustrate, and upset staff members.

Thinking of administration in relation to power that connotes authority or control is easier than seeing it in relation to caring. Most administrators will recognize the importance of caring among staff, and others, and that it is crucial for good teaching, learning, and working to occur; however, power, authority, accountability, and responsibility are also directly addressed in conjunction with the role of administrators and leaders, whose job is to ensure organizational needs are addressed and officials are responded to promptly and competently.

Strong desire and action to change bureaucratic structures will be required to enable care for each other and the community as a whole, where collaboration is the norm. Many leaders today are advocating a team approach modeled on the merits of the five disciplines of organizational learning (Senge, 1990, 2000), but given the pressures and demands of the day, they can expect to experience many obstacles and barriers that limit opportunities to bring about and sustain meaningful change. There are contradictory messages from administrators and agendas imposed from above that undermine values of collaboration, trust, and sharing. Often having to function in the midst of frustration and isolation means that caring requires more than understanding feelings. It requires understanding the ambiguous nature of roles and how that ambiguity affects what can be accomplished. It requires understanding that collaboration and support are necessary from entire staffs within organizations.

Embracing a social justice perspective of equality, I question whose interests are advanced and whose views are legitimatized through the focus on organizational learning. Current school reform efforts focus on partnerships that require a balance of authority and control through decision making and management—shared with educators, administrators, students, parents, and various other government and community groups (Grogan & VanDeman Blackmon, 2001; Sheppard, 2000; Taylor et al., 1997; Williams & Sparkes, 2000). The aim is to develop more people-oriented, relational, and collaborative ways of working where people care about one another (Shields, 2003; Valentine, 1995; Zimbalist, 2005). This is consistent with feminist notions of alternatives to bureaucracy and hierarchy to develop organizations that are grounded on an ethic of caring (Brunner & Bjork, 2001; Held, 1995; Noddings, 1992, 2002). When one looks at struggling organizations (including educational institutions), the effects of corporate managerialist agendas, and increases in apathy among some employees, it is apparent that the time has come to lay aside demeaning ideas about people in workplaces and treat them instead with dignity and respect. But this will be more complex and difficult to achieve than it appears. The central question is whether caring, as exemplified by the work of Tronto, Noddings, and others is compatible or even possible within the current educational system.

Senge (2000, 2006) cautions us to consciously examine our mental models and what we too often take for granted as real or true, for example leadership as control over others. If schools become professional learning communities, the hierarchical authority-based relationships between principals and teachers must be replaced with a collaborative relationship characterized by co-learning interdependence among professionals. For this to be successful we must revisit our mental models of school leadership because "leadership figures as the most significant set of beliefs and values within schools" (Brien & Williams, 2009, p. 20).

I work from the position that "social relations are a central aspect of leadership work" (Blackmore & Sachs, 2007, p. 7). My focus on caring leadership in education is precipitated by the discourses of globalization, education reform, "corporate managerialism," social inequalities that have impacted me and many others as we worked in various leadership positions in education. I often feel stuck between a democratic and collaborative model for decision making and the traditional patriarchal, authoritative, and top-down one. I struggle with processes that on the one hand advocate equity, shared decision making, and social justice agendas and leadership styles, but on the other practice the lean, mean philosophies of the corporate world that are about measuring, counting, balancing, cutting, and competing.

Reflection

The foundation and theoretical base for discussing and understanding the issues addressed in the book examine different theories and perspectives that currently impact people working in educational organizations in positive and negative ways. The relationship between theories of care and practices of education reform discussed seems to offer no empirical evidence that demonstrates the potential of more caring policy and practice in education to change the status quo. Rather, a myriad of structural and contextual variables prohibit and constrict possibilities for positive change.

Nevertheless, more caring work environments and more caring relationships would contribute to a more socially just and inclusive education system, which should be the result of transformative practice. The remainder of the chapters address further significant issues.

- How the narratives of those who experienced education reform can be instructive for leaders who will work through other subsequent reform processes.
- What it was about the professional and institutional as well as historical, cultural, social, economic, and moral context that empowered some and disempowered others.
- How leaders in formal and informal positions of leadership in education (in schools and districts) experienced and negotiated the contradictions, paradoxes, and turbulence arising from the process of education reform.
- The potential of more caring approaches to deal with people to improve not only the morale of those affected by radical change but also create positive effects for their organizations.
- How leaders can act in more democratic, transformative, and socially just ways.

I am committed to promoting more humanistic approaches to leadership predicated on social justice and the possibility of transforming the world of education into a better "place." I hope what I say in this book leads to dialogue and debate about our values and the goals of education.

2

A Researcher Practitioner's Personal and Professional Narrative

If

If you can keep your head when all about you
Are losing theirs and blaming it on you,
If you can trust yourself when all men doubt you,
But make allowance for their doubting too;
If you can wait and not be tired by waiting,
Or being lied about, don't deal in lies,
Or being hated, don't give way to hating,
And yet don't look too good, nor talk too wise:

If you can dream—and not make dreams your master;
If you can think—and not make thoughts your aim;
If you can meet with Triumph and Disaster
And treat those two impostors just the same;
If you can bear to hear the truth you've spoken
Twisted by knaves to make a trap for fools,
Or watch the things you gave your life to, broken,
And stoop and build 'em up with worn-out tools:

Caring Leadership in Turbulent Times, pages 33–69
Copyright © 2014 by Information Age Publishing

33

If you can make one heap of all your winnings
And risk it on one turn of pitch-and-toss,
And lose, and start again at your beginnings
And never breathe a word about your loss;
If you can force your heart and nerve and sinew
To serve your turn long after they are gone,
And so hold on when there is nothing in you
Except the Will which says to them: "Hold on!"

If you can talk with crowds and keep your virtue,
Or walk with Kings—nor lose the common touch,
If neither foes nor loving friends can hurt you,
If all men count with you, but none too much;
If you can fill the unforgiving minute
With sixty seconds' worth of distance run,
Yours is the Earth and everything that's in it,
And—which is more—you'll be a Man, my son!

—Rudyard Kipling (1865–1936)

Throughout my growing up, my mother found many appropriate opportunities to recite at least a part of this poem by Rudyard Kipling. She had learned it by heart as a child in grade school, and it seemed to come back to her with ever more relevance as she passed through each stage of her life. Although there are other versions of the poem containing more gender neutral language, they fail to be as significant or meaningful to me as the original version.

This chapter is an autobiographical compilation of stories and experiences from both my personal and professional life, involving education, politics, economics, history, relationships, social interactions, and values. Over the course of my career, as a teacher, curriculum specialist, district administrator, and academic I have spent years teaching, evaluating, and writing about others—students, teachers, parents, communities, employees, and colleagues. Gloria Steinem explained that "most writers write to say something about other people—and it doesn't last. Good writers write to find out about themselves—and it lasts forever" (1992, p. 6). This writing experience has enabled me to be reflexive, not just about myself as a researcher but about myself as a person and all "my selves," the person needing tenderness and inclusion, the person I'm trying to become—at work and in my personal relations—and the person I have been: teacher, mother, wife, daughter, employee, leader, colleague, and friend. My professional life has been intrinsically personal and my personal life has supported the professional.

The approach I have taken in this chapter developed from a genuine desire to deal with real-life situations alongside the belief that stories about ourselves teach us much about our own lives and about life in general. I opt for "subjectivity as a strength of qualitative approaches rather than attempt to establish detached objectivity" (Wolcott, 1990, p. 131). My only concern with my strategy was considering how far I should go with personal revelation. I have attempted to distinguish between "revealing my feelings and imposing my judgments" (Wolcott, 1990, p. 131) and have discovered the power of personal writing to clarify my ideas, nurture conceptual development, and illuminate my research. My learning has involved personal (including affective) and social (including moral and ethical) elements (Hanrahan, Cooper, & Burroughs-Lange, 1999). Belief that dealing with the personal can enhance rather than undermine writing (Kamler, 2001) and seeing my individual production of knowledge as necessarily shaped by my personal place in my own cultural context, I have chosen to openly report relevant aspects of my personal context.

I begin feeling tentative, though, in my search for words because "my professional socialization and family upbringing caution me against disclosing the personal and speaking about what is presumed to be private" (Gumport, 1997, p. 183). Administrative work taught me to expunge emotion from my writing and led to a calm, impersonal, and institutionalized style. Reflexivity involving self-reflection on my research processes and findings, self-awareness of my social position and my values, as well as perspectives and self-critique of the effects of my words and actions on the individuals and group (Young, Skrla, & Skrla, 2003) I studied gave me opportunities to connect my work (how I do it, why I do it, and what I'm finding) with my values, commitments, and theoretical frameworks. It also provided an opportunity to examine the dynamics occurring between me and those I work with and to experience how these dynamics are affecting my work and other people. I have tried not to be timid and have asked hard questions of myself and others in different circumstances to shake up bodies of knowledge and institutional practices in important ways.

I drew upon scholarly work on narrative writing (Clandinin, 2001; Clandinin & Connelly, 1998; Clandinin, Pushor, & Orr, 2007) to help me detail my growth toward recognition of power and privilege in school district administrative positions. Working within our education system provided potential for critical engagement with hegemonic practice that positions me to do more authentic work toward equity and caring. What follows is the story of my progression from a naïve and protected young girl to an educational administrator and graduate student at first somewhat hesitant to label myself a feminist, to a university academic advocating for equality through graduate and undergraduate teaching of inclusive education, curriculum studies, and foundational education courses, where I now proudly pronounce my feminism (advocate for the equality of females and males).

My story is based on the bits and pieces, the incidents and reflections I choose to disclose; it represents my effort to shape perceptions. There are many developing intersections and critical incidents (Tripp, 1998) that have made me "me" and that give me strength and conviction, although even now, while I am freer than ever to offer my own insights, I find myself having to follow rules and expectations of fitting within the parameters defined for me by authorities and scholars, policies and practices. Feminists often feel boxed in, restricted, and confined by others who want to label, direct, influence, guide, or even prescript us (Blackmore & Sachs, 2007; Blackmore, 2011; Steinem, 1992). Certainly rules, guidelines, and policies are valuable and necessary, but they also have a tendency to become hegemonic devices, mechanisms of inclusion and exclusion that are often unexamined. Many who have tried to work within systems to critique them, or who have been kept out of them, understand and relate to this point.

I draw on my practitioner researcher knowledge and experience to suggest that educators or educational institutions (such as school districts) can work authentically toward equity and caring while recognizing their power and privilege. I first discuss my life history that has molded and influenced my thinking, to provide insight into some factors that have helped forge my moral purpose (Sergiovanni, 1992) as well as influence and direct my thoughts and actions throughout my career in education, and shaped the perspectives I share in this book.

The Early Roots of a Caring Disposition

I was born at the cusp of the sixties, the third child and first of two girls, into a hard-working business family in a traditional rural fishing community in Newfoundland on the Atlantic coast of Canada. My parents provided my siblings and me with a nurturing household that fostered a philosophy of caring and service to others. Before elaborating on our family values and the early childhood experiences that so significantly shaped the person I have become today, some details about my parents are pertinent to share.

My mother, born in 1923 and the eldest of nine siblings, was raised during the dreary years of the Great Depression. Newfoundland's confederation with Canada in 1949 led to significant improvement in the quality of life for families. Over the 86 years of her life, she experienced changes that took her from the brink of poverty to a more than comfortable lifestyle.

My hometown, Winterton, a small rural fishing village, was also my parents' birthplace. Although the population was less than 1,000, because my parents "belonged to" different Christian denominations and did not attend the same school, they had not known each other well until they corresponded during Dad's military service during the Second World War. It was after Dad's return from the war, while Mom was working, that they officially began their courtship.

After high school, my father had been employed as a clerk with the Department of Agriculture and Rural Reconstruction in St. John's but resigned to join the Air Force. He was rejected due to the detection of a minor heart condition. He then applied and was accepted into the Newfoundland Militia. A short time later he was transferred, as a gunner, to the 59th Newfoundland Heavy Regiment. During the Second World War, my Dad served a total of two years and 219 days and saw active duty in England, France, Belgium, Holland, and Germany. Following the war, he was appointed to another government position but his father requested he return home to work in the family fish and general merchant business.

On November 11, 1947, my parents married and spent their early life together in Thoroughfare, a scenic but remote fishing village "across the bay" from the base of the business in Winterton. They were young, energetic, and undaunted by hard work. Thoroughfare lacked many of the government services provided in other communities and was accessible only by boat, but my parents loved life there. They had little money but built a home, constructing the entire interior and then insulating it themselves to protect them from the harsh winds blowing off the North Atlantic Ocean. Dad started out early in the morning and worked late into the night to run the family fish processing plant and general store. Mom adored the wholesome peace and natural beauty of the place, the kind-hearted and cooperative people, and looked forward to her husband's return from work at the end of each day. My two older brothers were born during their stay in Thoroughfare.

The provincial government of the time announced a resettlement program and relocated residents from Thoroughfare and several other remote areas into other small communities that could be connected by roads, enabling them to avail of the comforts of running water, street lights, schools, medical and social services. I recall the heartbreak in Mom's voice whenever she told the story of how they were forced to pack their belongings, close their home and business, and relocate. Mom and Dad with my brothers returned to Winterton, where the business had been in operation since in the early 1900s, and where in 1958 I was born.

We lived in a comfortable three-bedroom home that my mother proudly described as having been "built by them." I was able always to see the goodness, unselfishness, generosity, and genuine caring of my parents. I was taught to respect differences and never think I was better than anyone else. Mine was a "low tech" world. Most homes did not have a telephone, television, or even a record player. For entertainment, my mother's father invited the men of the community to visit his home on Saturday nights to listen to the National Hockey League (NHL) game broadcasted on the radio. I benefitted from my caring family environment, feeling content and secure. I had all the essentials to a happy childhood and am amazed by those who are resilient in the face of hardship. It certainly was my parents' philosophical and spiritual views of life and family that informed and influenced my life and taught me foundational values and skills for living a productive and happy life.

In my hometown, caring was prevalent, but men were valued for what they did and women for how they looked after their family. Care, concern, and service to others were family values taught and practiced on both sides of my family. Grandfather Green was actually forced to declare personal bankruptcy during the 1930s because he extended too much credit to fishermen. He gave them their fishing gear in the spring with hopes of being compensated when they sold their fish in the fall, but many were unable to pay. This is not the typical story of greedy and insensitive shop merchants of the day who were perceived as ruthless and uncaring.

In all matters related to home Mom was a take-charge person. She worked the role of nurturer for the family and was always involved in many other nontraditional responsibilities as well. She had a keen interest and practical know-how when it came to fixing leaking faucets, completing home repairs, or discussing matters of landscaping, plumbing, electrical and carpentry work with the community tradespeople, who occasionally came to help with projects in our home. She was always a leader in our family, in our church, in our local community, and beyond. My mother was unique in her time.

During the fall of 1965, there were troubles for the family business when fire destroyed the fish plant and an entire season's stored production of salt fish, ready for market. With fortitude and memories of his father's resilience after bankruptcy, Dad rebuilt, equipping the plant for fresh fish as well as salt fish processing—a move that proved to sustain the plant's future through a time when others were unable to remain in operation. Another devastating blow was dealt to the entire provincial fishing industry in 1992, when the federal government declared a cod moratorium, a desperate measure to protect and strengthen a diminished cod stock. This time with my brothers' leadership, the business was again reinvented and survived mainly through diversification into secondary processing of alternate species.

Dad never questioned whether his boys could carry on the legacy of the family business, although he never seriously considered that either of his daughters would follow in his footsteps. Perhaps he thought we were not interested, but I believe he thought after we girls married and had children, we would not have the time or focused attention required to run the business. Thankfully times and these perspectives have changed! (I'm delighted that now my niece is the CEO of our fourth-generation business.)

Our parents believed, though, that we should each branch out beyond Winterton. They had each felt pressure from their fathers that had determined their careers and were resolved they did not want to limit our choices in any way. This in part represents why my sister and I are who we are today: both educators who love to travel. We listened to conversations at home and with the many visitors and guests my parents hosted (missionaries and clergy, businessmen, exchange students, relatives) and we were always interested in life beyond Newfoundland.

Although my sister and I grew up in a middle-class community with traditional understandings and expectations regarding gender roles, we were privileged to live the kind of lifestyle that enabled us to consider any career path. In both subtle and blatant ways, intellect was respected by our parents. Reading material—books, local newspapers, and magazines—were always abundant in our home. Among my relatives, one greatly admired was a university professor cousin who had published several scholarly papers and books (documenting and critiquing the history of India). Another relative, an uncle who had grown up in our little town, served as president of Queen's Theological College in Ontario, Canada, was nominated for the position Moderator of the United Church of Canada, and also published scholarly writings (about the life and teaching of the Apostle Paul). These two individuals were highly regarded, and their accomplishments proudly acknowledged and celebrated.

Mom often told stories of her school days and how she wished the circumstances had been different for her. Although both my parents were bright and capable, neither of them attended a university, even though they might have liked to. (The only university for our province, Memorial University, was not established until 1961 with an enrolment of 1,400 students. Now it has more than 15,000 undergraduate students enrolled with an additional 2,600 in various graduate and postgraduate programs.)

Mom had not had the opportunity to work outside our home for an income after she married, but she certainly communicated the expectation that my sister and I would. We grew up having as much in common with our male friends as we did our females friends, who were more traditionally socialized. We were constantly encouraged and supported to follow our dreams and desires. Our parents had great faith in us (notice the religious reference; see Chapter 3 for a discussion of the Christian denominational education system that permeated life in Newfoundland and Labrador). We were constantly assured "you can do it"; the result for me, as well as my three siblings, was that we have been fortunate to study, work, and travel extensively throughout our adult lives.

We had several strong, independent women in our family. Aunt Mary (Green) Guzzwell was certainly one. She stood at barely five feet tall but what she was missing in physical stature she more than made up for in personal fortitude and courage. After high school, she travelled to Montreal (then in a foreign country) to study nursing. Upon her return after completion of her studies she was issued a nursing contract with the Department of Health and Welfare along with an annual salary of $900.00. For years, she provided medical care, travelling by boat and dog team into remote coastal communities around northern Newfoundland and Labrador to care for the sick, deliver babies, and pull teeth. From 1944 to 1947 Aunt Mary served as the Superintendent of Nursing and helped to establish cottage hospitals throughout the country of Newfoundland and oversaw the nursing ongoing in them.

As a child I was awed by her story about the little girl who tripped and fell among a dog team that almost ripped her scalp from her head before she was rescued. Aunt Mary met the child with her family at the dock, took her aboard the ship, stitched her scalp back into place, and had the girl stay with her in her quarters for a week (to ensure infection did not develop) before returning her to her family on the ship's next visit to the port. Aunt Mary also described other serious medical emergencies, storms at sea, meagre medical supplies, and deplorable living conditions. After I became the sole female administrator working in a male-dominated environment, I came to more fully appreciate and respect Aunt Mary's caring, confidence, and competence.

From an early age, my siblings and I were taught the virtues of hard work and spent our summer vacations from school working either in the family's general store or fish plant. Our parents believed it was better for us to spend our summers stocking shelves, packing groceries, or filleting fish than swimming or riding bicycles as most other kids our age did. I'm proud to say I have worked for pay since I was 13 and was also expected to do volunteer community work from an early age. My sister and I canvassed our hometown annually to collect donations for the Cancer Society and the

Heart and Stroke Foundation (a couple of the charities our parents worked for as volunteers). By the time I was 15 and my sister 10, we were then also assuming many of the typically female domestic duties of cleaning, gardening, and caring for sick relatives.

Perhaps because of my father's role as the unofficial undertaker in our town, as a child I was fascinated by all that accompanied death: the flowers, the smells, the black clothing, closed window shades, the mourning, and all the other religious rituals and rites. My parents always spoke openly and candidly about their perspectives on death, so I grew accustomed to accepting death as part of a continuous cycle. Yet when the predictable and expected deaths of each of my parents actually happened (I was an adult with children of my own), I felt unprepared for the depth of the loss I felt. Although I had had the opportunity to discuss with each of them everything that mattered to us, still their departures from my life left significant voids. Now I focus on the linkages with my remaining family and friends and expend energy conducting research that matters to me and is consistent with the values my parents instilled in me. Throughout my formative years, I had limited exposure to multiculturalism as ours was a unilingual, white, Christian Canadian society. There was religious prejudice but I never witnessed blatant racism. As a matter of fact, visitors or residents in Winterton who had colored skin were assumed to be intelligent (likely doctors, businessmen, or university professors) and intriguing because they came from a different and more exciting part of the world.

Despite an inclusive environment at home, our communities in the 60s were not exactly open, respectful, tolerant, or appreciative of diverse approaches to life and living, particularly as they related to religious beliefs and practices. Communities in Newfoundland and Labrador were either predominantly Protestant or Roman Catholic; ours was Protestant with only a few Catholic adherents living there because they had married into community families. It was quietly conveyed that if Catholic and Protestant followers married it would only complicate life and cause unnecessary stresses and strain.

School, Not Always a Caring Place

For the residents living in my hometown in the late 60s, there were three schools for a population just over 800, one for each of the three dominant Christian faiths in the town: United, Anglican, and Salvation Army. This arrangement changed when I was in Grade 4 and when the Protestant churches throughout the province agreed to integrate their school populations rather than operate separate systems. (Roman Catholic and Pentecostal schools throughout the province remained separate.)

Using her old box camera, Mom took a picture of me in the front yard on my first day of school. I was full of hope and positive thinking, obedient, and proud that I was old enough, finally, to go to school. I looked forward to all the possibilities it would bring. As a child I learned about social structures without needing too much direct instruction. I could see the stratification for myself and others, the differences between the "haves and the have-nots." In preparation for school our parents bought us new clothing and shoes. Clothes were a recognized status symbol. Women distinguished themselves on Sunday by wearing their finest hats and coats, businessmen wore shirts and ties; the fishermen and tradespeople generally wore much more casual attire. Similar differences were evident among the children at school.

School inspectors from the school board visited occasionally and walked up and down the rows of our classroom. We were instructed to stand immediately and erectly beside our desks whenever an inspector entered the room and be prepared to answer any questions if asked. Our desks and belongings were to be kept in an orderly fashion and the inspector sometimes asked us to show him (they were always male) our fingernails as an indication of our personal hygiene. We were taught to respect authority, cleanliness was next to godliness, do what we were told, conform to expectations, and follow rules.

Although I did not experience academic problems in school, I was seldom thrilled by the learning experiences afforded me. I recall rote learning of spelling lists, poetry, and recitations. Some of the greatest learning for me actually happened outside the school, often during summer vacation when my cousin visited and we created concerts with other friends to perform for kind elderly ladies who were family friends. Berry picking with Mom was another pleasant and memorable learning experience. She loved being close to nature and being "in the woods." We replanted trees from the woods to our yard, she shared her awe of the moon and stars, taught me about wind directions, the difference between coniferous and deciduous trees, and we discussed weather patterns. There were rich opportunities for real-life, hands-on learning. I experienced it, not merely through talking or reading about it. Math did not become relevant for me until I started working at age 12 in Dad's store and I learned to add weekly grocery lists; total monthly accounts per household; weigh, price, and package cheese, potatoes, and nails; cut fabrics; and help during stock taking. I developed interpersonal skill, a social conscience, and responsibility through volunteer activities, including collecting for charities, helping the less fortunate, sponsoring foster children, supporting our church's mission and service fund, and participating in youth groups. Our parents appreciated the fine arts and had us take music lessons in the hope we would learn to play the piano. Occasionally we travelled within the province, even sometimes beyond, so our out-of-school geography lessons started with learning about our own immediate world and branched out from there. We ran, walked, or bicycled everywhere and played rudimentary ball games, hopscotch, and kick-the-rock. Our lifestyle was by necessity active and healthy.

A highlight during the school year was preparing for our Christmas concerts. Our teachers put great effort into helping us memorize lines, and we rehearsed for hours. School concerts were major events for the town as well as for all of us who participated. I remember the feeling of excitement and anticipation, as prior to our opening Christmas carol we nervously peeked through the stage curtain to view what appeared to be a sea of appreciative faces. There was much anticipation of Santa's arrival after the final performance. Every school child's name was publicly announced. It is amazing to me now to recall the pride, patience, and attention our audience had as they watched each and every child come to receive a gift. Indeed our entire village was raising its children and each adult felt it their business and responsibility to "keep an eye out" for us. We felt cared about by everyone in our community and dared not be seen doing anything we should not do. We knew our parents would be told of any misdeeds, and punishment was sure to follow. Misbehavior was not tolerated in our community at large any more than it was at home or at school.

Not all my memories of grade school are pleasant. I remember my Grade 5 teacher did not smile much. She was very strict and serious. I was impressed though and fascinated that despite having deformed fingers, her penmanship (a much admired skill in those days) was beautiful. She perfectly formed each word as she wrote notes on the chalkboard. Unfortunately for some of the boys, she did not have any more difficulty holding the big leather strap than she did her chalk. She demanded that we do our work and do it well. Even though I think she liked me, I remember feeling I had better "be good" or else I would hear the loud clap of that leather strap on my desk, or worse, feel it slap across my hands as some misbehaving classmates had!

In school, then as now, children learned about the real world and did experience difference. Some of these experiences at an early age gave me understanding and empathy for diversity, a term I did not know or use back then. Students with challenging needs did not usually attend school. They were either sent away to an institution or kept at home. Students with developmental delays were ridiculed, bullied, humiliated, not only by other students but by some teachers as well. Teachers then did not understand speaking out and were intolerant of and impatient with students who misunderstood what was taught. Cyberbullying did not exist, and the bullying that occurred then was different from now, but it was still hurtful. Being called "sissy," "stupid," "fatty," or "ugly" were seriously damaging words to a fragile self-esteem.

Harold was a short sixth grader who because of his appearance and nasal voice was constantly taunted by his classmates and even made the brunt of some mean-spirited teacher jokes. Harold was slower than the rest of us to learn most things. He wore thick black-rimmed glasses and walked with a unique gait. Back then the guys' haircuts were usually short, which did nothing to hide Harold's unusually large ears that protruded prominently from his head. Students, and even our homeroom teacher, often flicked Harold's ears as they walked past him in his row. Despite being ridiculed, laughed at, and humiliated he was most often pleasant and had managed to keep a good sense of humor. Harold had a kindness and gentleness about him, which instead of being valued made him an easy target for bullies. I remember feeling terrible for him and wondered how I could intervene. My mother told me I should tell the teacher about what I saw happening. But when I added that the teacher was as guilty as some of my classmates, I remember my mother said, "Well Mary, make sure you are kind to Harold, kids can be very cruel sometimes—*people* can be so cruel!" Harold began to miss more and more days at school and when the time came for us to take a bus to the high school, he was not with us. I never saw Harold again but often thought about him.

It is still shocking to me how children viewed as "different" are treated as "less than" by so many in our society. Months after writing these recollections of Harold, I discovered through a friend on Facebook that at age 56 he passed away. It certainly had not been easy for Harold or for his elderly parents who raised him. It is interesting how memories, people, and situations in life converge at unique moments to give pause, elicit reflection, and offer learning.

At the end of my eight years of schooling in Winterton, I was ready for the transition to travel 20 kilometres by bus to attend the regional high school in Heart's Content. There I began to take on leadership roles. I was never brilliant but I was among the top students in my classes. I thrived in some executive positions with a variety of clubs (Yearbook, Red Cross Youth, Reach for the Top, Public Speaking) and was a member of most of the school athletic teams. Those were the days when you did not need to have exceptional ability to make the team. There were so few of us in the school that if you expressed interest, then you could participate. I enjoyed the healthy competition and physical activity. Winning was fun but there was no humiliation in defeat. These were not exactly high-stakes competitions, but they certainly were friendly, social, and inclusive. I loved travelling to other schools, meeting new people, competing, seeing the differences and commonalities among us, and it helped me to develop self-confidence. I began to realize that my parents might be right: maybe I could become anything I wanted to be.

We built strong friendships, our teachers knew every student in the school by name, and although our facilities and curriculum were basic (less than basic in some areas), it was not until later that I realized how "good" our school was. We enjoyed and benefited from strong community support, plenty of opportunities to lead as well as follow, and much encouragement and caring.

These childhood memories of my family life and schooling had considerable impact on me. My parents taught me that I was not better than anyone else, but they also taught that I was as good as anyone else. All people were deserving of respect. I learned that I should always behave, do what I'm told, follow rules, be kind, caring, share, and "do unto others what I would have them do unto me" (*The Good News Bible*, 1976, Matthew 7:12). My parents constantly made me aware of my privilege (they often described it as being "blessed"). Because I was fortunate to be able to learn, I was given much more than basic necessities: I knew right from wrong, I was expected to be responsible, to make wise decisions, take care of myself, and take care of others.

I have come to realize that we become more or less smart depending on our teachers' vision of us, that we learn better when teachers are passionate about their subjects and expect us to be as well. Unfortunately, some teachers want to be right more than they want to teach students to do well. Teachers, and I would venture to say most students, know the level of competency of the teachers who surround them, but parents may not know who the best and worst teachers are. Students learn best when teachers are nonthreatening and demonstrate empathy and care. I and others are most comfortable and able to learn in less competitive, less high-pressured environments. Certainly, we need more caring male and female role models in schools.

Learning From Mistakes

In 1975 I left the shelter and comfort of my home, family, and high school to attend Memorial University and in short order was forced to deal with a harsh reality check. In my first term, I was truly humbled by my first failure, in a foundation chemistry course. I was humiliated and demoralized. My idealistic dream to save the world by discovering the cure for cancer was dashed over the weeks of that torturous class with an arrogant professor who seemed to feel no connection with me and who I believed did not care whether I failed or succeeded. I became overwhelmed, intimidated, and detached. Now I can actually thank him, for without him I may not have known the experience of failing in school. I eventually settled into a Bachelor of Education program, believing I could improve the world by influencing the lives of young people through a career in that field. Still, that experience of failure has remained with me; I believe it taught me how *not* to treat my students. It also taught me the importance of being empathetic and caring and teaching empathy. I'm convinced that without it one cannot be a good teacher. So I am thankful for the hard lesson I learned. The experience made it possible for me to relate to what it is like to feel all the frustration that goes along with not being able to do what the teacher expects.

Once I found my bearings, I managed to learn a lot while attending Memorial, but the work required of me in my first year, as a "frosh," often left me feeling panic-stricken. What was I, a young girl from a small rural fishing village, doing in the same classes as the "townies" from St. John's and international students from even more mysterious and exciting places? I realized how sheltered I had been and sensed I must have had a false sense of myself. Fortunately, my social skills worked for me and I drew strength from the friendships I was forging through my co-ed residence life. I weathered that first year of university with my worst ever academic record, a 58% average over 10 courses. Thankfully my parents did not give me a hard time about my less than stellar grades. They loved me, praised me, and continued to believe I could handle anything that came my way. They trusted me to be responsible and find my way forward. The world had opened up to me. I learned to love university life and was smart enough to realize I had to pass the courses if I was going to be able to continue to enjoy the environment and my new-found freedom. I stretched my wings and felt excited to be able to think and choose for myself.

Memorial University, although only a two-hour drive from home, seemed to be a totally different world, and I seized many opportunities to develop and grow. I played on most of the intramural sports teams, organized charity events, and "danced up a storm." I learned I was strong and that I could indeed balance my social life along with my academic pursuits. I must admit, though, that often it was consideration of what my mother would think of me (if she knew where I was and what I might be doing) that really kept me out of trouble! I never wanted to disappoint my parents. To my own credit I did manage to complete three degrees at Memorial that laid the groundwork for my career in education and for doctoral studies, which I completed in 2008 through the University of South Australia.

Early Career Insights

I cannot recall how many times during the early years of my career I heard pronouncements about the importance of establishing control and asserting that I was the boss in my classroom. It was what my own teachers had modeled, what I was taught in my education program at university, and the way I started out in my career. I was, after all, only 21 years old and had only slightly younger 16- and 17-year-olds in my classes. (In my first year teaching, one of my students was actually six months older than me!) Gradually, I learned to assert myself without having to be confrontational; I discovered that in all my dealings with young people it was essential to be flexible and open to change. Even after hours of lesson planning, it was often more effective to seize an unplanned and spontaneous "teachable moment" to explore a tangent, or sometimes even abandon altogether my original plan. I became comfortable with and open to surprise and after a few bumpy encounters with students who wanted more to test my patience than to learn, I relaxed and came to enjoy the privilege of being able to learn with and from my mostly happy and energetic teenage students. I worked to establish mutual respect among us through collaborative learning projects and emphasized all things positive to build confidence, rapport, and trust so that we could take on some difficult and personally challenging learning outcomes. I was fortunate to work with a range of student and colleague personalities. With some, I was challenged to discover what might motivate them, and with others I experienced pure joy as together we made new discoveries. Many made quite an impact on my life, and I will never forget them.

I taught David throughout his high school years; his story illustrates our need to be more caring, and how despite good effort and intent, we never really get to know what is on some students' minds or comprehend how complicated their lives may be. He was a tall, slim, outgoing student who was almost always energetic, often silly, and sometimes his behavior was borderline inappropriate. David would sneak up behind me as I walked down the school corridor during lunchtime supervision, suddenly grab my waist or put his arm around my neck and say, "How's she goin' t'day Miss?" He really meant no harm but each time it happened I explained how his behavior made me feel uncomfortable, was inappropriate, and that I wanted him to stop. He would laugh it off and say, "Oh Miss, you need to relax."

It took effort and patience, but David could be reasoned with most of the time. He was certainly bright, capable, and loved to participate in classroom discussions, but he was never motivated to do his best or to achieve his full potential. Where David shone the greatest was in Drama Club. Another teacher and I were the directors, and David excelled at putting his heart and soul into whatever character he was assigned. He took every role seriously and was never shy, self-conscious, or inhibited as many other students were. He comfortably displayed the full range of emotions expected in the various roles; actually, the stranger the characters, the darker the personalities and more eccentric they were, the better for David. I believed then and still do that he struggled to find "his place" in school, to feel comfortable with himself and who he was.

He seemed unlike other teenagers who we knew struggled with any number of identity issues; he certainly was unique. Back in the early 80s, there were aspects of students' lives that teachers often missed, personal struggles that were not addressed. Many of us felt something was "off" with David, but we could not put our finger on it. He certainly would never be considered a discipline problem. He attended class, completed his work, and participated in extracurricular activities; however, there were many times when we did not know whether we should get angry or laugh along with him. Around the school and during classes, he was constantly a joker. I think it fair to say that as a staff we viewed him as immature and silly and believed that in due time he would settle down and find his niche in life.

After David had graduated from high school and gone on to university, we were shocked to learn that he had died. There were mysterious details about what had happened. The events surrounding his death were very confusing and troubling. All who knew him, including his teachers, had many questions—it was a terrible tragedy! What had happened? Should we as his teachers have seen potential trouble? I often ask myself if we failed him. I had known David his entire life. He lived and grew up with his parents and siblings in the same small community that I did. I had also taught some of his older siblings. I felt I knew David well, but did I really know him? His death was a reminder of the complexity and fragility of youth and it made me realize that as teachers we often see through our own eyes instead of through our students' eyes.

Throughout my teaching career, I have been privileged to know and work with many amazing people. This next story about a great teacher I know underscores the importance to teach and model a balance of independence and interdependence and that the essence of teaching is about making connections and building caring relationships.

Sarah was a young, eager student of mine who enthusiastically used education as a stepping stone to achieve success in life. She was hard working, committed, reliable, and ever pleasant. I believe there was not a single teacher who did not enjoy having Sarah as a student. But her childhood had its challenges. She was one of several children born to her parents. There was much love and encouragement at home, but her family had only the bare essentials when it came to material resources.

What set Sarah apart was not simply that she was a bright, pleasant kid or that she would later graduate from university despite financial hardship. What made Sarah special is that she went on to a career as a teacher and became a wonderful role model for her students and colleagues. I taught Sarah both as a high school student and again as a graduate student. Later, she taught my son. I know Sarah has remained in contact with him and his group of friends throughout their university years. I felt pride and respect for Sarah when I saw her congratulatory comment posted on my son's Facebook page on the occasion of his university graduation.

Sarah has always been a "real" person and done a multitude of kindnesses for others who struggle with one thing or another. Sadly, while still teaching, Sarah was stricken with illness and continues her uphill battle. Throughout it all she remains ever-positive and upbeat; she blogs to chronicle her experiences and keep her connection with her huge circle of supporters, including former classmates, students, and colleagues, as well as family and friends. Now hundreds of people pour love and concern on Sarah and try to return to her some of the care, compassion, and strength she gives to others. I wish there were thousands of Sarah's in our world! Of all the teachers (friends and colleagues) I know and have taught, I rank Sarah high on my list of who I would choose to teach my children.

Another important source of motivation and learning for me was the women's movement. It made me aware of some constraining norms that directed my life. Reading feminist literature about housework, parenting, equality, and balancing the personal with the professional were significant and empowering. It helped me through a process of rethinking who I was and who I could be. I had married a man who believed in me but held some restricting assumptions about gender, work, and study that were common in our generation. I am thankful that he encouraged my pursuit of a Master's degree. After almost 10 years of teaching high school students, I wanted to know what new strategies were being explored, what fresh approaches I could bring to my students. I do not think I was as aware back then as I am now of the reasons why study mattered so much to me. It satisfied my personal curiosities and helped me to search for and find women who had been able to do things I wanted to do. I felt restless at that time, some things were distressing me, and I needed both the structure and the freedom that the Master's degree afforded me.

Graduate studies enabled me to rethink most aspects of my life. In particular, the relationships I forged at that time provided welcome opportunity to expand my mind, to travel and study in England, and to strengthen my confidence. I felt rejuvenated and awakened to exciting possibilities I had been missing. I had always thought being a wife and mother would be the centre of my life but discovered there was more I could be and do. I started my career in a profession predominated by women except in key leadership roles, but I had come to comprehend so many reasons why that imbalance needed to change.

Transitioning Into Other Leadership Roles

After 10 mostly content years teaching high school students and completing a Master of Education, an opportunity arose to work at the district office as a language arts coordinator for Kindergarten to Grade 12 programs. Apparently my efforts were recognized and I was asked to apply and interview for the position. I welcomed the opportunity and felt ready and motivated to take on a new challenge. I was on maternity leave from my teaching position at the time, had just applied and was interviewed for the vice-principalship at our school. With two young children and because I did not consider myself capable, the program coordinator position was not one for which I would have applied. It required a one-hour commute each way and included evening meetings most weeks. Thankfully, a district administrator encouraged me.

> My professional life, like that of many other women, has not been the result of linear projection and orderly plan. Rather it has been the result of various accidents and an awareness of opportunity. Between awareness and actualization, of course, there also has been discipline, hard work, and lots of other external and internal factors. (Noddings, 1997, p. 166)

A newcomer as a curriculum consultant, I was fortunate in many ways to have a superintendent who helped orient me, but he also tested my commitment and my ability. I noted first-hand how hard women had to work to prove themselves in leadership positions to be taken seriously, and men were automatically credited with authority once they took up new positions. I felt overwhelmed at times, invigorated at others. I accommodated new practices and priorities expected of my "boss," the institution, and my position, while I also sought to maintain valued relationships and ways of working that were consistent with my principles.

Gradually, I learned to do what I thought was best; I tried to be myself and sought opportunities within my work to advance agendas important to me. I managed to build dynamic relationships among our program staff, and collaboratively we planned and implemented meaningful professional development programs for the teachers throughout the district. I chaired meetings, had control of agendas but included input from others, used consensus decision making, and built understanding, ownership, and support for each other's work. We were an effective team working from the premise that we must give teachers respect and freedom to be professionally responsible rather than hold them accountable through evaluation, standardized curriculum, testing, and rigid regulations.

Within two years, I absorbed a great deal and was again successful in my application for the position of assistant superintendent. It was during my tenure as a district administrator with the school board in 1990 that a Royal Commission on Education was appointed by the Government of Newfoundland and Labrador (see Chapter 3 for explanation of the provincial policy direction for education reform). My colleagues and I saw much potential for improvement to our education system and were hopeful as to what the Commission would report. I did not realize it then, but I was gaining important experience that I would bring to subsequent positions.

A Gender Equity Committee, the first for school boards in our province, was initiated by my (male) superintendent who had me establish it and direct its projects. I worked with trustees, principals, teachers, and students and was trusted to do work that I felt was important and necessary. It provided me a relatively safe first step into a political arena that validated and strengthened my feminist perspectives.

Later involvement in my first arbitration case gave me more valuable experience and insight. The superintendent had disciplined one of our principals for sexual harassment of two female teachers, and it became our personal as well as professional mission to see that justice prevailed. Through the process I learned to manage my emotions, think quickly, speak clearly, avoid speculation, and carefully document everything.

Evolving Leadership in Gendered Contexts

When I started working as a district administrator in a formal leadership position, "managerialism" (Blackmore & Sachs, 2007; Franzway, 2005) was the dominant paradigm rather than a culture of shared decision making and democracy. Authority came with position and as assistant superintendent my duties and responsibilities included the organization and delivery of a professional development program for teachers employed by the school board; determination and supervision of the curriculum initiatives undertaken by district office personnel; development and monitoring of budgets related to curriculum and instruction; deployment of regular teaching units to schools; and the implementation of changes directed by the Department of Education. I also coordinated the facilitation and delivery of Regional Student Support Services shared among four school boards. These services included educational psychology, itinerant services for students with visual and hearing impairments, as well as guidance and instructional resource supports.

At the time, provincial and local consultation sessions and numerous meetings among educators were occurring throughout the Royal Commission on Education's information gathering stage. Most of us working in the district offices experienced mixed emotions. I recall feeling optimistic and eager to learn what the actual changes to the system would involve. I and most of my colleagues supported education reform; we had developed collaborative ways of working across our denominational lines and agreed that significant improvements were possible, change was necessary. We were excited by the potential to shake up the system, but at the same time, we lived through agonizingly long months of job insecurity and concerns about how the system, which we had given our careers to work in, might be dismantled and reconfigured.

On March 31, 1992, the Commission submitted its report to Government. The report outlined 212 recommendations for monumental change, including discussion of a new nondenominational model for education in the province (Williams et al., 1992) (see Chapter 3). In my early years as a district administrator, I was easily swayed by the opinions and suggestions of my "superiors." My bosses were all male, and I tended to respond well to their coaching to be strong, unapologetic, directive, and decisive. At first I did not resist. I do not think I was mindless, but I was young and not reflective enough; I focused on completing the work that was expected of me. This changed as I read more and gained more experience.

There was an occasion I thought the superintendent crossed the line, when during one of our meetings he made personally demeaning and derogatory comments about one of the principals. He spoke negatively about a colleague who was not present to defend himself. I and the three other assistant superintendents remained quiet. What a dilemma: I felt I was a part of it because I allowed it, felt silenced but wanted to speak out as I believed a person's character was being slandered; should I speak up and risk the superintendent's wrath or punishment, get frozen out and then be unable to influence the outcome, or keep quiet, allowing the wrong to continue.

Some women who understood the challenges I was facing expressed thoughts to me such as, "I don't know how you do it," which caused me to pause and ponder: they did not want to work in positions like mine. Some women were deterred from principalships or other senior district positions for a variety of reasons, two being because they did not want to make the personal sacrifice of time away from family, or they did not aspire to the increased visibility, accountability, and pressure. With restructuring, redistribution of jobs meant a loss of power for many. I recall thinking that some needed to lose it and others needed to gain it. There were aspects of managerial power I was uncomfortable with, which restrained and constrained me, although I often enjoyed using the power of my position as an assistant superintendent (and later as a member of the Royal Commission Implementation Secretariat) because I was able to give voice to teams, networks, and other important collaborations.

Through reflection and reflexivity, I was learning much about myself and others, making mistakes and experiencing successes. There were times I felt powerful and others times powerless. I think I often appeared to be in control but I did not feel that way. I was my own toughest critic, constantly reassessing myself and my performance as I tried to figure out how to work strategically and ethically. I was beginning to get the sense that I was under constant surveillance, as a woman and an administrator. I often suffered from the " impostor syndrome" (Jeong, 2011; Wells, 1999) and felt unsuited for the job. The persistent battling and confronting made me feel awful. I tried to stay upbeat and pleasant, positive that my work had meaning and value, but deep within I believed there were more effective ways of working and being a leader that were not valued, much less implemented.

I welcomed any opportunity to network with other women in similar positions across the province to share experiences, find support and encouragement, and ultimately feel secure. I joined an ad hoc group of women educators from which we each gained important personal insights. Whenever there were provincial meetings, we found ways to meet. While the men did their thing, we did ours; we would rather find our own ways to get together, build in important leisure and networking opportunities, whether it was over a coffee break or the occasional bottle of wine. At first the men were ambivalent about our get-togethers, but within two years they had become intrigued. Some male colleagues even expressed interest in being included in our outings and conversations as a refreshing alternative. I found it inspirational and affirming to have these rare conversations with women who I believed to be pioneers in our province. We soaked up our invaluable conversations and one another's advice about political situations, ways to advocate for ourselves and build support, what to avoid, and the "games" people play. I respected their years of experience and understanding of conservativism and progressivism. They encouraged me to read the pulse of different situations we faced. As we shared our issues and concerns, it felt good to be trusted and treated professionally rather than judged. I listened with care and brought our wisdom to the issues, which gave me confidence to express myself. Spending time with that group of professional women helped me problem solve and encouraged my intellect. With genuine support from this group of colleagues, I came to trust my emotions and intuition, a validating feeling!

In 1996 I was seconded from my position as assistant superintendent in the district to work as Curriculum Projects Coordinator with the Royal Commission Implementation Secretariat at the provincial Department of Education. My responsibilities included the creation and coordination of seven provincial working groups to devise and implement curriculum plans related to Royal Commission recommendations. I developed and tracked budgets and timelines, liaised with all department divisions, organized symposia for the professional staff, and met with groups of educators and parents throughout the province to discuss reform initiatives.

When the term of my secondment was coming to a close, I returned to my position as assistant superintendent. On September 3, 1996, I received correspondence informing me that my position had been declared redundant. I was being re-stepped to a program specialist with the transition board, appointed in the interim, until the new consolidated board could become operational. (About this time all district administrators throughout the province received a similar letter declaring them redundant.) In my role as program specialist, I oversaw the professional development programs, developed and implemented curriculum, assessed teacher performance, and organized various working groups.

Jumping Into Turbulence

On November 1, 1996, the new district commenced operation. I was hired as one of four district administrators and accountable for the development, implementation, supervision, and evaluation of program matters from preschool through senior high school, including student support services, student evaluation, local courses, formal testing, teacher evaluation, and professional development. The program division at district office consisted of an administrative assistant, six program specialists, a partnership coordinator, four educational psychologists, two itinerant teachers for the visually impaired, two itinerant teachers for the hearing impaired, four speech-language pathologists, and one occupational therapist. Together we worked with 80 school administrators and 756 teachers in 60 schools (10,966 students).

I was actually ecstatic in 1996–1997 when the denominational school boards were consolidated to become nondenominational. I looked forward to greater efficiencies, elimination of duplication and of segregation, and less religious prejudice—more opportunity and inevitable benefits from the diverse perspectives—change was going to be good. I had experienced years of frustration under the old system; now we would get some previously "undiscussables" on the table. A significant shakeup was needed, not just tinkering at the fringes of the system. Unfortunately, my optimism would turn to disillusion and my enthusiasm to silence. Too much happened too fast.

I found myself making too many personal sacrifices and was constantly having to prove my worth. I was disgruntled that the new director seemed to have his favorites who were prepared to carry out his directives without question. Two unofficial groups developed within the office that made people compete for our limited resources. The environment shifted to little trust, collaboration, or caring. I expected my district and provincial positions would afford me freedom and flexibility; I found some of that, although I learned I also had to be politically correct and constrained. The message was subtle but clear: I had to act in certain ways, and I found myself working in the turbulence of power and politics.

My actions contradicted my values, and I felt conflicted when I experienced inequity and discrimination. I grew increasingly troubled and resistant to top-down directives that affected me but had not involved or even sought my input. What I wanted was to foster more collaborative and participatory forms of leadership and decision making. My mother's words resonated in my head, "Have the courage to stand up for your convictions," as did Rudyard Kipling's advice to his son from his familiar poem "If." How ironic that I was a woman in a male position, being coached by men to act like men, and even my own mother's words seemed to reinforce acting more like men. I had to find my own way through. "We make progress by a constant spiraling back and forth between the inner world and the outer one, the personal and the political, the self and the circumstance" (Steinem, 1992, p. 8). I found there was little open dialogue; our strengths and weaknesses were not acknowledged, much less addressed. There was a focus on power and position I had never experienced. Through analysis of critical incidents that occurred at the time, I have illustrated the serious frustrations many of us working in education felt (see Chapter 5).

Traditionally, we see promotion as leading to more opportunity to delegate, more freedom and autonomy; unfortunately, in too many workplaces it also involves intensification of work, pressing deadlines, increased demands, practices that conflict with values, and feeling one must put work first, home life second, and self last. I remember when I spoke out of turn during a board meeting. I was supposed to speak only when called upon by the director. If he needed background or additional information related to an issue or program, he called upon me for elaboration. I well recall the reprimand I received after spontaneously jumping into the dialogue around the board room table. The discussion related to my immediate area of responsibility. I felt passionate about the subject and wanted to infuse some energy and tempo into what I thought was a dull and detached dialogue. Following the meeting, the director privately informed me that I was never to do that again. He said the board chairperson perceived it as an indication of the director's inability to control "his" assistants and that it made him look "bad." I acted on my first instinct and apologized. In hindsight I wish I had thought more quickly before speaking. I should have seized the opportunity to talk about how the meetings were more hierarchical and bureaucratic in nature than facilitative of genuine dialogue about what was important for education in the district. Sadly, even if I had been more assertive in my response to stand up for my convictions, I might have landed myself in even more trouble.

There were similar occasions when I attempted to discuss education priorities openly and forthrightly, and each time I was reminded that we (the director and assistant directors) were to provide direction, make decisions, but not engage in dialogue. If we did otherwise, we would be perceived as weak and unsure of the correct course of action, or we would risk allowing people to speak out of turn (out of line), thus control would be lost. We were always to understand and respect the lines of authority that had been established. I was to know my place and only speak when called upon.

Then came my initiation in the process of closing schools. I felt nervous. I knew difficult decisions needed to be made, and no matter how well considered and necessary, they would be unpopular. There would be ill feelings, and some people would be angry no matter what the result. I and the other two assistant directors each led a team with other district personnel to map out strategies and options. We discussed our values, what we wanted to protect, and what we could not do without. The political pressure was intense. I remember feeling stressed and having a heavy heart as we prepared to present our options in the public meetings (refer to critical incident in Chapter 5 for a fuller description of public meeting proceedings). The public sessions were to present the options and receive input from various community groups. All suggestions were entertained. It was a difficult time for me and for my family.

Prior to the chaos of the reform process, I knew I was making positive changes by the encouraging reactions and interactions I was having with staff, parents, other district employees, some board members, and colleagues throughout the province. However, the increased intensity of dealing with board consolidation meetings, navigating strike-related demands, weekly nighttime meetings after full workdays, part-time doctoral studies, and time away from my family all created a heavy burden. I was losing the balance between work and my personal life that I had always tried hard to preserve. Although I was capable, I felt weary and worn down. I believed there was another way to lead but I had no chance to apply it.

I had been a relatively successful insider, but I could only go so far. Most districts were not ready for female leaders as was evidenced through our limited acceptance with predominantly male school boards. Predominantly male boards hire personnel like themselves (Brunner, 1998, 2000a, 2000b). I had the credentials, knowledge, skills, and experience to do the job of superintendent: two bachelor's degrees, a Master of Education, and most work completed toward a Doctor of Education when I applied; over 20 years working in the district as a teacher, community leader, curriculum specialist, and assistant superintendent, plus other work experience at the Department of Education and with the Royal Commission Implementation Secretariat. "Successful women in high-stakes leadership, aware of the dangers of naming the barriers to women's progress, hesitated in doing so, despite significant evidence of the permanence and impermeability of the organizational 'glass ceilings' and the 'boys' clubs" (Blackmore & Sachs, 2007, p. 11). Most often, beliefs and dominant values in organizations and in images of leadership are defined as forms of masculinity.

Doctoral Pursuits and Revelations

A novice researcher but also an experienced professional, I gradually discovered the direction for my doctoral research as I struggled through the implementation of education reform in the school district. By 2000, I had seen many people hurt, discouraged, disillusioned, and disheartened through the course of school reform processes. It was that lack of a caring relation among people in work environments that inspired my research questions and inquiry.

Initially, I was humbled by the intellectual scholarship that surrounded me, and I wondered if I could be successful in that environment. I developed my own voice, and I believe I came a long way from where I started. Steinem hoped her readers would "look beyond the specifics of the situation to the heart of the experience, and thus take from stories told by people of a different gender, sexuality, or ethnicity what is universal and true" (Steinem, 1992, p. 9). "This process of self-reflection was a critical aspect of identifying oneself in relation to those involved in the teaching and learning of social justice" (Solomon, Singer, Campbell, Allen, & Portelli, 2011, p. 169).

Struggles in my job revealed that my instincts and responses in many situations were dissimilar from those of my colleagues. I became aware of differences in my priorities and approaches. Specifically, I found myself wanting to collaborate with others and involve them in the process of making decisions that affected them. Others worked more from an authoritative stance. Our notions of what constituted "good" leadership differed. Some believed that being an effective leader meant one was decisive and able to take prompt action to implement their decisions. On the contrary, I believed a leader sought input and involvement of others as much as possible, and worked to achieve a consensus that could be supported by the majority. In some management meetings, I found our differences in approach came to a head. When I wanted to collaborate with others and requested time to share information and consult, it was perceived as indecision on my part, a lack of strength, and ultimately an ineffective leadership style.

Doctoral work exposed me to *Pedagogy of the Oppressed* (1970) by Brazilian educator Paulo Freire and I gained new understanding of the relationship of power to knowledge, particularly between those who are privileged and those who are powerless (the oppressors and the oppressed). Freire advanced a theory and a method for becoming literate based on the process of *conscientization* (knowing with purpose, reflection, and action). In order to know, one needs to confront one's own concrete reality. This means being able to identify and give expression to one's daily life. Freire's thinking enabled me to realize the urgency for us in the district to change how we were working and treating people. Thanks to Freire, I began to look at my work in the district through critical eyes with a critical perspective. I experienced inequalities between the levels of our hierarchy and across its divisions. I witnessed the way we discriminated against and silenced particular voices. This drove home the fact that my research needed to be oriented to social action. Rather than do research to satisfy the requirements of academia, I wanted to write something that could be used by leaders in education to help bring about real change.

A Second Wave of Reform

In the period between November 1996 and August 2003, phenomenal changes took place throughout the district I worked in that affected every employee, school community, and family included under the jurisdiction of the board. There were layoffs, reassignments, resignations, school closures, changes in department and district leadership, strikes, public demonstrations, and on and on it went. Topping all of that, just as the dust was beginning to settle and people were establishing themselves in the new ways forward, the government announced a second wave of reform.

I was in the fortunate position then to be on educational leave. The director, school board, and government had awarded me a unique opportunity to continue, full-time, my doctoral studies that had I begun part-time in January 2000. Although I was able to remain at home to complete most of the work through distance learning, I remained close to the system when the second radical school board restructuring took place in 2004. This expedited reform lacked the planning and consultation of the first. There had been no Royal Commission of Inquiry; rather, the province had seized on the opportunity and ability to cut government deficit by a significant $6 million (Galway, 2011).

On a fateful day in 2003, I sighed deeply as I read the director's email with attached correspondence from the Ministry of Education officials. I had just received notice that the second school board consolidation would be taking place, and upon my planned return to work it would be my responsibility to follow directives. After all that had transpired during the first round of reform, I felt less than eager to take on another one requiring still more intensive energy and commitment to accomplish a job few would understand, much less appreciate. We had come through a complex process that merged different school boards and schools with diverse policies, philosophies, priorities, and practices. Colleagues were going to be upset again, just as a new sense of "normalcy" was developing.

I wondered how I might equip myself to manage more public consultation sessions with their accompanying outbursts that could potentially become violent. There would also be more spontaneous meetings that would take us well beyond the hours of a regular day. There would be upsets for students, union concerns, and endless lists of email questions that would require attention. I would be expected to continue to muster the enthusiasm to develop every imaginable school reconfiguration scenario that would be a probable plan to provide quality education in an assigned area of the district amidst people steeling themselves for another school board consolidation.

There were many philosophical debates about how we could possibly justify another radical school board reform. Staff as well as community members and parents were questioning how we could argue the reform was in the students' best interest. This was purely an economic rationalist agenda: government wanted to cut administrative costs in education (Galway, 2012). The mandate was nonnegotiable; how could that be fair to anyone? Our only input was in helping to determine where the cutbacks were to occur. Most people affected by the changes interpreted the directions to cut budget and tighten belts as ill conceived. Saving costs to equip and administer three school districts as opposed to 11, the plan pitched by government (see Chapter 3), was a move to trim back middle management. The public would support that notion because few actually understood district work. In fact many perceived our positions as expensive and unnecessary extras, consuming resources that could be better utilized in classrooms.

Districts had all taken a beating through budgetary restraints, increased standardized testing, and a loss of autonomy (and now they were accountable and reported directly to the Department of Education rather than to elected school boards). The dust had not settled and the wounds had not healed (Fagan, 2012). We agonized over our duty as educators to help and care for all students, but we also had to consider the drain of emotion, intellectual and physical energy, and the effect on our home lives. I had to ask myself if I should return or find an alternate life plan for myself.

The school board that granted me the educational leave to pursue my doctoral studies no longer existed. I wondered whether it would be unethical not to return to repay the new district for my much appreciated opportunity for professional growth. I considered what an ethic of care might be from a district point of view. Honestly, I felt little more than a pawn for the new order, a manager to carry out the government's agenda, certainly much less than a genuine educational leader. I would be kept busy "tinkering toward utopia" (Tyack & Cuban, 1995).

As a female middle manager I often felt alone and frustrated; I experienced a lack of horizontal collegiality and support. Along with others in administrative positions, I worried that I might soon be unemployed. I was trying to change from an old network, to fit in, communicate, and connect, but I felt I had few support networks left from the previous system to share experiences with.

Upon return, I would again have to compete with colleagues for a position, for funding, and for respect, while also relying on them for follow-through to act on their commitments. I felt it was "them" against me. Fracturing relations between divisions and among peer relations, for a woman in a male-dominated environment, were unpredictable. I had worked hard and had to become careful about promoting equity. We were all under closer scrutiny than ever before. We felt alienated.

I felt my very soul was in jeopardy; I wondered how to keep true to my values and work with others who also felt demoralized and devalued. I believed my ethics and morals would again be questioned. I would be challenged to use my team-building efforts to renew, find a way forward, consult, focus, and move toward a common sense of purpose. There was lots of double thinking and double speaking—allegiances were being undermined—and our relationships of trust and co-operation were redirected toward compliance to government mandates and directives from officials.

Oh, how Kipling's words resonated with me at this time!

> If you can keep your head when all about you
> Are losing theirs and blaming it on you,
> If you can trust yourself when all men doubt you,
> But make allowance for their doubting too;
> (www.kipling.org.uk/poems_if.htm)

That first radical reform process disrupted even the most experienced and confident educators along with almost every community in the province. This second school board consolidation was undertaken to help the government balance their budget and to make administrators more fiscally responsible and accountable to government rather than to elected school boards (Dibbon, 2012). This reform aimed to have minimal impact at the school and classroom level.

Strategies to Calm the Turbulence

During my studies, I was able to reflect on and critically analyze education across the province, specifically how those of us working in the system were experiencing the reforms and sensed a need for *strategies* to calm the turbulence of education reform. Opportunities to develop and foster a constructive sense of ourselves and positive self-esteem within our workplace were essential to providing a strong, professional basis from which to improve the school system. In response, I was well into writing *Caring Relations at Work: A Case Study of One School District* (Green, 2008) as the topic of my doctoral research, analyzing the data I had collected. I invested time to read extensively and think critically about how care and caring could be practiced in an organizational setting. I also became increasingly aware of how the changes in education in our province were being influenced and driven by global neoliberal policy trends as well as the local conditions in our province. Through three interconnecting research studies I examined the contradictory ways in which educators, including myself, managed our competing agendas and explored how care and its potential were experienced or not by leaders implementing education reform.

During my tenure as a senior district administrator, I had worked with three very different male superintendents/directors of education. Their personalities, strengths, weaknesses, and educational priorities certainly were dissimilar. However, there was one characteristic they shared: each in their different ways tried to teach me to respect line authority. One director in several district professional development sessions instructed assistant directors and principals as to the circumstances and manner in which it would be appropriate to challenge his views on educational matters. Unfortunately, even when the rules were followed and dissent was expressed, invariably he perceived it as insubordination, a lack of respect, or "troublemaking" (Blackmore, 1999), an attempt to usurp the power of his position. Each of the men I worked with as a superintendent or director (it is relevant to consider the implications of the root words *super* and *direct*) felt personally threatened and uncomfortable presenting anything other than that they knew what to do, what the appropriate next steps should be. They did not want to jeopardize a perception of them as strong leaders, in charge, and able to maintain control of their subordinates.

There was a pervasive social class hierarchy in the province, district, and schools: teachers were viewed as the working class and administrators deemed themselves of a higher socioeconomic class. To the contrary, I aimed to treat all with respect, believing that we worked in various capacities and that our diversity was beneficial and necessary. I began with the understanding that acknowledging and working with diverse people is fundamental to making any changes in the schooling system and beyond. In order to be more caring and socially just, a systemic focus on how we all (individuals and groups) worked together—the interrelationships among us, the dynamics between us, and how we affect the teaching and learning in the classroom—was needed. To achieve this focus, we would have to work together to create the best possible learning opportunities for students and teachers and use a nonreductionistic approach that was inconsistent with many of the policy directions current at the time.

To move forward, we needed time to think critically, to process the contradictions and conflicts experienced among individuals, groups, and communities. We had to learn with and from others, and grapple with incongruities of shifting frameworks and ambivalent or resistant perspectives. Building trust and positive caring work relationships were necessary so that together we could create a more progressive and socially just school system. We needed to learn about, question, participate in, and experience democratic principles in action through anti-oppressive teaching and learning tactics to modify the status quo in response to contextual needs of our communities, district, and province. These contextual needs were informed by key variables such as socioeconomic status, geography, culture, religious background, and demographics (refer to Chapter 3).

Working in various positions throughout the education system has taught me many things through experience; in particular, I learned by challenging my assumptions about work in education. When we accept the challenge to work in educational leadership positions we run up against and sometimes become a part of contradictory perspectives and practices that detract from, rather than contribute to, the attainment of equity. We must be prepared to challenge assumptions about what educational leaders can and cannot do to help promote and establish equity. Individuals who advocate for the disabled, promote diverse cultures, inclusive environments, and gender equity have made significant contributions; still, social justice crises happen (Ryan, 2006).

I have been reminded of the way others view and treat females in senior administrative positions. Becoming an academic has helped me to interrogate our assumptions and practices, and reflect critically on what it means to be a feminist who promotes equity in educational workplaces. In the senior administrator pool of Newfoundland and Labrador, females have been few and dominated by patriarchal, bureaucratic structures. Our critiques of the education system remind me forcefully that inclusion of women and treatment of them has not gone smoothly. I always thought I acted as a feminist who promoted practices supportive of equality, but now I reflect on my work in the school district and see it differently. We think we are equitable, inclusive, and supportive but in fact we have not been as progressive in those regards as we would like to think. Incredible challenges face the women and men—the individuals—who are attempting to make equity and inclusion the lived reality in our educational work lives.

It is critical that we know our history, stories, successes and failures, and discern lessons from them (Apple, 2010; Behar, 1996; Blackmore, 2006; Czarniawska, 1997; Solomon et al., 2011). I believed I organized my work and teaching to advance equality for women through recruitment, participation in professional development, volunteering, and activism. Although I sometimes regret having been silent when I should have spoken up and times when I should have acted on my instincts when I did not, I have settled my conscience that I did the best I knew how to do at the time; now that I know better, I can do better. I feel that through personal reflection and learning with the interest and support of colleagues, family, university supervisors, and friends, I have come to see emerging patterns in my life and found my voice. Now I see my career as an educator from the perspective of one who is caring.

Women in Educational Leadership

For the first 25 years of my career in education, I feel much of my work was done to support an organization that valued patriarchal perspectives, many of which were not sitting right with me. It was frustrating to watch male educators with less experience than me and other females get positions of interest to us. I was excluded from meetings, particularly those related to plant maintenance, facilities construction, and finances. I was reacting more than acting (often doing things I already knew how to do and often saying things I had said before). I found myself contradicting my personal values and "biting my tongue" when I really wanted to speak out (see Chapters 5 and 6).

The problem for women is that the current climate will not be conducive to improving on our underrepresentation in leadership positions (at high levels). Most well-educated young women no longer suffer the "true woman" syndrome. Instead they suffer the "true professional" syndrome. Many ask whether it is possible to have both a profession and a family life; often, highly successful women say it is not. What their perspective means is that it is not possible to plan a professional life in the single-minded, linear masculine tradition and still marry and raise children. Indeed, to admit longings for home and family raises suspicion about one's professional commitment. But who says that the traditional masculine way is the only path to professional success? And, for that matter, "why should success be defined in terms of money and percentile rankings? Life can turn into a dull and drab composition if it is planned with only competitive goals in mind" (Noddings, 1997, p. 172). It is not about women's lack of ambition or ability/capability, but rather the "consequence of the limited opportunities created by the systematically gendered, cultural, social, and structural arrangements that inform women educators' choices and possibilities relative to their male colleagues" (Blackmore & Sachs, 2007, pp. 12–13).

Women leaders are positioned within popular discourses about women's styles of leadership and women leaders being caring and sharing (Blackmore, 2006; Brunner, 2000a; Grogan, 2003). However, the actual capacity to undertake democratic practice is shaped by political, institutional, and cultural contexts that are more conducive to authoritarian leadership practices—perceptions and structures that work in inflexible ways for women (Blackmore & Sachs 2007). "Leadership practices that silenced oppositional voices, another affective and effective trap of the performative organization," (Blackmore & Sachs, 2007 p. 194) forced me to learn the skills of a chameleon—when to blend in, when to assert my differences so that I could fit what was required of me in various situations. I had to be strategic about when to be strong or gentle, soft-spoken and nurturing, or determined and unyielding. I had to moderate myself. I discovered "there was the entrepreneurial discourse in which winning the game at all costs was the key to success" (Blackmore & Sachs, 2007, p. 194) and found it difficult to assume this discourse unquestioningly because of the exposure to risks and costs.

The penetration of work into family life and private life had been significant. Leadership work during education reform is especially difficult to do if you are a parent. I always felt torn between the competing demands and emotions of work and home. I sought balance. My work was important and gave me a professional sense of identity but placed a far second in my life when stacked up to my familial responsibilities and relationships. I found it no wonder that "women in formal positions still tend to be single, divorced, or sole parents more than male managers" (Blackmore & Sachs, 2007, p. 135).

Throughout my childhood I was led to believe that I had power within me as well as what I witnessed outside of me, but I came to see that many of my friends had problems perceiving power as within them. I was well into my 30s when I began to comprehend my internal centre of power that I had been neglecting. Those *without power* tend to be much more aware of the machinations of power while those *with power* are often unaware that they have it (Delpit, 1995). I comprehend better now how power is back and forth—between self and others. "While recognizing this right to manage, and sometimes being prepared to wield this acquired authority, the preference of most women was to work through persuasion" (Blackmore & Sachs, 2007, p. 167). I have learned more about power and how to maintain and share it rather than use it through my position. Power is about creating change by working with and through others and questioning the status quo. I have also moved beyond choosing silence as a response and aim to provide thought, space, and opportunity for myself and others to challenge taken-for-granted assumptions.

I have challenged my own path and believe I have become more authentic in the challenge. Remembering incidents and people at particular times made me believe things happen for a reason and we can always learn if we are attentive and reflect on our surroundings, the people, and situations we encounter along life's way. In the brief aha moments of life, similar to my remembering Harold, I felt as if several aspects of my present life, past memories, and my future were all converging to reinforce the direction I am pursuing. First, I decided to leave the education system in

Newfoundland. It felt odd, as if I were walking out and giving up, but at the same time it was inspiring and rejuvenating. Now I'm living in the Annapolis Valley in Nova Scotia, Canada, and work in the School of Education at Acadia University. I enjoy a new collegial work culture, supervising undergraduate students who are practice teaching, and learning with graduate students in face-to-face and online courses. I also enjoy collaborative research. Now, in the academic world of a small but lively university, I can more freely converse with others to disagree, construct, recreate, relate, and "model learning rather than authority" (Peterson, 1997, p. 222).

Gradually, I have discovered that

> walking out is an act of bravery, one that requires companions, compassion, determination, and perseverance. Yet if we're brave enough to take that leap, we are richly rewarded. We walk out of confining ideas and places, remove the limits and barriers—and our world becomes wide open to possibilities. We feel creative again, sometimes outrageously so. It's intoxicating to feel this alive. And it's wonderful to discover we are not alone, that the world is filled with interesting, courageous Walk Outs. We have companions for the journey. (Wheatley & Frieze, 2011, p. 227)

"Reflection without a critical and theoretical stance that locates personal experience within wider relations of power, and how those relations of power produce particular leadership practices, does not 'transform'" (Blackmore & Sachs, 2007, p. 148). In my experience institutional and personal power is accommodated in some instances and resisted in others. "Relations of power are therefore simultaneous processes of resistance, reproduction, and transformation" (Blackmore & Sachs, 2007, p. 167) that "work against demoralizing institutional technologies by tactically taking up submerged and lesser discourses mobilizing other aspects of the 'nonunitary' self" (Thomson, 2001, p. 15). Women often feel like strangers in a familiar world dominated by men. Our gender leads to a range of cultural processes of assimilation, ghettoization, and positioning as the "other" (Brunner, 1999; Blackmore & Sachs, 2007). Although I disagreed with the dominant managerial discourses, I was "framed by them" (Blackmore & Sachs, 2007, p. 167). I was steeped in dominant, white, middle-class, neoliberal values and social mores.

The male-dominated culture of education administration often silenced my female views and perspectives, structured work conditions, and prevented me from speaking out. I felt silenced for years and couched things I needed to say in male terms: used logic, structure, rationality that squashed my emotionality. A man or woman who becomes a superintendent is shaped by the discourse of the superintendency—molded or subjectified by a discourse in the sense that we learn to make meaning of our own experiences according to the dominant values and beliefs expressed within the discourse. Discourses teach us what to do and how to do it. Foucault uses the term *discourse* to help us understand how we are positioned as subjects in different relationships with others (1980). "There are rules within a discourse concerning who can make statements and in what context, and these rules exclude some and include others" (Carib, 1992, p. 186). In education administration those with the voices and power to define practice are male. A woman superintendent may experience tension and stress as she tries to reconcile the discourses of educational administration with that of mothering because the two make very different demands on her (Grogan, 1996).

Now I think beyond obvious ways in which students, employees, and people are marginalized or diminished and about the subtle conditions that occur with little or no notice. I think about the insidious ways in which people are disregarded and become subservient to the dominant, mainstream culture, and the manner in which token inclusion serves more to exclude than to empower.

I have engaged in a critically reflective confrontation of myself that has been both exciting and upsetting. I have been reflexive about my personal perceptions, ideas, beliefs, values, experiences, and I comprehend how these have shaped who I am and what I bring to my work. They impact on how I perceive and interact with others. I have learned many valuable lessons: how to survive, that I was personally committed to public education, that it was crucial not to lose sight of what is important, and that there are many ways to settle differences. I believe that in order to repair the hurt done in turbulent organizations struggling to change, there must be focus on (re)establishing caring relations. I often sought the input of others in making decisions that affected them rather than making decisions unilaterally. I also experimented with conforming to rules but discovered that the rules I valued in my private life were also the way I tried to live in my professional life.

My core value is an inclusive rather than exclusive one that devalues competition and enhances the value of collaboration. Generally, I dislike confrontation and believe the pressure of competition and measuring achievement on test scores leaves much to be desired and deserves a much diminished focus in our classrooms. As respected philosopher and educator Nel Noddings explains:

> Today I have little interest in "professional" standards, teacher accreditation, and the host of stuffy, silly, and rigid regulations endorsed in the name of accountability.... To induce that sense of truly awesome responsibility in

teachers, we must give teachers respect and freedom and allow them to experience the joy that goes with the responsibility. (1992, p. 175)

We need to move toward interconnectedness and relationships, collective and collaborative effort, care, concern, respect, and shared decisions with more positive trusting attitudes from the top. People generally want to do well and they want their organizations to succeed. We need less blame, and more patience, persistence, and opportunities to express our thoughts and perspectives so that our differences no longer make any difference.

I have learned through "taking some knocks," experiencing disenchantments and disappointments, but also I have enjoyed numerous opportunities for growth. I expect my future work will continue to intersect with my personal life. Knowing that it requires time and reflection, I aim to build trust and relationship and believe it is well worth the investment.

Reflection

Through story (Clandinin & Connelly, 2000) I have acknowledged that my life has been privileged and has created paradoxes between my educational administration background and my understanding of the possibilities of "other ways of knowing"(Ball & Reay, 2000; Belenky, Clinchy, Goldberger, & Tarule, 1997). I now comprehend that I helped to perpetuate hegemonic ideas of structure and function, which have no doubt influenced my work in education both as a practitioner and as an academic. Paradoxically, the structure and function of educational institutions and organizations (such as universities and school districts) aim to support diversity and promote various ways of knowing, but they limit those same aspirations.

I have tried to illustrate how the personal, professional, and academic aspects of my life are connected. At some points I felt as if my personal life was being crushed under the weight of the professional, but I have worked hard to keep perspective, seek balance, and not allow my life to become fragmented. Now, as I approach the years comprising the final third of my life, I want to return my attention to where I started. I want to record the oral and written histories of my family members, their thoughts on how people can live and work together in peaceful and respectful ways. I plan to immerse myself in collaborative research projects that are consistent with my values and that help to advance humane approaches in workplaces; document the processes and practices of unequal education; argue for more humane/caring approaches to education reform rather than the accountabilities and attention to fiscal bottom lines that often accompany reform;

and uncover and name practices of exclusion and discrimination that are institutionalized in education.

I trust this description of my personal journey records how people cope with imposed change and how life experiences, both personal and professional, are relevant and meaningful. Writing my personal account helped me to learn more deeply and allowed me to draw more useful conclusions than I otherwise would have. It also helped me to integrate my new learning with practical experience in a way that was exciting and challenging and opened up new avenues for my professional development. When I started my doctoral studies I kept a reading journal, which evolved to serve many purposes and functions. It became one of the frameworks through which I was able to make sense of my research, and in part at least, document my process of developing knowledge.

What I chose to research was inevitably something I felt strongly about but still presented me with problems. My early writing was never intended to be seen by anyone other than me. It represented my uncensored versions of reality on the paper before me; once I had expressed my multitude of ideas and feelings, I could then see and sort through what the main issues were, and what the evidence for and against them was worth. Having had the chance to express my personal concerns and values allowed me to see more clearly, to understand my concerns and what was more generally important about my findings.

3

Global and Local Contexts

We have to slow down. Nothing will change for the better until we do. We need time to think, to learn, to get to know each other. We are losing these great human capacities in the speed-up of modern life, and it is killing us.

—Margaret Wheatley

In the context of economic, technological, and social changes at the global level, workplaces are facing new challenges and undergoing massive shifts. Employees in all types of organizations report an intensification of work in a context of job losses and expectations from their employers to work harder. Most managers still believe that caring about employees' needs and meeting organizational needs are mutually exclusive rather than mutually reinforcing (das Dores, Abrantes, & Pereira, 2004). Priorities appear to be highly conditional upon global, national, and organizational contexts, as well as the values and experiences of management personnel. Caring relationships are difficult to maintain, much less develop and nurture, when people feel pressured to work harder and faster while silenced from critiquing or challenging top-down authority and direction.

Governments and businesses alike have been straightjacketed by a downsizing mentality evident in the shift in focus to effectiveness, competition,

Caring Leadership in Turbulent Times, pages 71–98
Copyright © 2014 by Information Age Publishing
All rights of reproduction in any form reserved.

and accountability that marks the policy direction in current times. These are also the "universalizing tendencies in educational reform" (Halpin, 1994, p. 204). Corporate managerialism—a rational output-oriented, plan-based, and management-led view of educational reform (Sinclair, 1989)—includes a demand for smaller government and belief in market competition, that old bureaucratic structures are inefficient and expensive, and that they are unable to respond quickly (Taylor, et al., 1997). Newfoundland and Labrador (a focus of this chapter), like other Canadian provinces and other countries, must compete in the global marketplace where economies and competitiveness are paramount, populations are transient, and there is competition for scarce resources (Williams & Sparkes, 2000).

This chapter addresses the influences of globalization and neoliberalism on national and provincial education policy in Canada and provides other contextual information about the Province of Newfoundland and Labrador. The province's historical, economic, political, and social conditions are described with particular attention to the education system that has recently undergone radical reform. The chapter also includes a description of the ASD as relevant background for the perspectives and experiences following through Chapters 4, 5, and 6.

Globalization and Policy Sharing

Globalization acts as justification for government policy, and educational policies are developed by governments in response to broader social, economic, cultural, and political changes taking place around the globe (Apple, 2001). Consequently, in this period of globalization, many workplaces are restructuring, particularly within government agencies (Blackmore, 2000; Gee, Hull, & Lankshear, 1996; Taylor et al., 1997). Globalization is accepted as inevitable and as justification for centrally driven educational policy that is closely linked to economic needs and productivity gains; perceived local autonomy in schools is controlled through strong accountability frameworks, including performance management of principals, teachers, and standardized testing; and greater intensification of teachers' work, increased scrutiny through accountability, and loss of autonomy and respect (Apple, 2000; Blackmore, 2000; Burbules & Torres, 2000).

There is a sense that in the face of overwhelming forces of globalization from above little can be done to stop it (Taylor et al., 1997). "Hope and confidence is [*sic*] the potential of progressive pedagogies, and social movements have been severely shaken by the successes of the ideological, political and economic projects of neoliberal globalism" (Franzway, 2005, p. 265). Franzway also notes, "It appears impervious to human effort, and at some levels, the anonymous forces of the political and global economy are destructive of communities that imagine themselves tied exclusively to some geographic or political locality" (2005, p. 277). "Government decision making has been captured by and reflects the interests of the world's powerful elites, who are not directly accountable for these decisions, and yet they have real effects on people's everyday lives" (Reid, 2005, p. 286). The accountability bandwagon is converging on education and is bringing with it a focus on control, efficiency, and testing (Anderson, 2001).

Education policy has risen in stature to become the vehicle for the delivery of the mandates of the globalized economy. In this paradigm education has become an extension of broader economic policy with restructuring and devolution dominating policy direction. A shift to central control of policy direction, consistent with this trend, brings tighter control of decision making and financial control with educators subjected to greater accountability resulting in a loss of professional autonomy and local control (Blackmore, 2000). Students are seen as future workers and must be given the skills and dispositions to meet the needs of the marketplace. Teachers are drawn in line with strict accountability measures, and the curriculum is narrowed to market utility. Theorists believe that a state of crises has been created through a concerted attack on schools and educators with alarms raised about high dropout rates and a decline in functional literacy skills (Tucker, 2005; Williams & Sparkes, 2000; Williams et al., 1992).

Neoliberalism and Corporate Managerialism in Education

Like other places in Canada, and around the world, Newfoundland and Labrador's policies have been influenced by global forces acting not just on education policy but affecting all social and economic policy. The rhetoric of globalization has been used to promote a neoliberal agenda that emphasizes economic rationality as the preferred ideology and education's role to prepare workers for the new economy (Apple, 2000; Burbules & Torres, 2000; Green & Tucker, 2011; Thomson, 2002; Tucker, 2005). Such dramatic ideological shifts challenged the very foundation that shaped education in the past and created substantive changes in the structure of schools and regulatory changes in governance and operations (Ball, 2008). There is a growing and alarming trend reflected in "an educational agenda that privileges, if not directly imposes, particular policies for evaluation, financing, assessment, standards, teacher training, curriculum, instruction, and testing" (Burbules & Torres, 2000, p. 15).

Although the problems of education have been laid at the door of teachers, their capacity for finding solutions has been taken away. The neoliberal version of the performing school (Ball, 2003) requires teachers and students to be followers. The rhetoric has been of empowerment, participation, and teams; the reality is that teachers have had to continue to do what they have always done—be empowered to do what they have been told to do (Gunter, 2001).

> The theoretical vision of education (including the aims of education), curriculum planning, as well as the power to implement school reforms, often emanate not from schools, principals, or teachers, but from business practices shaped by ideologically driven government policy-makers adhering primarily to dehumanized economic methodologies. (Solomon et al., 2011, p. 125)

People in educational institutions globally have worked with the apprehension that they may lose their jobs or be reassigned; public pressure has added further challenge, as the media ignore accomplishments and emphasize problems. Disputes with parent and community groups continue in print (Willick, 2013) and on the airways far more than positive reports about student achievement and other developments. "To be sure, the neoliberal plan to further centralize and confine power and capital to corporations and their government partners continues to gain momentum" (Solomon et al., 2011, p. 188).

Teachers "related again and again standards based educational reform works against the teaching profession, devalues learning in complex ways, and places further obstacles in front of those who are working toward a socially just society" (Solomon, 2011, p. 90). Standards-based reforms are well intentioned, but the motives for market-oriented and uniform standards for students, teaching, and teacher education may not guarantee positive effects in the real world of schools (Apple, 2000). Kohn (2003) calls for a refusal to accept the debate around standardized tests as it has been framed and insists that we must determine the source of the fierce demand for accountability and question its underlying assumptions. He maintains that it is especially important to consider who benefits and who loses when accountability, as constructed through the standards movement, becomes the primary focus of education.

Education Reform, "The New Work Order"

The institution of schooling changed relatively little during the twentieth century (Tyack & Cuban, 1995), but today there is considerable emphasis on the changing demands on the teacher, caused by a reduction in human and material resource allocations, the integration of students with special needs, pressure to meet multiple demands from society, innovations in education and changing pedagogy, and increasing pressure to add more and more to the curriculum. These mounting challenges, together with calls for further analysis and public debate, are the starting points for much change in education.

Current reforms have been based on a fundamental shift in how some educators and policy makers view the purpose of education.

> The shift in perspective, influenced by neoliberal and neoconservative ideologies as well as business interests... views the function of education as preparation for the workplace and the generation of capital. The current wave does not bode well for a progressive and democratically centered educational perspective where issues of social justice and equity are taken seriously. (Solomon et al., 2011, p. 70)

The management paradigm mobilized during the 1990s was more modernist than postmodernist. It was about "reengineering education in 'hard line' ways, promoting images of being tough, entrepreneurial, and decisive, sidelining the human costs, and utilizing demoralizing and dehumanizing strategies of downloading responsibility, downsizing organizations, and outsourcing or casualizing core work" (Blackmore & Sachs, 2007, p. 10).

Numerous amalgamations and closures arising from demographic shifts, economic hardship, and claims of student underachievement resulted. "In Canada, school boards are charged with the powers to carry out duties associated with formulating and implementing elementary and secondary education policy with their respective provinces and territories" (MacLellan, 2009, p. 117). In Newfoundland and Labrador the effects of reform were larger schools, fewer districts, elimination of religious control of education, and restructured relations among central bureaucracies, regions, and schools.

Devolution became the general trend and moved toward funding based on enrolments of individual schools through global budgets to facilitate local flexibility and the delegation of increased responsibilities for outcomes down to schools with stronger accountability mechanisms (Blackmore & Sachs, 2007). Similar moves have been taken in other parts of Canada as well as in Australia, the United States, the United Kingdom, and New Zealand. Mainstream initiatives to reform education put into practice standardized measures in an effort to increase the quality, rigor, and accountability of public education (Solomon et al., 2011), and meeting standards through the raising of test scores is a central focus. Accountability is in vogue. "There is a deeply entrenched mindset that standardizing education is a logical course of action that will improve the quality of schooling" (Solomon et al., 2011, p. 69).

In a globalized postindustrial service- and knowledge-based economy, productivity gains are to be achieved through the better managing of people, by getting more for less. Education reforms of the late 1990s were characterized by increased regulation, both internal and external, of educational labor in organizations, and regulation that was process and outcome driven, not learning centered (Blackmore & Sachs, 2007).

There are some positive perceptions about accountability—that it enhances teacher quality, school climate, graduation rates, and equity, and makes budgets transparent—all desirable to taxpayers. It has also brought extra work and expense and distracts from other important agendas. Schools and districts get judged on narrow criteria of success. Accountability maintains high-stakes testing and focuses on numbers, percentages, successes, and failures, which are all quantifiable. Unfortunately, an emphasis on numbers alone blames teachers, schools, and administration without considering other key factors, including poverty, drugs, crime, and socioeconomic status that negatively affect learning (Thomson, 2009). Those significant circumstances are not considered in the focus on test scores and bottom-line budget numbers.

A contradictory and "new wave" trend in school reform efforts focuses on building partnerships that require a balance of authority, control, and power through shared decision making and management. Decisions shared among educators, administrators, students, parents and various other government and community groups is transformative (Shields, 2003) and fits the model of empowering leadership (Grogan & VanDeman Blackmon, 1999). The aim is to develop more people-oriented, relational, and collaborative ways of working where people care about one another (Sernak, 1998). However, bureaucracy "sharply conflicts with our dedication to democratic principles which stress self-determination and a process for both sustaining autonomy and adjusting conflicts" (Purpel & Shapiro, 1995, p. 49). "There is a desire for control in our bureaucratized, computerized culture" (Shapiro & Gross, 2008, p. 167) where we value "work, productivity, efficiency, and uniformity over play, flexibility, diversity, and freedom" (Purpel & Shapiro, 1995, p. 48) and where controversy and critique are not desired.

> The increasing bureaucratization in the school climate ... has complicated attempts to integrate a diverse and equitable approach to teaching and learning in our schools. Rather, it has contributed to halting progressive education beyond simplistic and superficial attempts. The myopic focus on

standards, standardization, and outcomes has made it increasingly difficult
to fight for equity initiatives within this narrowly defined notion of school
reform. (Solomon et al., 2011, p. 133)

This limited concept of school reform has also caused educators to focus on
varied and questionable purposes, such as teaching to the tests and "dumb-
ing down" the curriculum (McNeil, 2000) rather than preparing students
to become useful and productive citizens (Kochan & Reed, 2005). "The
control-versus-democracy paradox being played out in schools warn[s] educators that accountability, at its extreme, can hurt students" (Shapiro &
Gross, 2008, p. 168).

Democratic educationalists offer "a principled defense of schooling
whose aim is to teach the skills and virtues of democratic deliberation within a social context where educational authority is shared among parents,
citizens, and professional educators" (Gutmann, 1999, p. xiv). A case has
been made for "deliberate democracy," asking all parties to come together
to discuss in-depth controversial issues and attempt to deal with them in
such a way that the problems can be resolved. It requires a more principled
educational debate on the difficult problems related to education with students learning about the civic values that make up their own country and
the moral purpose of other nations. This approach requires a great deal
from teachers and educational administrators and emphasizes tolerance as
well as critical discussions. To teach this type of democracy, there is really no
place for the back-to-basics movement. The curriculum is comprehensive
and broad-based, advocating a type of democracy where the process itself
is significant and must be taught and practiced (Shapiro and Gross, 2008).

In Canada, the 13 jurisdictions'—10 provinces and three territories—
departments or ministries of education are responsible for the organization, delivery, and assessment of education at the elementary and secondary levels within their boundaries. There are many similarities among the
provincial and territorial education systems across Canada, but there are
important differences that reflect the geography, history, culture, and cor-
responding specialized needs of the populations served. Newfoundland
and Labrador's school system operates within a Kindergarten to Grade 12
structure. Public education in Newfoundland and Labrador, since its beginnings in the early nineteenth century, has been shaped by two factors:
religion and the economy (McCann, 1998). Until 1997 the governance of
education was shared between government, through the Department of
Education, and the major Christian churches, through Denominational
Education Councils.

Central forces shaping the nature of school boards in Canada include critical changes in school demographics, shifting governance structures, stricter accountability frameworks, and the greater regulation of the teaching profession (Corbett, Wright, & Monette, 2007). "A move to restructuring and reforming education across Canada during the 1990s involved a range of initiatives and system changes; common among many of these reforms was the reduction in the number and size of school boards" (MacLellan, 2009, p. 122). "Education systems have undergone significant changes that reflect a systemic shift in how education is governed. . . . In fact, school board restructuring has often topped the list of educational restructuring initiatives within Canada" (MacLellan, 2009, p. 117).

> One reason school boards came under the restructuring knife is because they are composed of elected officials with varying sociopolitical agendas, and their leadership is often complicated by dynamic social, economic, and policy contexts within which their schools are situated. (MacLellan, 2009, p. 118)

Because of these and other factors, "the changing role of school board leadership in relation to Department/Ministry of Education and individual schools is an increasingly important issue in Canada's provincial and territorial education system" (MacLellan, 2009, p. 118).

The following four trends listed by Dunning (1997, p. 4) are common in most of the 1990s educational restructuring initiatives across Canada's provinces and territories:

- reduction in the number of school boards,
- redefinition of school board powers and responsibilities,
- centralization of power at the provincial/territorial level, and
- redirection of some responsibilities to school boards, parents, or community advisory councils.

Newfoundland and Labrador: Canada's Youngest Province

Newfoundland and Labrador, Canada's easternmost province, consists of almost 410,000 square kilometres, 17,500 kilometres of rugged coastline, and over 7,000 small islands. The population is just over 500,000 and is distributed primarily through hundreds of small rural and outport communities. The Strait of Belle Isle separates the province into two geographical divisions: Labrador and the island of Newfoundland.

Archaeological evidence suggests that the first human beings to arrive in Newfoundland and Labrador were the Beothucks, a nomadic people who relied heavily on the sea and lived by hunting, fishing, and gathering.

Their descendants were in Newfoundland at the time of the arrival of the first European settlers in 1001, when the Vikings came from Iceland to Greenland and then to Baffin Island, Labrador, and Newfoundland. In 1497 John Cabot arrived and claimed the land for the British. In 1610 the first colony in Newfoundland was established at Cupids. As a fish exporting society, Newfoundland was in contact with many places around the Atlantic rim, but its geographic location and political distinctiveness also isolated it from its closest neighbors in Canada and the United States. Newfoundland's history is intricately linked to religion, with family life, community life, and schooling the basis of its traditional social order. All these conditions affect the culture and generate a wide variety of unique customs, beliefs, and dialects. Our history is one of struggle and hardship, but also one of courage and caring.

The First World War had a powerful and lasting effect on the society and on the history of Newfoundland and Labrador. From a population of about 250 million, 5,482 men went overseas, nearly 1,500 were killed, and 2,300 were wounded. On July 1, 1916, at Beaumont-Hamel, France, 753 men of the Royal Newfoundland Regiment went over the top of a trench and the casualties were staggering. The next morning only 68 answered the roll call.

As throughout Canada and the United States between 1934 and 1946, Newfoundland experienced the harshness of the Great Depression, with its accompanying unemployment, poverty, disease, and hunger. "By 1932 starvation was a real possibility for many in Newfoundland" (Smallwood, 1981a, p. 612). On February 16, 1934, Newfoundland's dominion status was suspended and returned to rule by appointed nonresponsible government officials as an attempt to rescue the country from possible collapse, to instill new hope and confidence in the people, and to improve conditions so that they could at least earn a livelihood (Government of Newfoundland, 1933). The most important task the Commission of Government set for itself was to improve substantially the general level of education in this island (Government of Newfoundland, 1933).

In 1935 the Commission of Government appointed supervisors to carry out a general survey of educational conditions in Newfoundland. There was a great deal of hardship involved in travelling from one isolated community to another. "Between October 1 and December 15, 1935, the 10 supervisors had visited 1,153 classrooms staffed by 1,209 teachers" (Andrews, 1985, p. 222). According to Andrews, their survey did not include the schools on the Northern Peninsula or in the city of St. John's. They found that only 50% of students were adequately supplied with textbooks. Of the schools visited 85% did not have a single reference book, few settlements had a library, and only 40% of the classrooms had desks that were satisfactory. The school grounds were for the most part rocky or boggy, with little space for games or outdoor activities. One of the survey tables showed that of the 873 schools visited only 260 had toilets in reasonably satisfactory condition. It also indicated that 25 community schools had no teacher and 65 communities had no school.

The supervisors' survey also found that the teachers were unprepared for education with only 89 of the 1,209 teachers having any university training. Although there were some teachers with summer school training, 344 had no training at all. In 1938 the *Statistical Report of the Department of Education* outlined the development of healthy citizens as one of the primary concerns. The Departments of Education and Public Health and Welfare co-operated closely, providing nourishment to the schools and promoting physical education as part of the regular health curriculum.

As prosperity returned to Newfoundland, the Commission was able to carry out some educational reforms. It changed the curriculum, and made textbooks and school supplies available. Schools received Cocomalt in an attempt to improve the health of students (Smallwood, 1981b). The government increased grants to school boards as well as teacher salaries. It created a Teacher Training Department at Memorial College and offered a summer school program to teachers. Correspondence courses, the Travelling Library, the School Car, and radio broadcasts increased educational opportunities for teachers and students in remote areas. It appears, though, that much of the improvement in education was visible only in the larger centers of Newfoundland. Not much had changed in rural education. *The Book of Newfoundland* gives a rather scathing account of the Commission's efforts.

> [A]part from St. John's, Grand Falls, Corner Brook and perhaps a dozen other larger centers of population, there was no essential difference between the type of education enjoyed by children at all levels and that which had been available seventy years before. The schools were small, ranging from one, up to six or seven classrooms. They were wooden buildings, primitive in construction and appearance, heated by wood or coal stoves, improperly ventilated, lacking auditorium, gymnasium, library, and laboratory facilities. Most of them lacked running water either for drinking or sanitation, the only concession to the latter being decrepit and obnoxious outhouses. Vast stretches of the Province lacked electricity and where lighting was provided kerosene was the medium. In the smaller of the schools teachers generally lacked training, apart perhaps from what training they might have got in one or two summer sessions at St. John's. Even in the larger schools the majority of the teachers had not spent more than one year at University. Out of the 2,375 teachers in 1949 only fifty-seven had degrees and these, of course, were for the most part in St. John's and the larger centers. School

transportation as such was nonexistent. Out of 1,187 schools 778 were "sole-charge," that is, one-room schools, and of these 778 teachers over 700 had not spent even one year at University. The median salary to teachers in 1948 was $981.00. (Smallwood, 1967, p. 114)

The obstacles that probably defeated the good intentions of the Commission Government are summarized.

> The real enemies to an efficient education system in Newfoundland appear to be the same as existed a century ago—isolation, small villages and hamlets, dependence on a precarious occupation, and the general poverty of the Province. . . . Changes, to be really effective among a people whose philosophy and outlook have been so peculiarly nurtured and molded by centuries of history, economics, and geography, must be evolutionary rather than revolutionary, especially where such changes are likely to impinge upon religious scruples or prejudices. (Rowe, 1952, p. 140)

During the Second World War, prosperity and self-confidence returned to Newfoundland. In 1949, after intense debate, the people voted to join Canada. Since then poverty and emigration have been recurring themes.

In the mid-1960s, the Warren Royal Commission was established to examine education in the province and inform government policy. Newfoundland had been a province of Canada for less than 20 years and was in the midst of adjusting to the political realities. This report emphasized the social forces influencing education in the late 60s, which included technological developments, the growing recognition of the economic returns from education, the growth of knowledge, and rapidly changing personal values (Warren, 1967). The focus was on a human capital approach to education with the aim of economic prosperity. The future for the uneducated and undereducated would be bleak in the new economy with education regarded as the key to personal success and a prosperous economy. Along with the recognition that education was intricately linked with economic prosperity, there remained evidence of the values inherent in a liberal education. In a period of relative social and economic stability, which was influenced by the welfare policies of this period and a newly educated teaching force, progressive views of educational theorists dominated policy. Educators played an influential role in the development and implementation of policy (Tucker, 2005).

A significant factor in the history and economy of Newfoundland and Labrador was the abundance of cod fish that was available off the Grand Banks. In the 1960s the cod harvest ranged from 350,000 tons to 800,000 tons per year (Herendeen, 1998). Then disaster hit. The northern cod practically vanished—they were reduced to 1% of their historic spawning biomass (Herendeen, 1998). In 1992 the cod fishery was shut down by the Canadian government and cod fishing as a way of life came to an end for 30,000 workers (Higgins, 1998) after a 500-year history as the economy's mainstay. The sudden collapse of the cod fishing industry was a terrific blow: the already precarious economic base of many towns further eroded, and large numbers of Newfoundlanders left the province. This, together with a steadily declining birth rate, exacerbated the situation for schools. There was a pattern of significant student enrolment decline that subsequently led to teacher cuts and pushed the need for schools to close and students to be consolidated. As the effects of the crisis were felt throughout the province and established supports were weakened, tourism was embraced as a way of restoring the shattered economic base of many communities. Despite historic cultural and political tensions, a new spirit of a unified Newfoundland identity emerged through songs and popular culture.

In 1992 a second Royal Commission on Education was established in Newfoundland and Labrador and heightened the challenges for education policy makers in the coming years to ensure that "children obtain the skills, knowledge and abilities essential to survival in a fast-changing highly competitive world" (Williams et al., 1992). Requiring "fundamental changes" in the preparation of young people to meet the changing nature of future demands, the report gradually shifted educational philosophy and policy direction. Liberal views of equality of educational opportunity, as well as modernist views and economic demands, all found their way into education policy. Along with greater political involvement there was increased emphasis on economic efficiency and restructuring with the role of educators changing from integral to advisory, from shaping educational policy to carrying out directives (Tucker, 2005).

The provincial government's agenda was one of cost-cutting and restraint. A massive provincial debt had been accrued and the newly elected government expressed intent and determination to reduce its deficit and get into a healthier fiscal position. During the 1990s, "restructuring became the key means by which government could simultaneously reduce expenditure while linking education more tightly to the economy" (Blackmore & Sachs, 2007, p. 32).

> The current economic outlook for Newfoundland and Labrador does not offer much encouragement that provincial revenues will increase significantly in the short term. Consequently, spending on education is not likely to rise despite demands by the education system for greater resources and by society for higher performance. Such demands, coupled with already difficult fiscal restraints, are forcing educators to rethink how they deliver programs

and services in this province, and questions are being raised about the value received for the education dollars spent. (Williams et al., 1992, p. 3)

The mandate of the Commission was to investigate, report on, and make recommendations regarding all aspects of the organization and administration of the province's school system.

Specifically, the Commission was instructed to hold an inquiry into the organization and administration of primary, elementary, and secondary education in Newfoundland and Labrador and make recommendations concerning appropriate and realistic courses of action that government and administrative groups in education should adopt in order to realize the most effective, equitable, and efficient utilization of personnel and financial resources in the continued effort to deliver quality educational programs and services at all primary, elementary, and secondary students. (Williams et al., 1992, p. 5)

Some of the specific tasks set out for the Commission (Williams et al., 1992, p. 5) included:

- to examine the organizational and administrative structures for delivering school and school-related programs and services at the provincial, regional, school district and school levels;
- to examine the extent to which school districts could be consolidated and the costs associated with such consolidation; and
- to examine the extent of duplication resulting from the denominational system and the costs associated with it.

The reform mandate was supported by a majority vote (73%) in a constitutional amendment and also by a majority of educators throughout the province. Most people recognized the economic reality and social context and supported the change, believing it to be in the long-term best interest of the education system and students in the province.

The Commission report indicated that other societal changes had placed demands on the province's social institutions:

Chronic and perhaps irreversible changes in our traditional industries, the changing nature of the workplace, the introduction of new technologies, changing population characteristics, changing family structures, increasing strains on economic resources, new expectations, and a heightened awareness of the rights of individuals and groups whose liberties have been constrained in the past. (Williams et al., 1992, p. xv)

The report clarified the province's challenge to ensure "children obtain the skills, knowledge and abilities essential to survival in a fast-changing highly competitive world.... [F]undamental changes are required to create sensitive, responsive learning environments capable of preparing our youth for the future" (Williams et al., 1992, p. xvi).

The First Wave of Reform and Restructuring 1997

Based on the recommendations of two Royal Commission Reports, the first round of reform in 1997 eliminated all denominational school boards and districts and ended the division of students within communities. The various church councils (Integrated, Roman Catholic, and Pentecostal) had established a great deal of power and influence in education and exercised their legislated powers through their Denominational Education Councils (DECs). Government developed and prescribed curriculum and allocated funds to the various Christian denominations that in turn provided governance, funding, and regulation to districts and schools. Despite commonalities within Christian denominations, they had diverse traditions and different priorities that collided with government and each other. They had often worked together to respond to various government policies and initiatives, but on the Commission's recommendations related to creating a nondenominational system, they were divided.

The Williams report, like every major study in the past, recommended a restructuring of the province's governance structures to eliminate the costly duplication of services resulting from the provincially funded denominational education system. Historically the churches played an important role in the provision of education to the hundreds of small rural communities, but in a time of declining populations and harsh economic realities, the duplication of services proved to be a burden and a model of inefficiency. Given the province's history and church control of the school system, this was a highly contested recommendation which caused divisions in families, communities, and political and religious groups. The unique set of local circumstances along with dominant global shifts conspired to advance an agenda that accomplished a radical restructuring that fundamentally affected all levels of the education system as well as the internal dynamics experienced by administrators who implemented the significantly changed policy directives.

The educational restructuring plan that followed saw the elimination of all 27 districts, and the boundaries for 10 new districts were drawn with new interim boards tasked with creating the new governance structure. One of the most fundamental and polarized educational reorganization exercises in recent history was the 1997 restructuring of Newfoundland and Labrador's education system (Galway & Dibbon, 2012a). By a "constitutional amendment, the 150 year old denominationally-based system of education was replaced by a public system. The issue was highly sensitive, both socially and historically, bitterly divisive, and politically radioactive" (Galway, 2011, p. 9). Well over 100 district administrators were declared redundant and 40 were hired or rehired and tasked with the mandate to restructure the schools within their boundaries along nondenominational lines (Tucker, 2005). In the three years to follow, 150 schools would close with numerous others restructured, affecting virtually every student, teacher, and administrator in the province (Dibbon, 2012).

The restructuring of school districts and closing and reorganization of community schools between 1996 and 2004 affected virtually every family and amounted to catastrophic social upheaval in a province clinging to its traditional roots. How and to what ends the changes were managed by government and districts remains questionable and are the focus of Part 2 (Chapters 4, 5, and 6). The mandated policy and the radical nature and pace of change left little time or attention for adequate resource allocation; many of the "unexpected effects" were left for those responsible for implementation. The mandate to implement legislation, with conflicting ideologies that involved social, economic, political, and religious interests, created the context for the tumultuous times that followed. Within the first three years, implementing government's economic rationalist reform agenda, entirely new school boards equipped with an administrative infrastructure one third their original size proceeded to reorganize and/or close all the province's schools.

The process drew a great deal of unfavorable public attention; public demonstrations against school consolidation plans and picket lines at the entrance to schools were commonplace. Myriad newspaper articles featured the struggles ongoing within and among communities as well as with the school boards. There were disputes and court proceedings appealing board decisions, and the public generally felt ignored and disregarded. Parent groups and community leaders presented arguments during public hearings that their schools were the heart of their communities and viewed the closure of a school as the beginning of the end for some small communities. It was difficult during these times of fiscal restraint and cutbacks to convince families and communities that closing the neighborhood school and bussing students to a nearby community would bring program enhancements for their young people. The province had strong unions and strikes were common. People relied on unions to fight for their rights and privileges and came to believe that government processes of consultation and collaboration were neither genuine nor productive for them. For an approximate 10-year period everyone in the system lived through a challenging process of downsizing and loss of teaching units and administrative positions. Small rural schools closed and students were bussed further distances to avail of improved programs and services at regional high schools.

Although the first policy mandate was highly contested with competing interests well represented and highly organized, the majority recognized the economic reality and social context and supported the reform for an anticipated long-term good. Many of us looked forward to greater efficiencies, elimination of duplication, elimination of segregation, and less religious prejudice. We expected new opportunities with inevitable benefits from the more varied perspectives. Old thinking would get shaken up. However, from the perspective of a critical policy analysis, which connects the relationship between policy and change as involving contestation, opposition, and power, central "questions remain as to how and to what ends change is managed, and in whose interests" (Taylor et al., 1997, p. 153).

The Second Wave of Reform 2004

"Most provinces delegate the operation of school systems to locally elected school boards of trustees or commissioners. The number of school boards, their size and their district boundaries are defined in the various provincial/territorial legislation concerning education" (MacLellan, 2009, p. 120). It seemed by 2003 changes were beginning to settle in Newfoundland and Labrador: the number of boards were significantly reduced and reformed from denominational to public; new policies and operational procedures were developed but only partially implemented; employee layoffs and reassignments were worked through; and many school closures had been accomplished. New work relationships and community partnerships were in their infancy. However, the dust had hardly settled after the collapse of the education system, when in 2003, a second school board consolidation was announced to take effect in 2004 with the aim to further reduce the number of boards to five. The first round of restructuring, based on the recommendations of two Royal Commission Reports, was supported with a majority vote (73%) in a constitutional amendment, supported by a vast majority of educators in the province, and by all of those interviewed for this study. The second round, which occurred six years later, was announced in a budget speech with no prior consultation or warning in the educational system.

Prior to the first consolidation in the 1995–1996 school year, there were 27 school boards with 110,456 students in 472 publicly funded schools. The province's school system had been in decline since the 1971–1972 school year, when the provincial student enrolment peaked at 162,818. The student population continues to decline. In 2002, after the first wave of consolidations and closures, there were 11 districts with 86,898 students in 326 schools. By 2006 the provincial student enrolment had declined to 76,763, and the number of schools had reduced to 294. Table 3.1 shows the statistical extent of the changes occurring within the provincial education system over that relatively brief period (http://www. gov.nl.ca/publicat/).

Some of my colleagues and I felt growing dissatisfaction with our new work order as we constantly dealt with changes and new demands. There was upheaval, insecurity, and a requirement to be "married to work." New routines centered around budget cuts, additional programs to implement with less personnel and resources, multiple accountabilities, less not more flexibility, internal competition for limited funds, entrenchment of positions, working smarter and harder with little respect for family life, and less and less control over our workloads. In too many cases all this led to lost sleep, more stress, compliance, silence, and secrecy—everyone became protective of their own bits of information, as information meant power. There was less investment in professional development of staff. We aimed for coherence and direction when actually our work was incoherent and fragmented; we pressed forward under the illusion of stability.

Staff feared losing their jobs, experienced uncertainty, trepidation, and frustration. Anxiety and compliance were exacerbated because of job insecurity. Even tenured senior staff wondered whether they could hold onto their jobs, and indeed, the day did come when many of us were declared redundant. It was a toxic work culture. There was less time for tolerance, difference, individuality, and we felt overt coercion. Behaviors of intimidation

TABLE 3.1 School System Statistics (Government of Newfoundland and Labrador, 2011)

	1995–1996	2001–2002	2005–2006	2011–2012
School Districts	27.0	11.0	5.0	5.0
District Administrators	193.5	90.0	n/a	50.0
Schools	472.0	326.0	294.0	268.0
Teachers	7,259.0	6,264.0	5,485.0	7,935.0
Students	110,456.0	86,898.0	76,763.0	67,933.0

from the hierarchy were evident and power-over tactics developed a culture of bullying that disallowed criticism with frequent reprimands and orders to "toe the line." It generated a "chilly" work culture, and we had to get used to it or leave. "While women were used to chilly cultures during the 1980s, constant restructuring in the 1990s produced a volatility in organizational life that shaped social relations in debilitating ways" (Blackmore & Sachs, 2007). We were under contract and vulnerable to changes in government. We were seen as either too compliant or too resistant, and in an unenviable position. Disruption was seen as something to be stopped as opposed to a necessary part of the process.

The Third Wave of Reform 2013

The February 2013 budget speech came as quite a shock to the educational community when the provincial government announced that effective September 2013 the school boards would yet again be consolidated. In this wave of restructuring—the third within a 15-year period—the school boards would be further collapsed from four to two with one English and one Francophone board to serve the entire province (Antle, 2013; May, 2013a). This third round, as for the second, was initiated merely as a cost-cutting measure and not as a means to qualitatively improve education. The Minister of Education, Clyde Jackman, explained that Government's intent was to reduce expenditures without affecting the teaching and learning occurring in classrooms. The minister reported that since the last school board consolidation in 2004, student enrolment declined by about 14,000 students (17%) while the "Provincial Government investment in education has increased by 42%"; however, "even if there had been no fiscal challenge this year, it would have been necessary to examine the school board administrative structures and supports we have in place to serve this reduced student population" (May, 2013a).

The budget speech contained several other surprising cuts across various departments that prompted a flurry of negative reaction from around the province. In fact, within a couple of weeks and following strong lobbying from professional and community groups, it became clear that government had acted in haste and without consultation. It was evident that some of the cuts were radical, unwise, and would negatively impact important programs and services. As a result of the backlash, government retracted some proposed cuts, specifically those planned for within the Department of Justice.

At the same time, a group of retired school board CEOs came together to seek answers and encourage public debate regarding school board consolidation. They issued a news release on April 10, 2013, titled, *School Board Consolidation: Government Delivers Another Blow To Rural Newfoundland & Labrador.*

> The Government's recent announcement that it intends to consolidate the four school boards into one provincial board with headquarters in St. John's deals another blow to already besieged rural areas of the Province. Some have stated that such a decision is a simple numbers game.... It is correct that 60% of students reside in the eastern region of the province. This is not a new revelation. The majority of students have always resided in the eastern region. However, the delivery of K–12 educational programs is primarily based in the operation of individual schools, and not as an individual service to students, for the most part. In order to ensure that each child has reasonable access to provincially sanctioned educational programs, which is the right of every child no matter where she or he lives, the conventional means of delivery is through a school. The school, where students gather in varying numbers, is the focal point in the delivery of programming, and in Newfoundland and Labrador there are currently 268 schools. From the perspective of schools, there are 95 on the Avalon Peninsula. However, the greater number—173 schools (65%) are located in much more rural settings, more removed from the mainstream economic centers of activity, and where the challenges in delivery and access are more complex. (Retired School Board CEO Action Group, 2013a)

In the same news release, the retired CEOs further argued that

> to move to a provincial school board based in St. John's (the capital city) which is far removed from rural settings puts the students in these 173 schools at great risk of not having equal access to provincially sanctioned educational programs. (Retired School Board CEO Action Group, 2013a)

The education community considered Government's action was ill advised and ironic, especially given that on January 9, 2013—one month prior to the announcement about the elimination of regional school boards—the Canadian School Boards Association released research arguing that school boards are a successful and effective model of governance of the public school system: "A particularly important historically recognized role of school boards is to ensure that the governance of public education reflects community and regional values and priorities" (Sheppard, Galway, Brown, & Wiens, 2013, p. 10).

Other serious public criticisms surfaced on April 16, 2013, when a petition was circulated, calling for the premier of the province and her entire Government to resign and call a general election. The petition included charges that "there has been nothing but manipulation, secrecy and lies, along with fiscal mismanagement resulting in massive job cuts, higher taxes and horrendous danger to Newfoundlanders' and Labradorians' well-being" ("Dunderdale Must Go," 2013). On the same day, a news release was issued from the central school board stating:

> The Trustees of Nova Central School Board want to express their strong opposition to the Government's decision to abolish school boards in rural Newfoundland & Labrador, and establish one new school board located in St. John's. The Trustees feel this is an ill-conceived decision that was undertaken with little planning and no real consultation with anyone outside the Department of Education.
>
> After the initial shock of the announcement, people across the province are now starting to realize the impact of this attack on public education in Newfoundland and Labrador.... We call on all school board trustees, school councils, mayors, chambers of commerce and parents to stand up and be counted. It is time to fight for our local education system and time to fight for rural Newfoundland & Labrador. (VOCM, 2013)

This tumultuous week of public opposition prompted a sparring session in the provincial government's House of Assembly between the Leader of the Opposition and the Minister of Education. Opposition demanded that current and former elected school board trustees and former CEOs be given an opportunity for input before the proposed consolidation took place, asking "our preference is that you [Government] would revisit the school board amalgamation," and asking that legislation be brought into the House "so we can have public input before we merge those school boards" (Leader of the Opposition, 2013).

The next day, the Nova Central School Board trustees added their voices to the mounting opposition. A Board trustee reported: Their (the Board's) "aim was to see government reverse its decision to amalgamate the four English school boards in the province to one" (Canadian Broadcasting Corporation, 2013).

The Leader of the Opposition's release (2013) also reported:

> Government is removing 160 positions from the education system and the impact of this is going to be felt in every school across the province.... We have School Board Trustees, school administrators, and a group of retired school board CEOs speaking out about these drastic education cuts; something is wrong. Government is failing to commit to introducing legislation to amend the Schools Act that will allow them to merge the boards. This is yet another example of Government not having its head wrapped around just how detailed and sensitive this process is. Their lack of preparedness

could have been avoided had they consulted with key players to see if this procedure and timeframe was actually doable.

On April 18, 2013, the Minister of Education responded to some of the questions and clarified information about the decision of Government, stressing that "educational programming services provided to students and their families, and to staff, will continue to be offered in regional areas, as they have been in the past" (May, 2013b). He elaborated:

> There will be one CEO ultimately responsible for all aspects of educational programming and operations, instead of four, as well as senior executive staff responsible for programs and corporate services (e.g., financial operations, facilities and human resources) located at a headquarters in St. John's. It is important to note, however, that school board offices will remain open in Happy Valley-Goose Bay, Corner Brook and Gander. The difference is that they will be staffed with executive, management and staff who will be the day-to-day decision makers on issues specifically related to educational programming and related services to students and teachers—not corporate services. (May, 2013b)

In their April 23, 2013, news release *School Board Consolidation: One Giant Board To Rule Them All!* (Retired School Board CEO Action Group, 2013b), the retired school board CEOs continued to express alarm that "the Government is pushing ahead with its ill-conceived plan to consolidate the four regional school boards into one giant provincial school board headquartered in St. John's." To substantiate their concern, they shared information comparing the proposed Newfoundland and Labrador education system with those in other Canadian provinces:

> One school board for a province with an area of 156,000 square miles is tokenism. Prince Edward Island has one school board, but it only has nine high school systems in a relatively small and compact geography. Its area is less than 2,200 square miles, not much larger than the Burin Peninsula. Newfoundland & Labrador is 70 times larger than Prince Edward Island. Newfoundland and Labrador is more than five times larger than Nova Scotia. Yet Nova Scotia has eight school boards. A more reasonable comparison is with the provinces of Saskatchewan and Manitoba. What these two provinces have in common with Newfoundland and Labrador, more than any other provinces, is a huge land mass, numerous rural communities dispersed throughout its huge territory and, more importantly, a population density of less than 2.3 persons per sq. km. Newfoundland and Labrador has a population density of 1.4 persons per sq. km. Yet Manitoba maintains 38 school boards, while Saskatchewan has 28. (April 23, 2013)

Other strong objections were expressed in the news release, adding to the pressure on the Government to stop the consolidation and take the time needed to either review their decision or ensure it was done properly. Educators throughout the province expressed the belief that delay would be a sound educational decision, especially in the context of the time with only four months to the beginning of the next school year, when the change was scheduled to come into effect.

> Why does the Government believe a single school board will, with 65% of its schools located in rural communities dispersed over a huge territory, be more effective located in the far eastern tip of the province?....One provincial school board to serve 268 schools in a province that has an area of 156,000 square miles, 3 times larger than the Maritime Provinces, is a sham.

The retired CEOs, along with several other groups and individuals, began to probe into other comparisons as a way to pressure Government to rethink their decision.

> Another comparison is to look at the province's electoral districts. There are 48 of them with 48 MHA'S [sic] (Members of the House of Assembly) which works out to be about one MHA for every 11,000 people. Applying the same logic to school boards, we come up with six school boards for 67,000 students. (Retired School Board CEO Action Group, 2013b)

There were ongoing requests

> that the Government cancel its arbitrary decision to abolish regional school boards...and establish an independent commission to determine the number of elected school boards needed to serve a province as large and geographically diverse as Newfoundland & Labrador. It's time for the Government to scrap its recklessly conceived plan. (Retired School Board CEO Action Group, 2013b)

Turbulent Reform in the Atlantic School District (ASD)

Having provided rich contextual information about the historical, economic, cultural, and educational conditions in Newfoundland and Labrador, I next describe the school district where I worked as a senior district administrator during the turbulence of the 1997 reform to set the stage for Part II (Chapters 4, 5, and 6). Insight into the history and culture of the ASD is critical to an understanding of the ways in which we as staff initiated, developed, and perceived care and caring in the context of our work. "School boards are on the frontline of educational change and their ability to respond effectively determines not only their success but also the schools they lead and that of the communities they serve" (MacLellan, 2009, p. 118). We struggled through turbulent years that tested our resolve and the very nature of our beliefs. As teachers and administrators, in the midst of significant educational change, we worked through the demise of a long-standing denominational education system and now live with memories of years of school and school district consolidations and closures.

With the first district consolidation in 1996–1997, four school boards— Integrated (Salvation Army, United and Anglican Churches), Roman Catholic, Pentecostal, and Seventh Day Adventist—were merged in the area where I worked to form a single district, the ASD. It was the second largest of the 10 major districts in the province. (The school board for French Language students covered the whole of the province, including the area served by ASD.) All schools were scattered throughout 127 rural and semi-rural communities with populations ranging from 7 to 5,600. When ASD began operations in January 1997 it consisted of 57 schools and a student enrolment of 12,915. By 2001 most of the schools and all employees had been impacted in some way. The number of schools had reduced to 35 with a total enrolment of 12,000 students. Almost without exception schools were working with redefined attendance zones, different grade configurations, staff changes, new curriculum, and facility renovations. It was a struggle to establish a student-first philosophy and sustain focus on the teaching and learning occurring in classrooms while dealing with diminishing human and material resources, two strikes of public employees, court challenges related to school closures, significant pedagogical and curricular change, new achievement standards, and expectations to integrate technology into all aspects of the district's operations.

At first, the short period of aggressive closures and consolidations between 1997 and 2001 were a blessing. We had a momentum that other districts could only dream of: we were focused on achievement and teaching and learning, exhibited a strong work ethic, had a strong leadership team and committed staff. The school board was supportive and allowed administration room to move and make decisions. For the first few years of the reform, operational savings from the closure of buildings were redirected to enhance remaining schools. In short order government proceeded to make further cuts to budgets and improvements became less evident, hampering the success of the reform process and the realization of positive results. Rivalries between communities resulted; the district's elected trustees and professional staff took the brunt of much public and private criticism. The incidents and events that were disturbing ASD affected all the people employed there. As an administrative team, there was much pressure on us, but at the time we seemed to be able to absorb it and not get taken off track.

By 2001 most of the district's schools had been changed in some way. Now, upon reflection, I understand and feel the toll it took.

Promises did not materialize and there were not the program enhancements we expected. For those of us who spent a career promoting the ideals and philosophies of a nondenominational, collaborative, and caring system, the experience of consolidating school boards and schools was a shock. District administrators were often politely listened to but not taken seriously. Many, including me, were "grieving the demise of collegiality, care and cooperation" (Blackmore & Sachs, 2007, p. 210) and no longer felt attachment to our organizations. The focus of our efforts shifted from teaching and learning issues and concerns to school consolidations and closures, job protection, and survival. We struggled with poor communication among offices of senior administrators. The focus shifted to power and position.

All district office staff were organized and belonged within one of three distinct divisions: Finance and Administration, Programs, and Personnel. The organizational flowchart of positions indicated the director at the top with each of the assistant directors who oversaw and managed the divisions falling under the director. This arrangement magnified the split, not only between the leadership and members of each division, but also among members within the divisions. Social stratification by position existed within the organizational structure: director–assistant director; assistant director–program specialist; executive assistant–administrative assistant; administrative assistants–secretaries; district administration–school administration; school administrators–teachers, and so on. Each level was accountable to the one above, and few decisions were made without approval from above.

This organizational structure, determined and to a large extent staffed as a result of government allocations, contributed to the various groups' perception of positional power and led to the establishment of alliances and separations. Often relationships were adversarial; any changes in policy or practice coming from the administration evoked suspicion and distrust. Power struggles were provoked when the administration was leading an initiative to share decision making.

The hierarchical features of a large government bureaucracy became more and more evident as the school board navigated through new and previously uncharted territories. An attitude of winning rather than compromise prevailed between management and labor and between communities and the school board. Turmoil, confusion, mistrust, and chaos abounded.

Education reform in Newfoundland and Labrador was a time of great personal tension when it became obvious that our personal lives, our schools, our communities, and our province were all directly affected by the process. Everyone felt vulnerable, tense, and stressed with early retirements, relocations, redundancies, and other disruptions causing anger and astonishment. We had to "regulate our feelings" (Crawford, 2007, p. 92) at the time, and given that I still mull it over so many years later makes it obvious that it touched many of us in significant ways. If people really are our greatest resource, and if the global economy really is moving from an industrial/capital base to a knowledge base, then I believe committing to making people central in our workplaces is warranted.

Even our district office site evoked consternation at the time. To many, the building appeared less than approachable and was described as a maze. It was divided and subdivided to provide individuals and groups designated work areas and offices. There was also a windowless meeting room on the main level. It contained an oversized board table surrounded by large swivel chairs. A few plants and displays of student artwork added colour and a touch of softness to an otherwise institutional and impersonal building. Downstairs housed a warehouse, technology centre, large conference/meeting room, and staff kitchen. A large back parking lot provided overflow parking and space for teachers' vehicles when they attended professional development sessions. The surrounding neighborhood was comprised of modest houses, lawns, and gardens all bordering the coastline of the Atlantic Ocean, a quaint, quiet, and safe rural community.

In the reception area of the district office an institutional and hierarchical signboard indicated the names and positions of the educational staff—rank-ordered with the director at the top. A pleasant and welcoming receptionist sat inside the front doors of the district office and behind a prominent reception desk. She enthusiastically greeted anyone entering the building and offered assistance with directions to the appropriate office or individual.

Offices reflected their occupant's individual styles and tastes. Those higher up in the hierarchy occupied the larger offices with windows, and people with temporary or lower level positions had the smaller offices in the inner core of the building. The furniture in each also sent a message regarding the positions people held. The director's office was complete with mahogany-stained matching furniture—impressive desk, bookshelves, round meeting table and covered chairs, the latest technology, numbered prints of artwork by local artists, and higher grade carpeting. Other offices were devoid of artwork or posters and contained uncoordinated and often dysfunctional furniture and computer equipment.

Following the school board consolidation of 1997, the district office became known as "the Taj Mahal" within the province's educational system.

The then director acquired the newly formed school board's approval to carry out a major renovation with the intent that the building would become the Professional Development and Conference Centre of the region. It was designed and decorated by professionals. Although many of the changes were necessary, at a time of fiscal restraint some of the renovations were deemed extravagant. Innovative and colour-coordinated concepts influenced the renovation with state-of-the-art and attractive but often superficial features. The intent was to establish a sense of the new district as polished, professional, businesslike, and "on the cutting edge." Unfortunately, the school board and administration were perceived as putting ourselves ahead of student needs. The luster of the newly renovated district office was secondary to what was in the hearts and souls of many people within. Ironically, these physical changes were made at the central office at the same time the school board adopted a student-first philosophy. This all seemed to communicate an air of superficiality and lack of commitment to what education was really about: teaching and learning and the interactions in classrooms.

A newcomer to the district had been selected by the school board to be the first director and CEO. Despite significant challenges and opposition, he managed to consolidate and close many schools within the first 18 months and was able to avoid taking the board through lengthy and expensive court challenges. He advanced his technology agenda and managed to reorganize the schools throughout the district. Senior district administrators each worked long hours and made personal sacrifices. We often felt unnoticed and unappreciated during that period.

People believed that if their school closed and they moved their children to another school, then they should experience improvements in program offerings and facilities. In some cases this happened. Although at first operational savings from the closure of buildings were redirected to enhance remaining schools, annual government cuts to school and district budgets eventually overshadowed improvements. All this change happened shortly after completion of the renovations at the district office, which exacerbated the perception that the top people looked after themselves and did not care about others. There seemed to be a double standard that only the best was good enough for everyone at district office while schools, students, and teachers were going without basic needs. As well, technology labs and classrooms were being equipped with new technology but library budgets for books and classroom allocations for curriculum materials were cut. In addition, a tremendous amount of professional development was required to assist teachers with implementation of the technology in their teaching and learning practices, but without an implementation plan, accompanied with the resources to support it, the expensive technology was often left underutilized.

A second director was hired in 2001, bringing hope of a fresh new focus, and ASD attempted to redirect attention to teaching and learning after a period of tremendous chaos. As mentioned the cutbacks continued, and yet another school board consolidation was mandated and implemented in 2003. People at the district office and throughout the schools worked with the apprehension that yet again they could lose their jobs or be reassigned. All this affected the attitude of the staff toward making substantial changes. Some people supported change, hoping to keep their jobs and schools open, but others refused to attempt innovation because they thought it was not worth the effort. Teachers found it almost impossible to get their volunteer requests for transfer to other schools listened to or acted upon. Often they were reassigned involuntarily from schools to fill vacancies in others. These attitudes had a significant effect on the attempt to establish shared decision making and organizational learning as the approach to school organization and leadership.

The district seemed to be fighting a losing battle because of factors beyond its control. The media ignored the district's accomplishments and emphasized the problems. How could the district pursue an ethic of caring in an organization that had been fraught with so much struggle and turmoil? Having to function in the midst of ambiguity increased everyone's feelings of frustration, isolation, and distrust but caring required more than understanding their feelings. It required understanding the ambiguous nature of roles and how that ambiguity affected what could be accomplished. It required understanding that collaboration and support from the entire staff were necessary.

Reflection

The situation in our district and province was unique in many ways and responded to some extraordinary local needs. We continue to struggle with similar dilemmas that any significant education reform is likely to involve. As has been discovered in Newfoundland and Labrador, if our work environments are in flux, so, too, is our sense of identity (Lowe, 2000). The resulting unease could be most effectively addressed with an ethic of care, which I explore in more depth in Chapters 5 and 6.

It is essential for educational leaders to move away from a top-down, hierarchical model for making moral and other decisions and instead turn to a leadership style that emphasizes relationships and connections (Beck, 1994; Wheatley, 2005, 2010). Policy makers and administrators need to encourage collaborative efforts between faculty, staff, and other groups within the education community to promote interpersonal interactions, to deemphasize competition, to facilitate a sense of belonging, and to increase individuals' skills as they learn from one another (Wheatley, 2002). This does not simply mean handing over tasks but making certain that everyone is involved in the process of education and feels as if they are of worthy, heard, and valued.

It would be wise to reflect on solutions, make decisions that show concern for others as part of the decision-making process, and consider the consequences of decisions: who will benefit from them and who might be hurt. We ought to consider and weigh the long-term effects of the decisions we make.

PART II

One Canadian School District's Turbulent
Reform Experience

4

Neoliberalism and Caring in Policy

The smallest act of kindness is worth more than the grandest intention.
—Oscar Wilde

This chapter examines the relationship between education policy in a particular school district and conceptualizations of caring. In the turbulent context of the historical, social, political, cultural, and economic conditions of the times, I examine the constructs of care and their implications for practice through three policy documents. Specifically, the policies I analyzed were the ASD's *Our Vision for Teaching and Learning*, its *Teaching and Learning Decision Making Matrix*, and the *Teachers' Personal and Professional Growth and Development Policy*. My analysis is framed using a critical discourse analysis (CDA) perspective as a form of critical social research that begins from questions such as: how do existing societies provide people with the possibilities and resources for rich and fulfilling lives, and how do they deny people these possibilities and resources (Fairclough, 2003). I describe the theoretical tools I used to guide the policy analysis, the specific policies reviewed, the CDA methodology that guided the analysis, and conclude with discussion of my findings with recommendations for how the direction of future organizational policy development and implementation might be

Caring Leadership in Turbulent Times, pages 101–130
Copyright © 2014 by Information Age Publishing
101

changed. In essence, I found multiple and contradictory meanings of care within the policies, and although they endorse an ethic of caring, they fail to provide sufficient opportunities and resources for the implementation of that ethic.

Policy Study in "New Times"

Recent policy shifts are aimed at preparing people and nations to be more globally competitive. According to some, moving in this direction will be in everyone's best interest (Taylor et al., 1997). The knowledge society and global community for which we hope to educate our children and ourselves exist because advances in information and communication technology have removed barriers previously imposed by location (Sheppard, 2000a, 2000b). Changing bureaucracies are emphasizing strategic plans, outcomes and efficiency, the devolution of financial responsibility to increasingly isolated schools and colleges, a focus on entrepreneurialism, industry relevance, and quality measurement and self-funding in the higher education sector. As well, they are focusing on the development of human capital and on vocational training in all sectors of education. Institutions are under intense pressure to operate as if they were a business. "The corporate model, based on head-to-head competition and survival of the fittest, is the prototype for all government and, more recently, educational institutions" (Barlow & Robertson, 1994, p. 94).

Public policy in education has two main functions: to provide an account of those cultural norms of what is desirable in education, and to institute a mechanism of accountability against which students and teacher performance could be measured (Taylor et al., 1997). Policy is a bureaucratic instrument with which to administer the expectations that the public has of education. Vision statements respond to the global trends toward increased testing and accountability in specific areas of the curriculum as a way to produce literate graduates capable of coping in the world of work. "The desire for control and to reduce risk by executive management and governance alike has led to increased surveillance of professionals in the name of accountability and a trend toward standardization" (Blackmore & Sachs, 2007, p. 22).

The study of educational policy is the study of change, how it occurs and how it impacts those who are most affected (Tucker, 2005), and is important because policy is the way that governments seek to produce and manage change (Taylor et al., 1997). Such policies are developed in response to broader social, cultural, economic, and political changes taking place around the globe. Taylor et al. (1997) suggest the way we as policy analysts judge the changes that have (and have not) been produced is highly dependent on our own ethical/political positions. My decision to undertake an analysis of policy documents arose because they contribute to the understanding of care in education and in any organization.

> This is both a good and bad time in the world of educational policy. On the one hand, there have been very few periods when education has taken such a central place in public debates about our present and future. On the other hand, an increasingly limited range of ideological and discursive resources dominates the conceptual and political forms in which these debates are carried out. (Apple, 2005, p. 209)

Purpose and Intent

I examined district policies in terms of conceptions of care drawn from research literature (Chapter 1). I was concerned, and continue to be, with how educators are treated and treat each other within a large bureaucratic and hierarchical institution, especially when the organization and people in it work under chaotic, turbulent, and stressful conditions. I witnessed, and myself experienced, the "exasperation felt by teachers and administrators as they try to respond to the policy imperatives of the new times" (Taylor et al., 1997, p. vii). I offer this chapter as an opportunity to rethink what caring means in educational policy with intent to seek new ways of informing practice within organizational work environments. To accomplish these purposes, I developed the following questions to guide my study:

- What discourses of care are reflected in the school district policy statements?
- To what extent do competing discourses, contradictions, and multiple perspectives exist within the policy texts?
- Who was involved in developing the texts? Who was not involved?
- What are the implications of the policies on caring practices?
- How do these documents work to change peoples' work in education?

Critical Discourse Analysis

The nature of the questions being asked requires a departure from traditional, empirical methodologies. This inquiry requires the use of discourse analysis, a relatively new analytic tool.

> Discourse analysis is the study of talk and text. It is a set of methods and theories for investigating language in use and language in social contexts.

> Discourse research offers routes into the study of meanings, a way of inves-
> tigating the back-and-forth dialogues which constitute social action, along
> with patterns of signification and representation which constitute culture.
> Discourse analysis provides a range of approaches to data and, also a range
> of theorizations of that data. (Witherell, Taylor, & Yates, 2001, p. i)

Discourse analysts examine language in use and trace patterns in the language. New meanings are created with language use over time, and are
dependent on context. The competition over the meaning of ambiguous
words, events, people, and objects has been called the "politics of representation" (Mehan, 2004). Discourse is structured by dominance (Wodak &
Meyer, 2001) and thus, investigating language use in institutional settings is
relevant. There are three concepts in all critical discourse analyses: power,
history, and ideology (Jager, 2001).

Critical policy analysis is concerned with change and reform, requiring
that attention be given to the processes of policy development and implementation. Issues of power related to whose interests are being served by
the policy and how those interests relate to social, economic, and cultural
forces within the organization need to be examined. Policy analysis in the
critical tradition is multilayered, cyclical. It examines underlying assumptions, process, product, implementation, and follow-up. The selected district policy documents are shaped by other texts that they are responding
to and by subsequent texts they anticipate. There is an importation of prior
texts and discourses, for example, Royal Commission Reports, and other
government policies.

Taken together, I explore caring in education as policy texts using a
critical discourse approach to discourse analysis. I began with Foucault on
discourse (1984) and modified it, and have been helped in my thinking by
Fairclough (2003), Mills (1997), and Witherell et al. (2001). My analysis is
informed by an understanding that dominant discourses are determined
by power struggles (Foucault, 1984). I have taken a reflective and critical
look at texts, which on the surface seem noncontroversial, but I argue that
there is a set of unexamined "theories-in-use" (Argyris & Schon, 1974) embedded in the ambiguities visible through an examination of the policy
documents. A fully "critical" account of discourse requires a "theorization
and description of both the social processes and structures that give rise to
the production of a text" (Fairclough & Kress, 1993, p. 2), and of the social
structures and processes within which individuals or groups, as social historical subjects, create meanings in their interaction with texts.

According to Fairclough (1992), there are three central considerations
for the analysis of discursive practices: *force* (what the text is being used to do

socially); *coherence* (the way in which it is interpreted); and *inter-textuality* (the way in which texts are drawn upon in the production of the interpretation of new texts, the way the text borrows from other texts). Fairclough suggests a three-dimensional structure for discourse analysis: textual analysis (a close linguistic analysis of the text); discursive practices (production, distribution, and consumption of the text); and social practice (broader analysis of the macro-structural context within which the text is embedded).

In this chapter I look for patterns within much larger contexts, such as those referred to as the "society" and "culture" of the district (Taylor, 2001). I identify patterns of language and related practices and show how these constitute aspects of society and the people in it. Controversy is basic to this form of discourse analysis. I examined powerful words, phrases, images, and also considered absences and read these as traces of the discourses operating within district policy texts.

Each of the district policy documents were statements negotiated within relations of power. They were identified as necessary by the district's senior administrators who selected the individuals, representing a cross-section of roles and positions to participate in developing the documents that were presented to the elected board of trustees for official approval and adoption. The policy documents were developed by professionals, who were authorized to write, express, and create based on current theory and debates in the field of education. These professional texts were prepared through a collaborative process and they borrow from, model, and transfer from the texts of other districts and provinces.

Policy analysis involves more than an examination of a single policy document or text; it is also concerned with the background and context in which the policies were written, including the historical antecedents and relationships with other texts (Fairclough, 2003; Phillips & Hardy, 2002). As education policy cannot be separate from political, social, cultural, and economic conditions that exist, I include background information, the context for understanding the events impacting the policies that evolved in the province, and subsequently, in school districts during the time of my study (see Chapter 3). Understanding policy involves examining contexts, texts, and consequences (Taylor et al., 1997). The contexts are the social, economic, political, and historical factors leading up to the development of a particular policy. The texts refer to the naming and framing of issues, which bring particular issues to the foreground, send some into background, and leave others out altogether. Consequences are the effects of policy.

I considered social interactions, organizational culture, and social relationships and framed the analysis in the following order: Firstly, I describe the overall context for the time period of the analysis, providing a general characterization of how caring in policy was created at the time. I discuss the implications of policy decisions and address other documentation that impacted the policy. Secondly, I explain the basis I used to select the documents chosen for analysis, providing a description and context for each, as well as information on how the document was developed and written. Thirdly, I carry out a document analysis with attention given to the surface features of each of the three policies, including layout and structure. I examine the values that are constructed (Kamler, 2001) and how students, teachers, government officials, and the school board are portrayed. I consider who produced the text, for whom it was produced, why it was produced, and what it is trying to do. I examine the general characteristics of the text, including its readership or audience and its political localization (Jager, 2001). Finally, I examine how caring has been defined and represented in the practices and values of the school district and the truth claims being made, the expected actions, and what is unseen and unheard. I conclude by offering reflections on the analysis and the extent to which the policies help us to respond to the needs of others (Noddings, 1999a, 1999b, 1999c).

Policy Context

A 1992 Provincial Royal Commission of Inquiry into the delivery of programs and services in primary, elementary, and secondary education published a report, *Our Children, Our Future*, that referenced profound political, social, and economic changes throughout the world as the impetus for educators everywhere to reassess the effectiveness and efficiency of their education systems (Williams et al., 1992). (Discussion of global trends in education policy, as well as other contextual information that informed my research questions, and the discourses that influenced district policy development and implementation are included in Chapter 3.) There was an established expectation that the district and each school would engage in an ongoing and continual process of growth and development. These were known to some as school improvement processes, to others as the effective schools movement, and in our district as "strategic planning." Components of those processes involved developing mission statements together with an implementation plan to make the vision, mission, and purpose statements practical, observable, and achievable.

At this time, the provincial government was advancing a much larger national and international policy direction and trend. It was emphasizing the need for schools and districts to improve student achievement indicators as measured on public examinations, and criterion-referenced tests and tremendous effort was being applied provincially to develop, field test, and report student performance on these tests (Williams & Sparkes, 2000). The administration of the district valued the data provided through these elaborate testing programs, but it also argued that other components of the school curriculum were equally important (Sheppard, 2000a, 2000b). The fine arts, health and physical education, and the social sciences were not being tested in the same way; consequently, they were not valued to the same extent. Through its vision statement, the district was attempting to balance the message that what gets measured gets valued with other important aspects of schooling that were not evaluated in the same way.

Administration believed instructional leadership at the classroom, school, and district levels was needed, and that with a vibrant and forward-looking professional development program for educators change in pedagogy could be accomplished. The integration of technology into all aspects of work was expected, as it offered a means for innovative instruction, evaluation, record-keeping, reporting, and professional development. The district also wanted to communicate to parents and the general public that the processes of teaching and learning had changed. The district hoped to use the vision statement as a tool for discussion by the general public, as well as for professionals. It was meant to be an instrument to foster educational dialogue and refocus attention back to the truly important educational matters in schools.

Policy Texts

I focused on policies that reflected the prevailing discourses of our new district, on texts that were purposefully designed to influence the work relationships among employees and the district's culture. The policy documents I selected for study were officially approved by the school board for implementation throughout the district, were widely distributed, and were statements associated with changing practice. They were promoted as constituting a snapshot of the current "negotiated consensus of the espoused best practices" (Anderson, 2001, p. 201) and thinking at that point in time.

Policy 1: Our Vision for Teaching and Learning

The vision statement articulates the district purpose and was developed in a highly political, social, and cultural context that also resulted in the development of other policies related to teaching and learning. Statements including a description of what the vision should look like when it was implemented, a plan for how and when the vision would be realized, and a checklist for teachers to determine how their teaching reflected the vision all emanated from *Our Vision for Teaching and Learning* (District, 2003a).

The vision statement addressed the central concerns of the district. "The purpose of teaching in the . . . district is to challenge and develop the learning and achievement capabilities of each student in a safe, caring, and socially-just learning environment" (District, 2003a). The policy represented a view of student learning, that there are multi-intelligences, and a broad curriculum. It acknowledged the importance of social, cultural, and citizenship learning outcomes and advocated a collaborative work relationship among colleagues.

A powerful vision is the first ingredient in establishing an outstanding organization (Bennis & Nanus, 1985). Effective leaders have a vision of what they want and first clarify personal goals before attempting to influence others (Zimbalist, 2005). Following this proven approach, the director began the process of developing a shared vision by first making public his personal philosophy through the district's newsletter:

> I believe that leaders must be committed to a philosophy of leadership rooted in respect for people. Consequently, my commitment to all those whom I will serve in this District in my role as Director of Education, is that my leadership approach will be collaborative and very much dependent upon the collective of the entire District community. It will always have the intention of inclusion and participation, and be based on a philosophy that is rooted in the most fundamental of moral principles—respect for people. (Sheppard, 2000a)

In formulating his personal vision statement, he quoted and built upon the district's stated beliefs: "Teaching involves the use of a variety of instructional techniques by caring dedicated individuals" (Sheppard, 2000b). He initiated a collaborative process that involved everyone in the district, including students, parents, educators, employees, and trustees, in the development of the vision statement. Various drafts sent throughout the district were accompanied with a call for them to be scrutinized. We were attempting to build a shared vision, one that everyone would have input into developing and ownership to see implemented. After several months of dialogue among individuals and groups, the current text was approved by the school board.

Our Vision of Teaching and Learning is organized in three distinct sections. Section one outlines the broad philosophical statement of belief within the district. In a single paragraph, it states the purpose of teaching in the school district, describes the process of learning, and the environment in which it occurs. Section two outlines how the vision is expected to be manifested by providing "images of our vision in practice" (District 2003a). It outlines the expectations of teachers, including lists of how they will demonstrate commitment to "making a difference in the life of each student," be held accountable for the learning of each student, engage students, organize their learning environments, collaborate with others, and reflect on the process of teaching and learning. Likewise, parents and other community members are expected to partner with educators in support of student learning. The third section addresses implementation and evaluation processes.

The document was to be used as a direction-setting text; the intention was that it would stimulate discussion within and among the various individuals and groups involved with education. Primarily it was designed to guide instruction in the classroom and was expected to be referenced in regular staff meetings and professional development sessions.

This is a "material policy" because accompanying it is a "comprehensive framework for action, illustrative implementation strategies, reporting and review arrangements and some funding made available for implementation" (Taylor et al., 1997, p. 48). The vision document refers to this as "Charting the Course," which involves self-assessment by individuals, schools, and the district. Questions are provided to guide each of the assessments.

> To what extent do(es) I/my school/all schools engage in the teaching and learning behaviours, norms, or practices that form the images of our vision? How much will a change in my/my school's/all schools' current practices toward the vision increase individual student learning and achievement? What is a reasonable time frame for me/my school/all schools to significantly change current practices so that our vision becomes a reality? (District, 2003a)

The policy recognizes the nature of knowledge is changing while teachers remain at its heart. "Teaching engages learners in dynamic, interactive, motivating, meaningful, hands-on, integrated, and creative learning experiences that include direct instruction, experiential learning, group work, individualized instruction, home study, and digital learning" (District, 2003a). The policy seeks a radical departure from the education system of the past. Students are viewed as individuals requiring unique and relevant instruction and attention. The policy represents an effort to serve children more effectively, prevent problems from developing, and identify barriers which stand in the way of addressing the needs of all children (Williams et al., 1992). The document includes an emphasis on developing social, emotional, and physical goals for all children, as well as academic or intellectual ability. Attention is also paid to the need for appropriate assessment procedures and intervention strategies for those students identified as struggling. "When individual students have unique needs that will require modification of standard provincial curriculum outcomes, teachers lead a team to appropriately modify the outcomes to meet those needs" (District, 2003a).

The curriculum is viewed as needing to be responsive to all students, to be more than academic, and to develop the "whole child." All courses of study are seen as equally important. The district vision statement attempts to emphasize areas of the curriculum that have not traditionally been in the limelight, for example health and physical education programs, "movement and healthy living" (District, 2003a). This reference is also responding to evidence in publications and media reports concerning the obesity levels of young people.

The document, constructed to be authoritative, legitimate, and efficient, offers the formal, official, objective position of the school board. The text aims to be applicable to various groups with something for everyone. The inclusion of such words as *democracy, participation, diversity, shared decision making, collaboration* are all examples of this. However, these words are often contradictory. A rational vocabulary is coupled with words like *visions, missions, values,* and *beliefs.* One intent of the *Vision for Teaching and Learning* document is to stimulate thought and dialogue; it also aims to force change and bring accountability and consistency with evaluation, surveillance, and power as underlying themes. Administrators must legitimate the organization to multiple constituencies (Anderson, 1990). Schools need discourses of democracy and equity just as much as they require discourses that reflect objective, scientific, research-based practices and reforms to socially engineer increased student outcomes.

The document incorporates a coercive form of power using language like "we will conduct assessments" (District, 2003a). Teachers, principals, and parents are the intended targets of the policy: "Teachers take responsibility," "Teachers are accountable," and "Teachers ensure." "Parents and other community members are considered partners in support of student learning" (District, 2003a). Responsibility for ensuring that curriculum goals are achieved rests with the teacher. The term *collaboration* sends a democratic message, but others like *effective* and *performance standards* send a marketization of education, deficit theory (Shields, 2004) message. Both discourses seem to be at work in this document, making it difficult to determine which is real and which is rhetoric.

Our Vision for Teaching and Learning aims to come not from techno-crats but from well-educated leaders, who use language not to offend any group but to speak to all. However, the vision statement is an example of a modern technology of control par excellence because it disciplines sub-jects while hiding the source of its power (Anderson, 2001). Although the intents of *Our Vision for Teaching and Learning* are to stimulate thought and dialogue, it is typical of this form of policy making with its contradictory goals, processes, and strategies to force change and bring accountability and consistency.

Elements of care and caring are explicitly and implicitly evident in this policy. A specific care relation is evidenced with individual students, as well as student groups, but there are mutual responsibilities.

> Teaching takes place in a caring, co-operative, nurturing, inclusive, struc-tured, resource-rich environment with routines of high expectations and mu-tual respect. There is an emphasis on the development of self-discipline and responsibility; however, appropriate consequences for violation of school and classroom rules and procedures are well established. (District, 2003a)

This is in line with Noddings's argument that equal quality of education for all students does not require identical education for all (1992). "Teach-ers design learning opportunities that focus on the learning needs of each student" (District, 2003a).

The policy suggests we think about a multiplicity of models designed to accommodate the multiple capacities and interests of students. The motiva-tion for caring for students is so that they are able to learn to their full po-tential. A broad curriculum should supply students with knowledge of other people and their customs, so we can reduce misunderstanding, stereotyping, and fear of strangers. "Cocurricular programs are designed to complement and support the core curriculum to ensure a focus on all of the Provincial Essential Graduation Learnings: Aesthetic Expression, Citizenship, Commu-nication, Personal Development, Problem Solving, Spiritual and Moral De-velopment, and Technological Competence" (District, 2003a).

The policy holds teachers responsible and accountable for student learning, and the needs of students are justified as part of their role as "re-flective professionals." They are also expected to discuss matters on which they have no specific training—"show sensitivity and attentiveness" (Dis-trict, 2003a) to students' current and future needs. In other words, a great deal is expected of teachers under the rubric of caring professionals.

Care is voiced for teachers as professionals who have their own indi-vidual needs. "The district will demonstrate its care for teachers and assist them so that they can continuously learn new strategies and techniques, meet instructional standards, and raise the levels of student achievement" (District, 2003a). But they, too, have a mutual responsibility and account-ability to contribute to the learning of their students. The district advocates a reliance on current educational research to help educators focus on and implement sound educational approaches to teaching and learning. All this is seen as a "challenge," where the policy recognizes that teaching is work that should push known boundaries and engage both teachers and students in thought-provoking and meaningful learning activities.

Policy 2: Teaching and Learning Decision Making Matrix

I selected the *Teaching and Learning Decision Making Matrix* (District, 2003c) document for analysis because its intention was to build collabora-tion among all groups and flatten the traditional hierarchical, authorita-tive model of organization within the district. It was designed as a tool to implement *Our Vision for Teaching and Learning* and a mechanism to dem-onstrate how shared decisions are made. The district's leadership team, the General Administrative Council (GAC), wanted to believe the development of shared decision-making matrices would bring a new way of working to-gether that was more democratic and less top-down, but it was ultimately interpreted as an autocratic, top-down, surveillance tool.

We engaged in an elaborate process of developing matrices to determine who had which powers and/or rights on specific issues of importance. Partici-pants were encouraged to openly discuss concerns and ideas and to feel free to honestly evaluate and critique suggestions. Although dialogue was welcomed during the developmental process, involvement in the process was mandatory.

This policy attempts to "suture together and over matters of difference between participating and competing interests in the process of policy text production" (Taylor et al., 1997, p. 50), a form of policy as settlement. Sharing decision making caused conflict among district administrators and some program specialists and principals who held strong antiestablishment views. The matrix sought to overcome these conflicts but resulted in further confusion. There was a lack of understanding and implementation of the matrix, and many did not use it to gain more control. It was an ambiguous and often confusing process. Despite striving for unity, fragmentation was the result. Unfortunately, we did not think of policy as a representation of practices inside the walls of an organization. Instead, it became more a rep-resentation of formal abstractions from these practices (Biesta, 2004). The shared decision-making process was contrived and imposed; consequently, the intent to build community was not realized.

It was difficult to work together supportively and in caring ways in the face of disagreement and adversity. Caring required us to communicate continually to understand each other's ideas and what needed to be done after a decision was made. The development of the district matrix was intended as a dialogue to help us work together systematically and confidently in supportive ways, but there was little attention given to supporting those who were implementing it or being impacted by it.

A series of dialogues and collaborative working sessions worked out negotiations of power and rights. It was an effort to share power and decision making and to demonstrate the complexities and intricacies involved with the process of working that way. The process began from the perspectives of care and justice, with commitment to persons, values, rules, and principles intermingled. Through the matrix, the district aimed to reduce the hierarchy within the organization and redistribute power downwards, thus empowering employees. Unfortunately, the district's commitment to establish a caring community became subsumed in the maintenance of power positions with language such as "right to be informed, right to veto or amend, right to advise." Participants often did not know the reason behind decisions made by the administration and this contributed to negative perceptions of the staff's relationship with administration. There was disbelief in the rhetoric about collaboration and shared decision making. Misunderstandings developed because administration failed to communicate their dilemmas to staff.

Discussing time frames, giving background information and reasons for some hasty decisions would have shown caring and evidenced trust on the part of administration for employees; however, the district administration felt significant pressure from community and from school reforms, and the extended time necessary to communicate in appropriate ways was just not there. Senior administrators ourselves felt little or no support from within or outside the district, and we were often criticized, which further frustrated us in our efforts to care. As administrators, we often gave mixed messages so that our collaborative, open, caring messages were contradicted by our authoritative and unilateral directions and actions.

Transposing the policy direction into action required the support of each educator at the district office with every principal. Supported by district personnel, the principals were counted on to lead changes at the school level. Lines of authority were used to enforce policy directives. Some felt that administration was inviting or persuading others to join "our" side. Some colleagues were silenced; others felt their positions were attacked. The sometimes heavy-handed attempt to introduce different processes was an overly ambitious approach, given the turmoil experienced throughout the education system. Through insistence, impatience, and sometimes even coercion, the administration's determination to complete the matrix development contradicted and undermined its own caring efforts. Unfortunately, because of mixed messages conveyed by district leadership, some felt cajoled and pressured into accepting the views and perspectives of others rather than expressing or standing up for their own. The contradictions inherent in the policies, and the policy development processes, only exacerbated the situation.

It became evident that we should not have pushed colleagues into behaviors and thinking they did not understand or agree with, as it brought out skepticism and complacency rather than energy, commitment, and action. When we live in caring relations, we must take responsibility for each other. "An ethic of caring does not sit in judgment and proceed by accusation and punishment" (Noddings, 1992, p. 120). "The best way to *care* for persons is to respect their rights and accord them their due, both in distribution of the burdens and benefits of social cooperation, and in the rectification of wrongs done" (Friedman, 1995, p. 71). The matrix represents formal relationships. This formality facilitates and sanctions control where there would otherwise be a lack of trust, or simply an inability to predict and plan necessary actions. Persons impacted by this are presented as competing for positions, and the effects of these relationships were negative for many.

Some principals usurped the authority of the administration, causing the director to revert to dealing in unilateral and hierarchical ways on some issues. There was a lack of faith that the matrix would actually work the way it was intended. A lack of trust prevented staff from caring and being cared for. There was much frustration and not enough tangible results.

In the context of our roles in the institution, it was difficult for the staff to consider district administrators as caring. We needed security that we would not be risking damage to our reputations with the school board and throughout the district and province. We were accountable for bringing about change and creating order and in the process were sometimes insistent, and impatient. That raised questions and caused people to doubt whether we really cared for others or merely used the rhetoric of care and shared decision making to promote ourselves.

Policy 3: Teachers' Personal and Professional Growth and Development

I chose the *Teachers' Personal and Professional Growth and Development Policy* (District, 2003b) for analysis because it represents a tangible attempt via policy development to demonstrate care for teachers and their learning/professional development. Its goal is to create an organizational environment in which knowledge is highly valued and ongoing learning is encouraged and facilitated.

The policy articulated a vision that breaks from tradition when the responsibility for maintaining teacher accountability resided with the administration. The responsibility and resources for teachers' professional development were shifting from the district and province to the school and individual. This offered substantial opportunity to create and support alternative and local initiatives that would value and give credence to the views and perspectives of educators at the local level. The process aimed "to create a pedagogical space that maximized collaboration, response and agency, a safe space" (Kamler, 2001, p. 122), where teachers could challenge dominant discourses and implement alternatives.

The policy was developed by a committee, including membership from the provincial teachers' association with district and school personnel. The initiative was research-based and invited input from within and outside the district. The committee completed the initial draft, sought feedback, redrafted and submitted the policy to the district administration who presented it to the school board for consideration and approval. This policy was closely related to the director's previous work and research at the university, and he influenced the committee through participation in meetings and by offering feedback on various drafts.

The procedure to develop and implement this policy direction employed the action research model (McNiff & Whitehead, 2000) that enabled members of the organization to write a personal plan in a systematic manner. Once developed, the growth plan was to be implemented by the individual with the support of a collegial team of one or two people. The essential steps involved in this process include: review the District Strategic Plan, review the School Growth and Development Plan, complete a self-assessment, draft three goals, select two goals for the current growth plan, write the Professional and Personal Growth Plan (Goals, Strategies, Timelines, Evaluation), share a copy of the plan with the school administrator, implement the plan with the support of one or two colleagues, and complete a year-end personal assessment of the plan with a colleague or school administrator (District, 2003b).

Concepts such as the knowledge society, lifelong learning, and the learning organization have become part of conventional business wisdom, but employers still do little to provide employees with adequate training opportunities (Lowe, 2000). This policy encourages responsible self-evaluation, where professional educators assess their work and draw on peers to participate in learning necessary new things. The policy assumes that the dominant training model of teachers' professional development—a model focused on expanding an individual's repertoire of well-defined and skillful classroom practice—is not adequate to achieve the new visions of teaching and learning. This professional development policy places classroom practice in the larger contexts of school and district practice. It is grounded in a bigger picture—the purposes and practices of schooling—providing teachers an opportunity to see connections between their work and that of others. Teachers are viewed as instrumental in the reform effort, although acknowledgement is made of the ways in which the entire organization is implicated. Principals and teachers had opportunity to play a significant role in the formulation of the policy. There was a district event to brainstorm ideas to be included, drafts were sent to schools for feedback, rewrites were done and then sent back to schools, more response was sought, and finally school principals and district personnel worked together in a meeting to process and finalize the draft that was presented to the school board for approval and adoption. This "rational, out-put oriented, plan-based, and management-led view of educational reform has been described as corporate management" (Sinclair, 1989, p. 389). The focus was on outcomes, access, and participation, with a balance of obligation and opportunity implicit in the policy. The expectation was that teachers and principals would develop their own policies, plans, and strategies to be consistent with the district policy. Then teachers were to identify their personal and professional goals, aligning them with the needs of the school and the district. This policy can be interpreted as a mechanism to control, to direct, and to put parameters on the professional development of teachers.

Much of what is called for in the current reform processes with respect to professional development is not skill oriented, because it cannot be expressed in specific, transferable skills. Instead it calls for authentic assessment of student learning, critical thinking skills, and curriculum integration. A skills approach to professional development would not be sufficient to accomplish the intellectual, organizational, and social requirements of teachers' reform efforts. Treating teachers as professionals, they are encouraged to find local solutions to discover and develop practices that embody their espoused values and principles, rather than demonstrate practices and skills thought to be universally effective (Little, 1994).

The policy is ironic given the province's history of major government funding cuts and the province's pervasive attitude that education needed to be trimmed and tightened rather than nurtured and grown. The limitations of financial resources placed constraints on the types of learning experiences that could be provided. The messy and often contentious forms of professional development to examine existing practice were often too expensive and time consuming before results could be measured or the process justified.

In response to the shift away from totally prescribing what government agencies and the district thought teachers needed to learn, the district moved to offering a menu from which they could choose. The sessions to be provided ranged from training in co-operative learning strategies to development and implementation of vision, mission, belief statements, and strategic plans, to classroom visits with colleagues in other schools and attendance at conferences. When teachers describe their preferred professional development experiences they say they enjoy sustained work with ideas, materials, and colleagues (Delong, 2002; Little, 1994; Williams & Sparkes, 2000). These types of activities require an organization to offer substantial depth and focus, adequate time, and a sense of doing real work as opposed to being talked at. The policy of the district aims to provide teachers with opportunities to meaningfully consult with colleagues and experts. "Teachers work collaboratively with other professionals to develop units of work and to improve practice" (District, 2003c).

Teachers as "reflective professionals" are held responsible and accountable for student learning and as with *Our Vision for Teaching and Learning,* a great deal is expected of them under the depiction as caring professionals:

> Because teaching and learning is a complex dynamic process, teachers constantly strive to gain more knowledge and understanding of the research about how the human brain learns in order to improve their teaching methods. Our best practices are based on research, and our vision for teaching and learning evolves accordingly. (District, 2003b)

There are contradictory discourses in the *Teachers' Personal and Professional Growth and Development Policy.* On the one hand, teachers are viewed as professionals who make their own decisions about what they need to learn, and how they should plan and implement teaching and learning strategies in their classrooms. On the other hand, the district outlines specific parameters and guidelines that must be followed in the development and implementation of each individual teacher's Growth Plan. There is the notion that teachers are autonomous, but also that they need to be monitored, checked on, and systematically evaluated. The policy is compatible with the organizational structures and cultures in which the work of the district happens (within the context of the district's goals and schools' goals).

The policy communicates a view of teachers as not only classroom experts but also persons engaged in a long-term career, who can make an impact in terms of perspectives, policy, and practice. The policy builds into the teachers' professional development program a focus and dependency on collaborative learning through networking with colleagues. The goal is to provide teachers with a broader network of professional relationships, small semiformal associations that extend beyond the classroom walls and exert influence on teachers' attitudes and practices. Partnerships among the Ministry of Education, teachers' association, university, district staff, and business community provide possibilities for valuable organizational activities designed and led jointly by teachers with others.

This policy is based on the pursuit of knowledge, the idea that educators, like students, are lifelong learners who need to be cared about and supported as we interrogate our individual beliefs and patterns of practice. The objective is to help employees to be knowledgeable, confident, and resilient and able to cope with multiple, often intense demands. However, this text contains contradictions as well. On the one hand, is the expectation that teachers are willing to generate knowledge and assess the knowledge of others, and on the other hand is bureaucratic restraint with the policy heavily influenced and dominated by district direction. Frequent use is made of the word *should*, indicating that action is imperative.

Each teacher completed an annual professional development request, outlining their needs, discussed it with school administrators to determine what could be provided at the local level, and then the requests were submitted and collated by district personnel who helped organize them and provide response. School as well as district funding was made available to enable the professional development to take place. In a time of serious cost-cutting, these efforts could certainly be recognized as meaningful ways to care for teachers. Care for teachers is tangibly demonstrated through the allocation of flexible funds to be used as the teachers, with their support team, deemed most appropriate. Former models of professional development provided standardized learning opportunities for teachers: what they should learn was prescribed for them by others. The provision of money in and of itself could never be sufficient or the lone solution, but it did provide unprecedented opportunities for teachers, and it demonstrated a real commitment on the part of the district to move away from old models of teacher training toward a more self-directed learning model.

Policy Consequences

All three policy documents studied represent an attempt by administration to socialize and conform educators within the new school district to the administration's preferred way of working. The policies are an effort to construct the work of educators and ensure compliance to policy mandates through dominance, coercion, pressure, position, and invitation. The district needed consistency and coherence across and among schools. New personnel were bringing new perspectives and priorities and a desire to separate from the past. Additionally, mandates from government, the ambition of individuals, requests from schools and individuals complicated our attempts to create order out of chaos. There was opportunity to build consensus and caring work relationships, but the result appears to be contrived collegiality.

There were multiple and sometimes contradictory meanings embedded within the district documents. Although they reflect current mainstream thinking in education and represent a set of espoused theories and values of what personnel in a school district need to know, and know how to do, the texts are also sites of struggle. They show traces of differing discourses and ideologies, and struggles for power and dominance.

Despite growing awareness among senior management of the importance of workers' knowledge, skills, and involvement in decision making, the fact remains that traditional work structures, management control systems, and an overriding focus on costs and profits make it difficult to nurture care in the workplace (Lowe, 2000). Resolving this contradiction remains a pressing issue on the human resource policy agenda. Despite our caring messages emphasizing lifelong learning, ongoing professional development, and shared decision making, the administration of the district was confronted with challenges from dominant processes of globalization from above.

The development of policy is a political and institutional process, involving contestation and compromise among and between differing groups and interests (Ball, Dworkin, & Vryonides, 2010; Ball, 2000, 2008; Taylor et al., 1997).

> In privileging the institutional and collective view however, the language of reform underestimates the intricate ways in which individual and institutional lives are interwoven. It underexamines the points at which certain organizational interests of schools and occupational interests of teachers may collide. (Little, 1994, p. 4)

It would be unwise for leaders to initiate change that is markedly inconsistent with the beliefs of the local community (Rhodes, 1990). Administration attempted to build a shared vision and implementation plan. We recognized that adequately providing teacher professional development was necessary to produce systemic change. There was an attempt to analyze current conditions, include community beliefs, and provide teacher professional development while business connections and change agendas were reinforced. The main challenges to the success of the policies were lack of resources to sustain implementation and persistent and constant changes in government and personnel at the district and school levels.

Structures can be understood as hierarchical relationships of power and processes that reinforce and subvert social relations. Organizations, for example, have a low tolerance for difference. There is a strong emphasis or similarity in understandings, language, and style, an expected commitment to corporate goals and to particular strategies and approaches (strategic planning, regulation, consistency, sameness, and conformity). "Symbolic power is a subtle form of control and domination that prevents this domination being recognized" (Blackmore & Sachs, 2007, p. 18). The district matrix illustrates this through promotion of individualism, competitiveness, and knowledge hierarchies.

Each of the policy documents emphasized the administration's preferred way of working. The "policies are an effort to construct the work of educators through their 'person-to-person and person-to-text' interactions" (Mehan, 2004, p. 347). All three policies could be interpreted as mechanisms, procedures, influences, pressures to invite, persuade, and silence opponents. "Neo-bureaucratic corporate educational organizations produce counterintuitive impulses that undermine, contradict, and even change what many educators described as 'the real work' the 'passionate work' of education, much of which is about social progress, creating opportunity, and 'doing good'" (Blackmore & Sachs, 2007, 199). The policies and guidelines were established to provide equitable opportunity and share decision making, but they also imposed limits and specified the participants to be involved.

The district's policies, procedures, and positional addresses did play a powerful role in clarifying the ambiguity of the early years of the district's conception and provided some consistency and a path forward for the educational community to follow. They were significant in socializing educators and others into the ways work was carried out in the district. Unfortunately, due to complex, imposed, and continuing changes to the education system of the province, there could be no orderly dialogue about or application and follow-through of the district's policies and procedures. As well, the dominant culture and situations at the time also created difficult working conditions. "When a woman's experiences of leadership do not fit that of the educational organization, they are positioned as not being ready or not appropriate, rather than considering that perhaps existing leadership representations and practices are not inclusive" (Blackmore & Sachs, 2007, p.18).

As members of the planning group, loyalty to district products and processes was expected from principals' meetings at the district, and most meetings were geared to advancing and defining the district plan. Individuals who pointed out problems were seen as negative and oppositional and soon understood they should be quiet; if they did not have something positive to say about the process, they should be complicit through silence. School and district personnel became "co-opted and self-divided, by institutionally coded governmental suppression of other virtuous dispositions" (Zipin & Brennan, 2003, p. 35) and had to advocate for and implement reforms that fundamentally they disagreed with, ethically and professionally. Inconsistency, misrepresentation, miscommunication, and perceptions of confusion and contradiction resulted.

People were encouraged to work together well and also expected to conform to organizational objectives, which meant navigating their way between control and support.

> What was most difficult was to move outside the parameters of the organizational goals and structures but still play the game, because the processes of consultation and strategic planning were tightly structured and monitored through centralized strategic planning.... [S]chool principals had to make their agendas fit with the district strategic plan, Directors had to fit within the provincial imperatives. Strategic planning was useful but also coercive. (Blackmore & Sachs, 2007, p.185)

The lines were being drawn between those who performed according to the expectations and those who did not. High-performing schools, districts, and teachers were identified, causing competitive relationships. The new accountability of professional management, together with outcome-based curriculum and assessment, reduced our capacity to focus on the individuals in our local situations (students, teachers, parents, etc.), and there was less room to be innovative outside the prescribed priorities.

It was a risky balancing act to perform in a global and local economy-driven environment while developing democratic claims and values. The exercises of performance management and accountability that focus on quantifiable outcomes fail to represent the complexity of teaching and what education is all about, yet they shape the nature of our work due to increased demands, standardization, and the narrowing of acceptable processes and outcomes. "Employees were to achieve predetermined outcomes without any guarantee that organizations provided the conditions of work that make such outcomes possible" (Blackmore & Sachs, 2007, p. 125).

Much of the focus of reform in the 1990s was structured with the devolution of responsibility for daily administration and outcomes to local levels in the form of self-managing, learning organizations.

> [S]tructured devolution had produced new forms of possibility but also new forms of constraint.... [W]hile there were [*sic*] discretionary activity possible at the level of the local decision-making unit...this was informed and shaped by the policies and contractual obligations imposed, on the one hand, and increased data collection, reporting, and auditing mechanisms back up that in turn delivered institutional and individual rewards and punishments on the other. (Blackmore & Sachs, 2007, pp. 112–113)

Ball (2000) suggests *performativity* leads institutions, and their leaders in particular, to construct institutional fabrications that are about escaping the gaze rather than being more transparent. This reduces the organizational capacity for meaningful evaluation and the ability to identify and resolve problems openly. Performativity is about representation and control, collecting data, producing reports, developing measures, best practices, comparability and a drive to constantly improve (Ball, 1997, 2000, 2003). The standardization of curriculum and evaluation "presents substantial role conflicts for teachers, pitting the reform's values of performance, efficiency, and academic achievement against teachers' values of care and investment in broader cognitive, social, and emotional development of students" (Vanderberghe & Huberman, 1999, p. 73).

Government's rationale, discourses, and measures of effectiveness were difficult to counter with "technologies of surveillance embedded in the hyper-rationality of corporate managerialism" (Blackmore & Sachs, 2007, p. 119). Most people in education were ambivalent, especially during the second round of reform, but felt that the balance between autonomy and accountability was weighed increasingly toward the latter. Although "governance is not about centralization or decentralization, it is about regulating relationships in complex systems" (Rhoades, 1996, p. 151); a sharpening divide grew between the policy actors that produced education policy reforms (politicians, consultants, bureaucrats) and the teacher and manager practitioners expected to implement them. Different games were played with their own logic and "truth"; players who wanted to stay in the game acceded, learned the rules, and made strategic moves as they deemed necessary. Contradictory tendencies were evident of centralization and decentralization, between innovation and maintenance work, and between care and compliance in organizations.

Care and Caring

Through its policies, the district aimed to go beyond the awareness and recognition that care is necessary (caring about) to actually assume responsibility for identified needs, and also determined how to respond to those (taking care of). There was action to address the unmet needs of those for whom care was given. Having recognized the professional development and ongoing learning needs of teachers, the district approved a policy complete with defined implementation procedures. The task of taking care of the teachers' needs went beyond that, and a source of time and money was allocated and support personnel coordinated. These are the taking care of tasks the district initiated, and in such a cost-cutting period, it was a real and meaningful demonstration of caring. It is impossible to determine through this policy analysis whether the needs were actually met, but substitute teacher time as well as an allocation of funds were assigned to each school to be used at the staff's discretion.

Some teachers did avail themselves of opportunities to travel to various schools and districts to meet with colleagues. Some teachers were supported to attend local and out-of-province conferences. Money does not solve human needs, though it provides the resources by which needs can be satisfied (Tronto, 1993). There is a great deal more effort required to convert a policy or allocation of resources into satisfying human needs. In the final phase of caring, the object of care will respond to the care it receives.

Conflict occurred over the focus on how to achieve what was an agreed upon purpose. Mutual respect, recognition, and representation of diverse interests and needs were necessary but difficult to accomplish in the environment where agendas were being mandated from above and where the time and resources necessary to adequately implement the complex decision-making process were not available. Shortly after its labor-intensive development process was finalized in 2003, the district was thrust into another provincially mandated consolidation. Given all this, it is clear the district had little chance to work beyond its initial implementation dips (Fullan, 1993) to realize the goals it intended. The district's bureaucracy seriously distorted and fragmented caring activities through the hierarchy of authority and power; its division of labor and the policies and processes did nothing to alleviate this barrier.

"Caring" is seldom directly referred to in the policy texts, other than in reference to teacher interactions with students and parents. However, a complication is that district personnel were to provide care for a number of other persons with conflicting needs. How the caregivers navigate these conflicts affects the quality of care and the perceptions on the part of those cared for as to whether or not they received good care. In this study, it is evident that the care receivers had a different idea about their needs than did the caregivers. The care receivers wanted to be more actively involved and directive in the kinds of caring they received. Educators carry out the work of developing and implementing policies related to teaching and learning, and through these routines and practices conceptions of care and uncaring became evident. Some calls for help were not answered, but others calls were responded to because they fit into particular parameters or agendas.

Discourse analysis of the three policy documents revealed that attempts to show care or develop care were central to the meanings the documents had for the district. However, responses to administration's attempts to develop and implement caring policies clashed with managerial discourses and neoliberal provincial restructuring imperatives. The potency of the discourses ran counter to the province's activities that were pressured by globalizing forces.

Complexity and Ambiguity

The reform initiatives in education presented a challenge of considerable complexity and ambiguity. There was an uneven fit between the aspirations and challenges of the initiatives and the practice and implementation. The reforms required a great deal in terms of intellectual and practical struggle as well as emotional engagement. Ways were needed to open up debates, construct real dialogue, and enrich the current array of possibilities for caring action. There was good intent and incremental steps were taken by individuals with progressive ideologies and principles consistent with the complexity of the reform task. Line authority was a strong influence as was illustrated through the development of the decision-making matrix. The chart with its distinct rows, columns, blocks, and codes were all ways of representing the lines of authority. It was not considered to be a truly collaborative process, and the chart did not represent the meaningful discussion and dialogue the process intended.

In fact, the document was developed from the director's standpoint. He needed a framework to provide apparent order to a very complex situation, and the business of the district needed to proceed. Although it was hoped the document would be a clear, concise statement that would remove ambiguity, others viewed it as ordered, hierarchical, top-down, not collaborative, and void of dialogue. The policies became formalized, rational, institutional representations that confronted the personal, common sense, and localized voices. Institutional representations are given higher status than the local ones. If, through the matrix development and implementation process the district was serious about moving away from top-down, command-and-control management styles, we needed more details on what the model would look like and how it could work. Because of the entrenched traditional hierarchy in education in the province, it was unrealistic to expect to create a new model that would work within the old one.

Reflection

We need to practice democratic and ethical educational leadership. We need a sustained process of open dialogue, a right to voice, community inclusion, and responsible participation toward the common good. We need honesty and openness in our approaches and the ability to see beyond our own agendas. This is a daunting project, especially during the turbulence of education reform. Caring relationships are difficult to sustain in work environments where individuals and groups are under the pressure of competing interests and demands. This study of caring policies revealed common concerns and identified and created the possibility of new alliances and alternative practices. Despite many pressures from above and challenges within, there are options emerging from the collaboration of groups and communities and the caring approaches and policies of leaders.

The effects of an emergent global economy are used to justify policy aimed at producing multiskilled, flexible, and more productive workers (Taylor et al., 1997). An implementation plan that does not adequately provide teacher professional development is unlikely to produce systemic change (Rhodes, 1990). Through these policies, the district attempted an innovation that encouraged employees to learn and contribute their expertise in all aspects of their daily work. This empowerment required change, not just in workplace structures and policies, but also in its culture. If the district was serious about developing people's knowledge and skills through continuous learning, then the quality of their work and work relationships needed to become a central issue, and there needed to be openness to make other significant changes. The education system's long entrenched hierarchical system with its top-down decision making and adoption of cost-cutting and restructuring directives were huge barriers to the district's ability to move forward, as they had negative effects on employees' morale, confidence, and productivity. Restoring a caring dimension to organizational management agendas may well be an important step toward ensuring future success.

More than caring intentions and decisions are necessary. We need continuing attention by leaders who listen, invite, guide, and support. Coercion produces resistance and weakens the relation (Noddings, 1999c). What is real, what is evident and relevant varies from person to person and position to position. Sometimes participants, as well as others not involved in the process of developing these policy directives, felt like faceless cases and complained that they were not cared for. Coercion signaled a lack of caring, and it would be wise to try to move from coercion to genuine persuasion.

It is possible to redesign jobs and organizations, to create a more people-centered working life, and to craft policies that encourage workplace innovation and increase meaningful work opportunities. Many believe that the strength of the economy lies in its knowledge workers and that continuous learning and adaptable skills are the key to prosperity (Lucas, 1999; Northouse, 2004; O'Toole, 1996; Popper & Lipshitz, 2000; Senge, 2006). The research literature is rife with calls for hierarchical organizational structures to be dismantled or flattened, and there are calls for employers and others in authority positions to get closer to their workers as well as the clients, students, or customers they serve. Workplaces need to become more humane. When workers/educators feel their needs are met, they will be more willing—and it will be easier for them—to meet the needs of others. A more complex notion of power, one not limited to hierarchical power, is needed; power needs to be thought of as a productive network (Franzway, 2005) that is woven into the fabric of everyday life.

It is evident that a network of power existed in relation to the development and implementation of each of the district policies. In the hierarchy, the upper levels were affected by other groups and how they were supportive of or reluctant to embrace the proposed changes. There seems to be an attempt in each of the three policy documents to flatten power but responses reveal that the vertical structures remained. True networks of power attempt to show that power is not static, and it does not exist only at the top. In our district's case, although there was still plenty of it at the top, attempts were made to make it appear otherwise.

A powerful outcome of the teachers' professional development policy was its impact on teacher professionalism. The organization was enabling teachers to participate structurally and officially in matters that affected them, and consequently, they could alter the ways the teaching profession was conceived and regulated. Teachers no longer had to labor in isolation. It became the obligation of teachers to closely examine their own practice and professional judgments, and this forward-looking document demonstrated care and concern for the voices and perspectives of teachers—it valued them as professionals. Teachers were given an opportunity to collaborate with others in their field. Through this policy, the district encouraged independent thought and judgment and participation in decision making. By caring about educators and acknowledging the importance of their intellectual capacities, and by crediting their contributions to knowledge and practice, such approaches could strengthen the enthusiasm they brought to their work and their interactions in the classroom.

Educators are promoting continuous learning as a way to build the knowledge economy—for workers to actively learn they must apply their knowledge in their work—but individuals cannot do this alone. It must be shaped by the collaboration among workers, employers, and governments. High-quality working conditions are necessary and fundamental to a democratic society: investment in professional development, support for family life and employee wellness, and the establishment of a co-operative culture of trust and openness. Policies to help create work environments supportive of a balanced life, setting clear expectations, caring for employees, providing recognition, and demonstrating to them that their opinions count (Flade, 2003) are all needed.

In this case, the caregivers were perceived as rational and autonomous. Consequently, the relationship between the groups was unequal, and relationships of authority and dependency emerged. Caregivers would be wise to consider and understand how their authoritative positions work in relation to those for whom they care. The power of the people in control played a huge role in these policies. Contrary to intent, I believe the relations of care were weakened rather than enhanced.

Global competitiveness and the interrelationship of global, national, provincial, and local organizations contribute to all sorts of intangible impacts or effects on practice in both the short- and long-term. Top-down policy and disseminated strategies for change and good practice in school will vary widely, depending on the people implementing them and the variety of interpretations they make of the policies. This document analysis can raise awareness and will help to reinforce and legitimate the need for shared reform in schools and other educational organizations. There will no doubt be different levels of initiative and commitment taken by different groups. I believe these have not evened out in the Province of Newfoundland and Labrador because of confusion and distraction caused by recent, ongoing board and school consolidations, and changes in district and provincial leadership. Despite this I believe that "the political and cultural economy of globalization presents opportunities as well as obstacles for progressive activism and new ways of working" (Franzway, 2005, p. 268). We need to start with what we have; what can be done may be discovered through a search for political possibilities, in this case examining the caring policies and practices of a district.

To find new ways forward in our globalizing world, we must seek to increase involvement in decision making at local as well as global levels by working to establish structures and processes that advance democracy and democratic work environments. If we are to find cohesion in our work lives, we will have to improve upon our processes of negotiating diversity within a commitment to care. These ends are especially difficult to achieve when governments and large organizations through globalization are moving us in the opposite direction.

Based on this analysis, I recommend that organizations undertake a policy review process every five years to determine how implementation is going. In this study, development of the policies with action plans was consultative and research-based, but because no other local models existed, the district struggled through the development process. As eager as change agents can be, we would be wise to be patient, allowing time to reflect as well as to plan and encourage and to guide negative employees and participants. We need to be prepared for others to make the decisions they want to make, not the ones we expect them to make. It is not the leaders' prerogative or responsibility to make all the important decisions (Pellicer, 2003); people naturally care more about the decisions they make than the decisions made for them by others.

The experience of this district provides an interesting study in the ongoing themes of power and authority of educators and the need for activists to respond to key local issues in the context of the global politics of education. With the aim of increasing community, by sharing decision making and participation in the management and direction of schooling, the district administration developed and implemented a number of reform policies that triggered considerable resistance but also created worthwhile discussion and opportunity for its education community. The pervasive effects of the provincially mandated consolidation of school districts pre-empted the district from working through implementation of its policies to experience the effects of their directions. District leadership made significant attempts toward attentive caring; unfortunately, these became confused with numerous other competing changes and directions. The complex demands of leaders to simultaneously respond to and respect others offer an illuminating and too-little noticed example of caring effort.

Attempting to care within an institutional setting is complex. We need to acknowledge that control and authority often are needed to effect caring. However, the effective use of power involves developing caring relationships with sensitivity, understanding, and compassion. Having to function in the midst of ambiguity only increased frustration, isolation, and distrust. Caring required more than understanding the feelings, understanding the ambiguous nature of roles, and how that ambiguity affected what could be accomplished. It also required understanding that collaboration and support were necessary from the entire staff.

The broader significance of and implications for care in educational (as well as other) institutions and organizations has, for the most part, been unexplored. One of the strengths that makes this study a worthwhile research contribution is that it brings together policy development and implementation analysis with the literature on caring. It helps fill a gap by documenting a clash between discourses of care and discourses of new managerialism referred to in various ways through the identification of contradictions and ironies in the policy development processes and in the documents themselves.

This is a case study of how the restructuring of the province—both as a funding body and as an education system—is worked out "on the ground." This study shows how difficult it is to juggle the two, and how the juggling is complicated by hierarchical structures and a mix of stakeholders that includes students and the broader community. This CDA offers opportunity to rethink what it means to be an educational leader and provide leadership for social justice. This examination provided space to critically consider what we had contributed to and what we failed to accomplish for others within a particular institutional setting. Each of the texts impacted the lives of educators and students throughout the district. What is the fit between reform and care for the people trying to implement it? To what extent does policy making rely on persuasion/coercion and regulation, or genuine dialogue and collaboration? In current care theory, caring refers to relation, not just to an agent who "cares," and we must consider the response of the cared for. Therefore, an organization might need to design multiple policies as guides through the maze of possibilities it encounters. It would be best not to use universal policies that require coercion; coercion produces resistance and weakens the relationship because it is a power technique.

When we turn to policy making, we see both the complementarity and conflict between justice and care (Noddings, 1999a). It is clearly not enough to make a just decision or to establish a just policy. One must follow up with caring implementation and with reflection guided by care to see whether the original policy has fulfilled its aims or has introduced new inequalities or harms. We need thinking that goes beyond the usual pattern of justice thinking, as justice orientations often prescribe formulaic remedies and then pronounce the problem theoretically solved (Noddings, 1999a). Justice draws to our attention the unfairness of a situation; care cautions us to look at the individuals before we recommend a remedy and to listen to those whose aspirations, interests, talents, and legitimate values may differ from our own (Noddings, 1999a).

Theory needs to describe what constitutes good caring in the context of work in organizations and the public domain. We need to rethink how particular circumstances (for example, how policies get developed) are socially constructed. We need to also consider the appropriate forms caring can take in organizations. Some schools and teachers have significantly influenced teaching practice—through acts of caring leadership and organization—not by being legislated, mandated, regulated, or coerced. A good question to explore is how can policy enable more of these actions? More study is needed in the area of top-down and bottom-up relationships. Consideration of the kinds of policy that could promote caring practices, as well as what happens to those who experience the consequences of decisions, are other areas deserving of further study.

5

Rationalism or Humanism

We are afraid to care too much, for fear that the other person does not care at all.
—Eleanor Roosevelt

It is important to be able to articulate a relationship between one's personal interests and sense of significance and larger social concerns expressed in the works and lives of others (Clandinin & Connelly, 2000) and a mistake to try to transform the educational system without revising our sense of selves as learning beings (Peterson, 1997). Reality is socially constructed (Czarniawska, 1997). There are many coconstructors of our world; therefore, rather than claim that my utterances are reality, I ask that others compare mine to theirs, since "good knowledge is what is judged by a relevant community (situated in time and place) to be useful, moral, or beautiful" (Czarniawska, 1997, p. 56). "To reveal one's own vulnerability in an accountability climate may be not only difficult, but also personally sensitive. Being asked to tell a story removes some of that danger, but risks being judged in a nonserious manner" (Crawford, 2009, p. 48). It is my plan that in constructing and reconstructing my self-narrative, the more broadly capable I will be in effective relationships (Gergen, 2004).

Caring Leadership in Turbulent Times, pages 131–166
Copyright © 2014 by Information Age Publishing
All rights of reproduction in any form reserved.

The purpose of this chapter is to present some everyday conflicts as demonstrations of ethical dilemmas in turbulent times. I examine two critical incidents that took place in our school district as my colleagues and I worked to implement neoliberal education reform policy legislated by our provincial government. I focus on our experiences and examine the extent to which our leadership was caring or not. The experiences also serve to highlight that "emotions cut to the core of people," (Denzin, 1984, p. 2), which only bolsters the urgency for establishing an ethic of care in workplaces.

> Leadership during education reform was linked to hard-nosed aggressive and authoritarian behavior, stereotypically masculine. The management paradigm mobilized during the 1990s was about reengineering education in "hard line" ways, promoting images of being tough, entrepreneurial, and decisive, sidelining the human costs, and utilizing demoralizing and dehumanizing strategies of downloading responsibility, downsizing organizations, and outsourcing or casualizing core work. (Blackmore & Sachs, 2007, p. 10)

A critical incident has been defined as a straightforward account of an everyday event that is crucial in its indication of underlying trends, motives, and structures (Tripp, 1998). Critical incidents contain an aha moment, leading us to question in whose interests we are working and how effectively (Mulhearn & Rogers, 2004). This chapter is derived from my day-to-day experiences working as a district administrator, collaborating with other district administrators, school board trustees, program specialists, school administrators, teachers, and community members. I discuss two such critical incidents to address the questions: what does caring offer to the reconstruction of work, and why is caring especially important for leaders struggling to work through the turbulence of education reform?

Through tacit stories of myself and my work world I examined some of my personal experiences of either giving care or withholding it, which helped me theorize about my life and work. I have written to explore the processes and culture of care (Tronto, 1993). Epiphanies, or "those interactional moments that leave marks on people's lives, have the potential for creating transformational experiences" (Denzin, 1989, p. 15). "Through story we can compare the worlds others create with our own representations, re-evaluate our own feelings and ideas, come to terms with past experiences and enter into the lives of others" (Booth, 1999, p. 3). I tried to step back, to distance myself, and after the passage of time be reflexive to determine what I could learn from the incidents in terms of our understandings, expectations, and efforts to care.

Analysis helped me analyze some of my dilemmas working as a woman in a male-dominated work environment during turbulent times. My writing is about balancing the demands and learning ongoing throughout the course of a multifaceted life that appears to be a challenge few have documented but many have experienced. Personal narratives of critical incidents are significant in illustrating my understanding of our continuing work in education and the practices of care that occurred, or did not occur, within it. I do not assume that everyone has had the experiences I describe, but taking my story and making connections with other experiences "allows us to particularize, to see and hear things" (Greene, 1995, p. 29).

I reflect on my work during the chaos of education reform amid a world of various personalities, issues, and circumstances and believe these critical incidents are relevant to educational leaders in various school settings. Common experiences convey values and significance that indicate how the people in organizations behave. This helps us formulate our beliefs and values, and we begin to understand why we are accustomed to speak and act in particular ways. My incidents are local stories about organizational life told to uncover the workings of our school district. The stories I share bring to life the ethical dilemmas that evolve from the complexities of working in these turbulent times in education.

In the climate of uncertainty, frustration, and a sense that we had compromised too far, even we tenured senior staff wondered whether we would have a job tomorrow. Indeed, all district administrators in the province did lose their jobs. For me it was September 3, 1996, prior to the first wave of reform in the province when I received correspondence declaring my position as assistant superintendent redundant. I was more fortunate than many of my colleagues: after a new recruitment process, I was hired in 1997 as one of the four administrators of the newly formed school board. It became commonplace to hear comments such as, "I don't trust the system and the people in it," "Everything is changing too fast," and "I'm not in control."

There was no effort to address the needs of those experiencing difficulty; as a result, people resorted to survival techniques. If pushed some pushed back; others attempted to preserve relationships with those in authority over them by agreeing when they really disagreed. They sat back and listened and avoided open conflict. They chose not to respond. Many perceived the lack of fairness and maltreatment of colleagues typical of other workplaces under restructuring. Several incidents fuelled distrust, and the process of public consultation articulated through this critical incident was certainly one!

District administrators had the power of position. Our location in the organization and community enabled us to act, but we felt pressure to act in detached, rational, and competitive ways rather than in collaborative, open, connected, and responsive ways. To survive we became enculturated into a hierarchical rather than democratic model of bureaucracy. I felt growing unease with the emphasis on bottom-line efficiencies and externally, top-down imposed agendas alongside discomfort with how I witnessed and experienced others and myself being treated.

A Case of "Severe Turbulence": Public Consultation About Education Reform

The first incident provides an opportunity to hear my self-reflective "inner voice" and speak about the cultural and educational world that has shaped me. This story addresses the power of location and status in the community and also the implications of the processes of education reform on personal and professional life. The incident occurred in the midst of an economic, political, and social process within the context of much broader political and economic change.

The ethic of care challenges the dominant and often patriarchal ethic of justice in our society and leads to discussions of empowerment, loyalty, and trust. An ethic of care leads us to consider the consequences of our decisions and actions (Noddings, 2001) and to contemplate such matters (Noddings, 1984, 1992, 2001, 2007; Shapiro & Gross, 2008) as:

- Who will benefit from what I decide?
- Who will be hurt by my actions?
- What are the long-term effects of a decision I make today?
- What is in the best interest of the student?
- What does the community think about this issue?

Shields's (2004) remarks upon the challenges of educational leadership only underscore the high expectations care generates.

> Educational leadership is widely recognized as complex and challenging. Educational leaders are expected to develop learning communities, build the professional capacity of teachers, take advice from parents, engage in collaborative and consultative discussion making, resolve conflicts, engage in educative instructional leadership, and attend respectfully, immediately, and appropriately to the needs and requests of families with diverse cultural, ethnic, and socioeconomic backgrounds. Increasingly, educational leaders are faced with tremendous pressure to demonstrate that every child for whom they are responsible is achieving success. (p. 109)

The narrative that follows explores and makes evident how people with formal leadership responsibilities relate to others. It illustrates the rigidity of positions, frequent inflexibility, ongoing personal sacrifice, lack of care, and winner/loser mentality typical of work in many organizations today. The current climate for educational leadership has actually been described as "greedy work" (Franzway, Court, & Connell, 1989; Franzway, 2001; Gronn, 2003). This incident taught me a lesson about how our jobs can affect our personal life. It caused me to question many things. I pondered how one can learn with others while not always agreeing with them and how one could create more caring relationships within which participants respect and value each other's opinions but also tolerate disagreement and diversity.

A PERSONAL JOURNAL ENTRY, OCTOBER 17, 2000

What a night! After a busy and full workday, I arrived at one of our elementary schools to sit through three hours of public hearings related to school closures and reconfiguration! One by one we listened to the presentations from angry, hurt, and disappointed individuals—parents, students, teachers, school council representatives, and community leaders—opposing the School Board's proposals to reorganize schooling for students in the school zone that I attended as a student and worked in as a teacher. I sat with the three other district administrators and the elected trustees behind a long table stretched across the length of the gymnasium. Rows of occupied chairs almost filled the room, and a lone podium with a microphone was positioned at the center of the room and directly in front of us.

A variety of speakers took their turn: some irate and irrational but provoked the audience to cheers and applause by personally insulting individual members on the panel of "dignitaries" before them whose role tonight is only to listen. Other speakers were calm, cool, and collected. They presented logical and well-researched arguments either in favor of, or opposing, various options. Some students spoke passionately about not wanting to be separated from their friends, others dreaded the breakup of their athletic teams and threatened that life can never be the same for them if they are forced to move to a different school. Parents of a disabled child pleaded with us not to change the school system because now their autistic child has just become accustomed to his teacher, classroom, and school routines. Mayors of municipalities accused us of contributing to the death of rural communities and to the out migration and resettlement of citizens. We all realize that a school is at the heart of these small towns, and if any new families move into the area they are likely going to choose to settle in a town that has a school for their children to attend. For any community to lose its school will no doubt be devastating.

I looked out over the sea of faces in the audience and unlike others on the panel, I recognized many of them. There were former classmates who graduated from high school with me, colleagues with whom I have taught, former students, and brothers and sisters-in-law, nieces and nephews with whom I shared Sunday dinner.

I feel a personal struggle as to what the right decision for schooling in this area can be, and no doubt so do many others who were there. The zone covers over 100 kilometers, has four inadequate high school buildings, four elementary schools between 20 and 25 years old, and a total K–12 student population of 1,200. Enrolments are projected to continue to decline for at least the next 10-year period. Everyone agrees that schools need to be closed and consolidated, but it can't be their school!

I sat there and made eye contact with some individuals who see me as an advocate for their cause. They expect me to lobby the trustees to vote for their favored option. Either because I am from a particular community, attended a particular high school, taught somewhere, or because I am related to them— they think they clearly know what the right answer is and that I am obviously "on their side." I think they are hoping that through a special link with me, they will be able to sway me to support them and use my position to their advantage. How can I be impartial, unbiased? I know the area and its people better than the other administrators working with me on this project. I know where the road conditions will be problematic on snowy winter days. My parents helped collect door to door to raise funds to support the construction of one of the schools now slated to close! I know many of the community leaders personally and have a good reputation and history with them. I consider these to be assets, but still I realize there are those who do not trust me to make the best recommendation. I made my connections to the people and issues in the area known to my colleagues and the board because I want them to be aware of my bias but also of my specific knowledge that could be an advantage.

Some of the trustees have little knowledge about the area that will be so significantly impacted by the vote they take. Others who, like me, either live in or have a more intimate knowledge of the zone, wonder what my influence on the decision will be: can I sway it in a certain direction, can I be objective? Throughout the process the trustees are urged to listen to and consider all the information presented and then make the decision that they believe to be best for our students. It will be difficult to vote to close a school in one of the communities they represent even if it is the most educationally sound option. Politics abound.

I tried to listen intently as the various speakers had their say. I felt as if we need[ed] to continually "turn the other cheek." It is difficult for many of us on the panel who have worked diligently and given many volunteer hours of service for the education of our young people to have our motives questioned and our personalities and credibility attacked.

My family and I have agreed that whenever we get together we would not discuss school-related issues. While I appreciate their willingness to give me a break from the "heat" rather than contribute to it, it is frustrating because I cannot vent some frustrations and receive some much needed understanding and support. While I often feel alone in this process, I do realize that back in our hometown community others pressure my family because I work at the board office and it is expected that they will get "favors" because of that connection. My brothers are unable to respond to some unkind commentary despite the fact that they understand and believe that I am trying to be fair to everyone. This isn't easy for any of us.

I am thankful to be part of an administrative team. Together we weigh all the facts and input gathered, then as a team, make a recommendation to the board. We are determined not to favor any community or group over the other but aim to do what is best for students and their education. However, when we bring our recommendation forward it enters the political arena, and anything can come out at the end.

There are so many factors to weigh:

- how to maximize program opportunities for the greatest number of students;
- how to most effectively deploy our human and material resources;
- bussing distances for students in this area;
- the condition of the current buildings;
- the cost of construction of a new building or renovation to older ones;
- community, parent, and school council preferences; and
- the history of communities and patterns of usual travel between them.

Even though a thorough, collaborative, public, and consultative planning process has been engaged in, there is no one answer that will satisfy everyone. In the end some groups and communities will perceive themselves as the winners . . . others [as] the losers. There will be demonstrations of protest, interruptions for schools and student learning, and media coverage. Some will perceive me as a traitor who let them down and others as a professional who challenged her own taken-for-granted assumptions and understandings and ultimately did what was best for education.

School boards are on the front line of educational change and their ability to respond effectively determines not only their success but also the success of the schools they lead and of the communities they serve (MacLellan, 2009). It had been intensive work to prepare and present professionals and our communities with various scenarios and options that sought and incorporated everyone's input. The process had been collaborative to a point, accommodating to a point. We believed that by seeking input through consultation, the reform objectives could be achieved in a manner acceptable to most involved and also accomplish the government reform directive. It was the hope of our district administrative team that a sincere and meaningful consultation process would make the unpleasant, and certainly difficult and painful process, also a respectable, open, considerate, fair, and democratic one.

Before beginning our rounds of public meetings, district administration first met with other office staff to brainstorm options and develop the scenarios. We entertained every possible arrangement we could imagine for schooling in each area of the district. We aimed to be objective, but of course we each brought our own biases to the task and expressed them in our responses to suggested arrangements. We fleshed out the details of each option complete with student enrolment projections, bussing distances, operational cost savings, and necessary renovation plans; we felt prepared for the public consultation sessions. We thought we presented them openly, forthrightly, answered questions, and invited other alternatives to be presented. We allowed time for communities and other groups to do some "homework" of their own before a second round of public meetings was scheduled to hear their responses and again receive input. We felt confident that we had considered and outlined every possible scenario. No one group or individual would get what they wanted. We attempted to circumvent favoritism and political interference; we aimed to be fair and just.

Still, some communities would lose their school, be required to bus their children longer distances, but in return receive the benefit of broader curricular offerings, have access to more specialist teachers (counselling and special education), enjoy improved science facilities and progressive educational technology. Either older buildings were going to be renovated or new schools would be constructed. We looked for opportunity and improvement, wanting reform to be about more than the loss of a religious-based system or mere downsizing; nonetheless, there were those who perceived us as trying to put a "positive spin" on a bad situation where some students, teachers, and communities would lose out and others benefit.

During the public consultation, teachers, students, parents, and community groups expressed significant opposition. Accusations of favoritism and unfairness were frequent. Board members and district administration were berated and accused of being inept, and there were myriad local newspaper articles featuring the struggles ongoing within and among communities as well as with the school board.

Although some scenarios were altered based on the input from the sessions, we were still accused of withholding some information. The process was perceived as political and not a true consultation process. We were accused of being insensitive and uncaring; we were blamed for upsets in communities, for individuals, families, and professionals. We were accused of not listening and not caring. Serious frustrations were expressed verbally and in writing, publicly and privately. Mistrust abounded, causing many to jump to unfair conclusions. Public outcries and demonstrations came fast and furious; people were often in tears as a result of their deep passion and the losses they perceived of long-held traditions and relationships. Everyone in the process felt marginalized in some way: parents, community leaders, educators, district administrators, and school board members. We all felt wronged.

A member of a town council spoke to oppose what he considered a grave injustice to close the school regarded as the center of that community with its rich history, traditions, fond memories, celebrations of graduations and achievements, and stories of victory and defeat in sports events. Everyone acknowledged that change needed to happen but asked that it be in another school rather than the one in their town. There was an abundance of posturing and self-righteous indignation as people campaigned to keep their schools open and close others.

Teachers were threatened with insubordination and letters of reprimand were issued to quiet them.

> The labor law generally states that employees may be disciplined for insubordination. Conduct which constitutes insubordination includes actions of employees that somehow undermine the authority of the employer. This includes off-duty conduct. Let's take the example of school reconfigurations and closures. It may be justified for a school board to take disciplinary action against a teacher who speaks out at a public meeting against the board's decision to close a school. While teachers, like all Canadians, enjoy the right to freedom of speech and expression, like other employees, they are subject to the limitations on this freedom in the context of the employer/employee relationship. This is often referred to as the duty of fidelity or loyalty to one's employer. The more closely an issue is related to the scope and nature of the teacher's employment, the more likely it is that the duty not to undermine the employer will outweigh the teacher's right to speak out publically on the issue. (Hobbs, 2007, p. 10)

Board members were personally attacked, berated, and accused of enjoying the power of position and not caring about the students they were elected to serve and support. District office personnel were accused of being incompetent as educators and removed from what was actually happening in classrooms and schools. Department of Education officials were accused of dumping their "dirty work" onto school boards, and district personnel were merely passing the pain along to people at the local level. Many people felt their integrity had been attacked. A few felt privileged, connected to the powerful decision makers, and expressed confidence that their preferred option would win out over the others. There were letters, phone calls, and behind-closed-door meetings that prompted tears, outrage, insult, hurt, and the feeling of being maligned. Our meetings were punctuated with hurtful words, full of sarcasm and pretense. We were all caught up in "severe turbulence" (Shapiro & Gross, 2008), despite the initial intent to involve people in a smooth, open, and democratic process. We ended the process with deep wounds that were far from healed when the second wave of reform was undertaken.

The morning after our public consultation had ended, I entered my office and readied myself to face the day. The first thing I always did was check email, listen to voice messages, and respond to immediate concerns. On that day, my inbox contained 14 new emails and my telephone showed seven voice messages. Even before I attended to any messages, I knew they were all going to be coming from angry and upset people, each concerned with how the reconfiguration of schooling in my assigned area of the district was proceeding. I prepared myself as I listened to the messages. Angry parent, after upset board member, after concerned teacher, and stressed principal stated how there were problems with the reform process, the direction it was taking, or the options. Over the previous two years, parents, community leaders, and educators had all become aware first-hand of the difficulties and complexities of school reform. Now that they understood how it worked, they were quicker to get involved, be proactive with intent either to overturn or minimally affect the ultimate outcome.

Many individuals and groups were struggling to reposition themselves in the new system. Some people felt silenced, beaten to submission, and exhausted by struggles like those represented through this critical incident. They felt the pressures of managerial coercion: there was little that could be done other than accept resulting decisions and outcomes. Those silenced did not speak out because they believed they could not change what was happening. Other people acted out and risked being viewed as a troublemaker (Blackmore, 1999). Once labelled a troublemaker, it becomes difficult to be taken seriously (Zipin & Brennan, 2003).

I struggled with caring in my work; even though I knew I could not achieve the ideal, it was worth striving for because it was—and still is—consistent with how I aim to live. I believed there was another way to lead, but I had no chance to do it. Although I tried to stay upbeat, pleasant, and positive about the meaning and value of my work, on many days it was a challenge to convince myself. I worked hard to accommodate the new practices and priorities expected of me by government officials and the district's director of education, while I also sought to maintain my valued relationships and ways of working. I "tried to learn and work strategically, through the webs of power and discourses of possibility that many, but not all, men take for granted" (Blackmore & Sachs, 2007, p. 146).

I had to discern the pecking order, the hot spots between divisions/departments and individuals, learn how to get information and give it, maintain relationships, and what I could and could not say to certain people. On the one hand, as district administrators we were teaching openness and the need to understand each other's work and roles as important features of a "learning organization" (Senge, 1990, 2000); on the other, I found myself always being careful with what I said and to whom. I wanted to be more trusting, open, to tell others everything I believed they needed to know, but it was about power—and information is power. I felt I could not be perceived as a dissenter within the district leadership circles, so I learned to compromise, to bite my tongue, and to bridle what I wanted to say. I wanted to speak up to power, but felt silenced once in power. I was told I had to comply or get out. I felt emotionally drained, exhausted, depersonalized, and reduced to being competitive, compliant, and alienated.

> Paradoxically, at a time when passion, creativity, and caring social relationships were necessary for individual and institutional survival, the tendency of education reforms has been toward technical expertise, standardization and uniformity, products of both markets that produce risk and the new managerialism that seeks to manage it. (Blackmore & Sachs, 2007, p. 2)

I understand this incident as representative of "the games we play." I do not use the metaphor of a game to disrespect or demean the process we undertook, as it was important and legitimate to give the people to be affected by change a voice; indeed, often the expressed voices had an impact on final decisions and outcomes. It is true, though, that many perceived the consultation process to be "a game" that wasted valuable time, a legalistic due process necessary to protect the school board from future potential court challenges. This was especially true for the people who felt they lacked the power of position that would allow them more possibility for action and for changing directions.

The board trustees and administration expected certain normative rules of "the game" to operate—norms that we hoped would give an opportunity to anyone who wanted to be heard. There were the official positions set up as a game board might be, with all players assigned specific places and spaces. Props were positioned—long tables behind which the officials sat, neat rows of chairs in front for speakers and spectators, and a microphone was stationed strategically between the two. There was a definite sense of "we" and "they," opposing sides, and various strategies were used by each side to advance their respective cause. Speakers appealed to the audience for support through use of placards and emotional pleas, while officials sought to maintain order and control through the use of time limits, precise procedures, and carefully crafted presentations.

Following the consolidation of school boards and schools, we all spent less time together as partners in the educational process—there were greater distances to travel, larger school populations, diminished resources, more contentious issues, and less opportunity to develop caring and trusted relationships. "The actual capacity to undertake democratic practice was shaped by political, institutional, and cultural contexts that were more conducive to more authoritarian leadership practices" (Blackmore & Sachs, 2007, p. 13). There was dissonance between my commitment to particular education values and the practices and values I was expected to espouse. We "voiced that we were being consultative and collegial but new managerial and market regimes restricted us from being so" (Blackmore & Sachs, 2007, p. 21). We had to keep on with the business of the organization. Unfortunately, by doing so, in too many cases we created more adversarial relations than those pursuing common goals.

This personal narrative helped me to illustrate the intersection of caring and power. Reflecting further on the "burden of care" (Bubeck, 1995; Fisher & Tronto, 1990), the reform process left me feeling that I place principles before people and that I am in contradiction with myself. No doubt, the director and the other administrators could share stories similar to mine, as we all felt conflicted. Ordinary incidents become critical when they make us question in whose interests we are working and how effectively.

To give the incident more relevance across education systems and jurisdictions, I explained the context and history of education reform in the province and district (see Chapter 3). The reforms undertaken are not unlike others undertaken nationally and internationally. They have affected structures, governance, and practice. Many governments have sought to redefine educational institutions in "economic rationalist" terms (Barlow & Robertson, 1994; Gee et al., 1996); consequently, individuals and groups are challenged by increased expectations to do more with less. Administrators are finding themselves caught in the middle of ethical dilemmas, feeling conflicted, and being compromised.

In the midst of all this turmoil it is difficult to work in caring ways and feel one's own work is valued. I speak for other administrators, as well as myself, when I say we felt silenced, in terms of being able to speak out about what was happening, because we felt little support. We were caught in a middle-management squeeze, trying to act with caring dispositions. Some colleagues around us could sense the dilemma and sympathized with us and the positions in which we found ourselves. We needed to find ways to augment our caring dispositions and "seek strategic and sensitive ways to overcome understandable reluctance" (Zipin & Brennan, 2003, p. 366). The changing conditions caused significant discord among communities, groups, and individuals about deep-seated core values and practices.

Consultation "sessions were more about how to implement what was pre-scribed...than discussion about issues or feedback on how programs or re-forms were impacting individual schools" (Blackmore & Sachs, 2007, p. 184). The focus of the meetings shifted to what was strategic from understand-ing and problem solving. Working as members of the planning group, loy-alty to district policies and processes was expected, and most meetings were geared to advancing and defining the district plan. Individuals who pointed out problems were regarded as negative and oppositional. Anyone who com-plained felt like a traitor (or a puppet of government and/or the director). We were "co-opted and self-divided, by institutionally coded governmental suppression of other virtuous dispositions" (Zipin & Brennan, 2003, p. 356). We had to advocate for and implement reforms that fundamentally disagreed with us, both ethically and professionally, a situation described as "managed professionalism" (Blackmore & Sachs, 2007).

I believed my ethics and morals were under question, and I felt alien-ated as a district administrator. I used my team-building efforts to move toward a common sense of purpose, but the double thinking and double speaking within the competitive social and work relationships where I found myself were challenging. My allegiances were being undermined and relationships of trust and co-operation were redirected toward compliance. Clearly, I needed to seek strategies to avoid "painful ethical self-questioning in fulfilling the dictates from above" (Zipin & Brennan, 2003, p. 364).

I worked to understand the larger goals of the director, the school board, and government and to mesh them with goals of our district's com-munities and groups. We tried to give support by the exercise of power as caring for the entire school district, but individuals interpreted our actions as controlling. Some could not recognize the connections between caring and power, or that power could be needed to effect caring that would help individuals as well as the district at large. Again, it is important to consider the historical background and how all this negatively affected people's perceptions of caring and power. There were unresolved feelings and tensions, skepticism, distrust, and a dominance of top-level decisions. Leadership and management focused mainly on dealing with crises, complex and rapid change, and less on leading, teaching, and learning. Leadership was more about line management and dispersing tasks to be done more effectively with less money; strategic planning as the center of systems, schools, districts, province; procedures to control aspects of reporting and competitive relations.

I became conscious that "in large organizations decisions would often impact detrimentally and unintentionally and collegiality and collaboration were not always possible" (Blackmore & Sachs, 2007, p. 213). Some colleagues became antagonistic and resistant because a transparent or evident rationale was not always provided. I believe "decisions, while difficult and unpleasant, when based on principles of fairness, openness and collegiality, were more palatable" (Blackmore & Sachs, 2007, p. 213).

Education reform was difficult to watch, be part of, and affect positively. I received signals from others that I, and others who worked with me, were being uncaring and were more concerned about our image than doing what was "right and good" for education. All of this was exacerbated by the structural and cultural divisions that forced competitive relations and social fragmentation rather than cohesion. I felt frustration and guilt when I was not able to do what others thought was best, producing inner struggles for me. Rationality was definitely seen as positive, be tough, stay calm; emotionality was viewed as negative, a loss of control, weakness. Yet, I witnessed several occasions when expressions of anger and stress were seen as acceptable, signs of strength and decisiveness—a real contradiction.

I feel strongly that in times of turbulence and rapid change, taking care of the rights of others is a leadership responsibility. Commitment to people and to particular perspectives is an important part of how I see our work, but I felt we were challenged to disconnect, appear neutral, to satisfy the political agendas. We seemed as a leadership team to spend most of our time putting out fires and responding to crisis situations, rather than being forward thinking leaders who cared about how we treated the people with whom we worked and interacted.

The incident described here is connected to significant decisions made by leaders in the organization and beyond and is subject to the emerging policy emanating from global trends, as well as government and school board leadership. As the new district administration, we were searching to establish a culture, develop procedures, and provide the best possible learning opportunities for everyone, while at the same time struggling to secure our own jobs. This account represents our attempts to provide education and care; unfortunately, it also reveals that people are sometimes seemingly treated in uncaring ways, even when the intent is otherwise.

Continuous reform produced confusion and a sense of a lack of control. Our "sense of disunity" was increased by a lack of time to nurture collegial relationships. Through attempts to uphold the rules and expectations of the provincial reform mandate, district administrators directed our actions away from a climate in which we could nurture each other. We ultimately "need to re-envision social institutions" (Fisher & Tronto, 1990, p. 56). I recommend our focus shift from leaders to leadership and from leadership to democratic practice as central (see Chapter 8) and that we move away from imposing decisions to a more "dialogic process of reform" (Blackmore & Sachs, 2007, p. 14).

Over a short number of years "a push for 'efficient management' has evolved into a runaway trend to 'rationalize' governance practices so as to privilege fiscal and other accountabilities" (Zipin & Brennan, 2003, p. 361). In our district and elsewhere, this push included a standardization of curriculum, hurried policy development, an interruption to planned activities, emergency meetings, limited resources, increased stress, new procedures, and intensified top-down restructuring and management. This growth of managerialism hampered our efforts to build collaborative relationships among our administrative group.

Caring About Rules, Regulations, and Policies Over Individual Needs and Concerns

The second incident illustrates the accountability theme at work in the everyday administration of the district and in our everyday interactions with others. This is almost a culminating activity because it illustrates just how pervasive the accountability theme is experienced in and throughout our everyday work. A set of complex rules, regulations, and procedures had been designed to ensure adherence to the district's budget, our "bottom line." We were all under surveillance. Government officials were monitoring, school board members were questioning, and colleagues were watching. Consistent interpretation of the policy was mandatory, despite its ambiguity. We were saying that program specialists would be treated as professionals with freedom to make judgments (as opposed to having to follow rigid rules), yet there was no room for interpretation and difference of application.

We were each expected to come to our work with the knowledge and skills to understand students, current pedagogy, strengths and needs of the system, to work collaboratively and to act professionally and responsibly; yet, we were not trusted to interpret a travel expense policy in any way other than the narrowest sense. There was no room for diversity, difference, individuality, or exception. It was a contradiction to me that the members of the program division were expected to demonstrate qualities and values that characterized the philosophical basis underlying the vision of the district—competent, ethical, and professional at all times—but they were not trusted to submit reasonable monthly travel claims without being scrutinized by several administrators. My scrutiny as their immediate supervisor was not enough. I was overseen as well, and the claims were further processed by at least one other district administrator. There was a high level of conflict over the situation, which was contradicting values espoused in the district's policy, *Our Vision for Teaching and Learning* (discussed in Chapter 4).

The travel claim incident—a communications nightmare—delves into the area of staff/ line relation, deception, undermining, and decision making. An important and relevant example, it illustrates the function/ dysfunction associated with working in a senior management "team," the (in)sensitivity of personal relationships, and the difficulty of trying to be a collaborative, caring leader in a bureaucratic, hierarchical structure.

In this case, balancing the budget was not good enough, shared decision-making processes contradicted the hierarchical system of power through position, and control took precedence over democracy. Although the travel claim policy and its accompanying regulations are completely understandable as a mechanism of accountability, the way they were applied created situations in which the interests of the people involved came into direct conflict. This dilemma can occur in any setting of this type—large or small, urban or rural.

The incident shows what can happen when the realities of accountabilities brought on through education reform clash with the everyday work of the people implementing the policies and reforms. This case demonstrates the dilemma of being forced through a process where contradictory value systems clash. How can the established values be balanced against the competing ethic? "Choices must be made not between good and bad but between one type of bad outcome versus another" (Shapiro & Gross, 2008, p. 154).

A COMMUNICATIONS NIGHTMARE, FEBRUARY 27, 2003

Reimbursement for meal expenses for program specialists who are required to travel as part of their work has been a thorny issue. We have a dynamic among the program specialists that is unique. There are often struggles with respect to decision making—who should have a say, when, and how?

The director reported that he had been requested to attend a meeting with the speech-language pathologists and their teachers' association representative to discuss the possibility of their being reimbursed for meal expenses. The director explained that it was not the practice of the district to pay such expenses and that we could not afford to start the practice. I interjected to indicate that routinely we pay meals expenses of program specialists. I said that there was no consistency in the claims that were submitted. Some program specialists claim very few meals, others three to five on average a month and some claimed whenever they visited a school outside the local area.

After participating in a two-day retreat with Admin Council and program specialists, I stopped in at the office on my way home to pick up a few things. That was my first mistake. My assistant quickly briefed me on what had been happening at the office during my absence and reminded me of several pieces of unfinished business. One included a meeting with some of the program specialists that I had asked her to set up. She had been unable to find a time that was convenient for the individuals involved. Now the last day of the month was upon us, and I knew the program specialists would be submitting their monthly travel claims on Monday. An uneasy feeling flooded over me as I recalled meeting with the Admin Council two weeks earlier, when I committed to meeting with the program specialists to indicate that I had been somewhat lax in recent months (and allowed a number of questionable meal expense claims to be reimbursed). This was outside the board's policy and because of the potential for other groups to expect the same benefit, I was to meet the program specialists and explain that we needed to adjust our practices slightly.

In haste I made the second mistake. My assistant and I talked about the time crunch we have been working under lately. I explained that I didn't want to have to turn down requests for reimbursements but wanted to act on the decision made by Admin Council and have the concern addressed in February, hopefully preventing a problem. Without thinking I jumped to accept an offer my assistant made to call each of the program specialists and explain the adjustment to them before they prepared their monthly claim. In retrospect, we both realize that this was an insensitive and untimely way to address an issue that we knew had a history and that I should have realized would cause concern and fallout. That Friday afternoon she stayed late to make the calls while I proceeded to attend to some other immediate matters on my desk. Unfortunately none of the program specialists were in their offices. My assistant proceeded to leave a voice message for each of them, which later was perceived as a cold and impersonal approach to the situation.

In the message, the board's policy was referenced and it was explained that I had not been following it as closely as I should. The policy indicated that meal expenses would not be reimbursed unless they were due to travel outside the district or under unique circumstances within the district, such as a required change in plans. It was not intended to be an "all or none" policy but rather a reasonable one. My assistant and I pressed on in haste to get a job done. We were not as mindful of people's feelings as we should have been. While I should have spoken personally to the individuals, I realize now that even if I had, there was still going to be a problem.

It was on Monday morning that I realized the harm I'd done. One of the program specialists came into my office to express total disgust for the way he was being treated. He explained that this was another petty move on the part of district administration that indicated a lack of regard and value for him and his work. He asked where the decision came from and elaborated on the point that for the last 17 years he had had meal expenses reimbursed. He thought that he was always reasonable in making his claims. He did not submit a claim for every day he traveled but felt that when he went to the more distant schools he should not be expected to take a bag lunch. He was visibly upset and I allowed him to express his points without interruption. At the time, the assistant director of finance came into my office to discuss another matter. I was relieved and hoped that he could help me to explain the context for the decision we had made but instead, the program specialist became even more enraged as the board's policy was explained. At this point I realized a number of factors were interacting to raise the concern: the challenge of cutting resources, the manner in which I conveyed the message, the history of the issue, a disagreement in the interpretation of the policy and the teachers' collective agreement, and the perception that this action was devaluing people and their work. The program specialist indicated that he would likely be filing a grievance with the teachers' association. Soon after, he left. Clearly he was unhappy and this would not be the end of the issue.

The day went on with everyone going their separate ways but there was a definite change in the atmosphere around the office. There was tension and discomfort, and program specialists were having one-on-one meetings with each other in their offices.

Five of the 10 program specialists received the voice message. They were the individuals who regularly claim some meal expenses for travel. The five who had not received the message were those who had not submitted their travel claims as yet for this year, or who did not claim for meals.

At the end of the day the director called the other members of Admin Council together to discuss an unrelated matter. I raised the issue of meal expenses. We talked about the manner in which I had communicated the message and how it was contributing to the problem. I agreed. We all wanted to resolve the concerns at the same time as hold to our decision and implement the board's policy. We all agreed that it was reasonable to expect that the program specialists might need to claim for three or four meals each month but that they would not on each occasion they worked in a school outside the immediate area of the district office, their headquarters.

Because so many of the program specialists were upset about our actions, we wanted to settle the matter as quickly as we could. It was agreed that all the program specialists be called to attend a meeting with Admin Council at 8:30 a.m. to hear them out and also address our concerns. Our aim was to work out a reasoned compromise. It was now 5:30 p.m. and most of the employees had left for the day. My assistant was staying late to prepare for a meeting that night so she was asked to call each of the program specialists to inform them of the meeting in the morning. I sent an email message to each of them as well. These communications proved to be a third mistake from the perspective of some of the program specialists.

That night I worried about how the meeting would go. I work closely with the program specialists and know how strongly some of them feel about the issue. I also know that different Admin Council members interpret the policy in slightly different ways. I'm caught in the middle.

As soon as I got to the office I went to the assistant director of personnel to determine from him what he thought the position of Admin Council was going into the meeting. He said he thought that our previous practice was fine because most claimed only three or four meals a month anyway. I explained that while for many this was true, some program specialists regularly claimed for a meal each time they were outside the area of the district office. Others rarely claimed a meal. I thought it important for us to state what qualified for reimbursement and what didn't, rather than say what was happening was fine. We agreed that this reasoned approach with meals being covered on exceptional circumstances would be the position we would take.

I then went to the assistant director of finance to determine his interpretation. He thought only in exceptional cases should we be reimbursing for meals when traveling in the district. I explained that we could not say that our current practices were fine and that we could continue as we were because there was little consistency in how program specialists were claiming. I wanted those who never claimed a meal to know that they should be able to, under certain circumstances, and that some who were claiming often should cut back on some of their claims. The assistant director of finance wanted to talk with the director before we went into the meeting to make sure we were "all on the same page."

At 8:40 a.m. the assistant director of personnel began the meeting with the program specialists and me in attendance. He explained that after hearing a number of concerns over the last 24 hours concerning the decision Admin Council had made, it was his assessment that what the program specialists were claiming all along was fine. I was shocked! He said he understood that they were within policy and only claimed occasional meals expenses. I reiterated what I had said to him privately and explained that this was not necessarily the case, some claimed more meals than others, and some claimed none.

It was at this point that the assistant director of finance joined the meeting, and about five minutes later the director joined us. The director started out by saying that a reasoned approach was what we were seeking. The board could not pay for all meals but there are legitimate circumstances when meal expenses should be paid. He asked that when we know in advance that we will be traveling to a school on a given day, that we take a lunch and eat in the staff room with teachers. It should not be understood that every time we travel to a school to do our work that all our expenses should be covered by the board. We hoped a middle ground could be found. If the board was forced through a grievance to pay the meal expenses of those traveling from district office to schools then other benefits, for example, professional development opportunities such as travel to attend conferences outside the district and province would be more limited. (Most of the program specialists are funded each year to participate in a national or international conference of their choosing. This benefit to employees is not required of the board but viewed as an important investment in the learning of each individual in the organization which contributes to their personal mastery and consequently to organizational learning.)

The program specialist who had come to discuss his concerns with me privately then powerfully expressed his feeling that this process did nothing for his personal mastery, rather it destroyed it. Another of the program specialists began to tell a relevant story and before he finished his voice wavered, he became upset, and left the meeting. A third program specialist was about to ask for clarification on the policy and an outline of what exactly she could claim but because of her colleague's emotional response, she could not speak.

The director apologized for the insensitive manner in which the issue had been handled and offered an explanation as to how sometimes even with good intent, we make mistakes in the haste of wanting to get work done and [then] we do not treat people the way they should be treated. He did not want to lay blame but instead offered to take responsibility for what had happened. At this point I quickly jumped to take full responsibility for the manner in which the telephone calls were made to program specialists and the message left for them. I acknowledged that it was not what should have happened, and I apologized. It wasn't my intent to slight anyone or to devalue their work.

One of the newest program specialists asked to have an explanation of what exactly qualified for reimbursement while another expressed that she did not feel very good about the way she was being treated and that there were only two meals she planned to claim this month. One did think he was being treated fairly by the administration and that he appreciated the flexibility provided to him. Another of the program specialists said that he had never been treated so poorly and that he planned to continue to claim for the meals that he thought were reasonable and if he was not reimbursed he would be filing a grievance with the teachers' association.

And what was going through my head and heart? Regret for how my colleagues, the program specialists, were feeling; betrayal by some Admin Council members; misunderstood by program specialists; disappointment with myself; regret for working in haste without thinking; feelings of being caught in the middle—acting in ways I didn't want to; compromised, hurt, and broken. Where was everyone's emotion coming from? Was it all precipitated by this incident related to reimbursements for meal expenses or was there something much deeper happening?

Individually, several of the group dropped by my office and made reference to the incident. Some did not understand how the issue so seriously affected some of the group. Others explained that they understood that I was acting on an Admin Council decision. They accepted my apology. Several expressed understanding for my position and sensed that I was caught in the middle of all this. One in particular tried to assure me that we would get past this.

So, as I reflect on the experience of work over the past few days, I prepare to take on a new day. As it happens, tomorrow is a "regular" meeting day for myself and the program specialists. No doubt we are all apprehensive about how things will go. Should we talk about how we are all feeling and what our next steps should be or should we move on with other business and allow time for the hurt to heal? I'm going to be chairing the meeting and I know there is a full range of sentiments in the group. Some don't get what the big deal is, some are concerned that other colleagues are demoralized, and some are perhaps despondent and withdrawn. Some definitely want to talk about it and others definitely do not.

Shock is too mild a word to describe my reaction. I had done my explaining, networking, and had little time in the meeting to do anything. I was upset, disappointed in my administrator colleagues, and angry that one in particular had let me down and misrepresented our conversations and negotiated position. I felt like I had been run over and undermined. After my preparations and individual meetings with the other administrators, I trusted things would turn out, but they acted carelessly with my trust. "In situations of interdependence when the outcomes you desire rely to some extent on someone else, you want to feel confident that the other person is benevolent, honest, open, reliable and competent" (Tschannen-Moran, 2004, p. 38). Unfortunately after this, I had the feeling one colleague in particular had taken advantage of my confidence to make himself appear as "the good guy" in our group; I was left feeling suspicious of him. Not only trust of the individual, trust of the organization, and a sense of safety at work, but also trust in my own judgment were all damaged.

> In times of mounting pressures and accompanying fears and frustrations, the maintenance of healthy relationships with one's colleagues is an emotionally demanding and even counterintuitive proposition. But it is where we need to go. We look to those we trust to care and to take care not to betray us, damage us, or wound us. If they do, we need to be able to trust that they will both honor the importance of our relationship and take the necessary steps to heal the wounds. The commitment to developing this kind of relational trust is core business if we are to create the collaborative culture that we need in our schools. (Beatty, 2009, p. 158)

How could I resolve the dispute and retain self-respect? How might I have used the heightened turbulence brought about by this crisis to the best advantage? If all sides believed they were working in the best interests of the education system, in this situation, how could we determine who was doing so most sincerely? To what extent did the individuals show care for those with whom we did not agree? What are the consequences?

This was a terrible time for us—our communities and various groups were set in fierce competition against each other—colleagues were competing for the same jobs, we all worried about our job security. It was inevitable that as the one who supervised the work of the program specialists, I was continually faced with the dilemma of judging the appropriateness of the travel claims and approving the ones that adhered to the policy articulated by Admin Council. The intensity of our experiences provided numerous opportunities for friction and conflict to occur. One specialist had been working for almost 30 years in the district, starting as a classroom teacher and moving through positions as a school principal, district administrator, and now program specialist. He had great job satisfaction and a high measure of respect throughout the district. His credentials and experience were unquestioned and he was used to supervising others but now felt slighted, insulted, and treated in petty and unprofessional ways when asked to change his claim for reimbursement. For him, this was about much more than a few lost dollars. From his perspective he felt disrespected and undervalued. I thought my relationship with the program specialists and my latitude as district administrator meant that I had some room to allow leeway in specific cases. I was hoping to be able to take time to work with the program specialists, discuss individually any exceptions to the policy, and over a couple of months be able to negotiate and dialogue with each to find more common ground. I was looking for some room to balance an ethic of justice with an ethic of care, and in this case, an ethic of professionalism.

Through written policy, and voiced in numerous professional and public meetings, our district leadership team promoted a philosophical focus on diversity, inclusion, and participatory planning—democratic shared leadership. *Ethical, caring, professional, open, diverse,* and *responsive* were all words commonly used in our various interactions within our communities. We were considered an innovative and progressive district, a "learning community" with e-learning and numerous collaborative networks *but* due to the contradictions of working with unrealistic and imposed timelines to accomplish education reform, our best intentions and philosophical positions could not be lived in practice. Our pedagogical framework was well grounded in research and attentive to the values of a liberal education with respect for the rights of individuals built in (see discussion of policy in Chapter 4). We had learning for students and professionals occurring online as well as face to face. Critical thinking was encouraged and emphasized. Students and educators were learning through analysis of our performance and discussion rather than by rote memory.

Years of successful building of trust between the program staff and myself could be lost if the situation described through this incident was not handled properly. My trust and relationship with colleagues caused me to reassess my commitment and willingness to take risks. I felt I had to check and recheck. I had no faith that my fellow administrators would be there to support me when I went out on a limb to take a difficult stand. We were deeply divided; it was a horrific situation. As a program division, we all felt the effect of mild rebuke and were warned to be careful with future travel claims. I wondered how that would affect each individual.

A number of questions and concerns flooded my mind:

- What level of turbulence were the other administrators feeling compared to members of the program staff and me?
- How might I have reduced the level of turbulence?
- What factors cascaded to cause this situation?
- In whose interest is the power over the travel claims being controlled?
- We were all morally and professionally responsible to maintain a financially stable operating budget.
- In what ways was care being demonstrated?
- How can these kinds of conflicts be avoided?
- Was there any positivity in this turbulence?

Facing internal conflict and wrestling with difficult questions makes for hard work. I had to think through my dilemma and choose among difficult alternatives that would define my own view of right and wrong. Facing this situation was especially difficult because I had the added complexity of my friendship with the group and also with the other administrators. "But if we merely obey authority, we are robbed of our humanity and the possibility of living in a democratic community" (Shapiro & Gross, 2008, p. 137). I had to decide whether to follow my own vision of ethical behavior and risk confronting the authority of my director or quietly acquiesce.

The issue was left unresolved. Without confidence that I could expect respect, care, and professional support, I was far less likely to take risks or take on new challenges. The culture and norms of our district office influenced the likelihood that betrayals like this would occur.

> Organizations characterized by negative internal politics, conflict over goals, and shifting coalitions lend themselves to a greater number of betrayals. The culture and norms may not always coincide with the personal experiences of an employee, thus causing intrapersonal as well as interpersonal conflict. (Tschannen-Moran, 2004, p. 64)

Betrayal is defined as a voluntary violation of mutually understood experience that has the potential to threaten the well-being of the trusting person (Elangovan & Shapiro, 1998). In this case my colleague made the choice to violate the expectations of my trust, what I thought we had agreed upon. It made me wonder what he had gained by alienating himself from the decision and making me look like "the bad guy." Obviously he felt justified in switching perspectives during our meeting with the program specialists, even if it meant harming me. I learned the hard way that I would have to be ever watchful of my words and actions in order to protect myself, and that one of my colleagues was not worthy of my trust. I had to move on. Clearly, I have never managed to forget, although I have forgiven.

I felt I had failed with my colleague and overall with the group. "*Collaboration* implies a strong commitment to both the relationship and the task, so that the parties negotiate a solution in which the needs of both parties are met" (Tschannen-Moran, 2004, p. 69). That kind of collaboration required creativity, a problem-solving focus, sensitivity, and skill; it seems we had lost even the essential underlying sense of trust necessary to successfully collaborate. I found myself in a relationship of interdependence with someone I could not trust, and I could not avoid it. I believed my distrust was rational and wise, given the situation, and wondered whether others felt the same about me. The whole issue made for an unpleasant and uncomfortable working environment.

The pressure was high, and I knew that all the program specialists felt the same way. I could understand the position each of them took; I felt truly torn. We were all good people, and each of the specialists could easily justify what they had done. I felt close to them; we worked as a team. Now I was pitted as an outsider, one of "them"—a mean-spirited administrator who cared more about balancing a budget bottom line—rather than one of "us" fighting for our cause. I understood why, as district administrators, we made the decision we did related to travel claim reimbursement, and I believed it was reasonable. The biggest issue was not having had the appropriate time to work through it with each program specialist individually and then together as a group. The decision and direction came suddenly and was perceived as a pronouncement from the powers that be. I wanted to be supportive and do the right thing. I felt as if I had been cut off; I sure could have used a little understanding and support myself.

I had been willing to deal with the difficult situation and attempted to communicate openly about it. I made a pros and cons list to help me look at all the outcomes in each situation and listed what I deemed pertinent questions. (Questions adapted from Shapiro & Gross, 2008, p. 141.)

- Was the policy clear? Why or why not?
- How did my thought process show care for my colleagues? For the district? For myself?
- To what extent was I placing the best interests of others at the heart of my thinking?
- In applying the ethic of care, what strategies could I use to diffuse the anger and frustration felt by the program specialists? Would justice be served?
- How could the director employ the ethic of care in this situation?

- How do the two sides demonstrate conflicting concepts of care?
- Who most thoroughly and convincingly speaks for the best interests of the district, or the program specialists?
- Why was the policy change stated to some and not all of the program specialists? Why did some get a call and not others?
- Considering the degrees of turbulence (Shapiro & Gross, 2008), how turbulent is this situation?
- How might positionality help to explain the differences in perceived turbulence?

We needed to combine pressing for the achievement of our goal with a demonstration of concern but lacked the time, wisdom, and sensitivity to discern how to balance our task orientation with a focus on nurturing relationships.

Often in my career I have been able to take the honesty and integrity of my colleagues for granted, but in this case the rush and insensitivities of education reform and do-more-with-less policy directions were destroying that benefit. We could not count on people to do what they said they would do, tell the truth, and keep their promises; trust was whittled away.

Although we each had to regulate our emotions in the meetings, the emotions expressed by the program specialists were stronger than any of us had anticipated. Given how much I still mull this over several years later makes it apparent that the incident touched me in particularly personal ways. My usual skills at reading others' emotions and using my intellect to prepare for the meeting and have everyone else adequately prepared were not "working" for me. To work this out required delicate negotiation, giving and taking, deferring, and repeating back to validate, application of resilience, endurance, and focus, as well as capacity to manage several things at once—all this was key to be able to identify issues and priorities and to communicate. As an organization we needed to provide time and space for discussion, to plan, reflect, and work as a team. Groups needed to get together to discuss and review what was happening and participate as equal players. It was clear that program specialists valued good relationships. Also, as experienced educational leaders they felt they should have been invited to provide input and have an opportunity to help work out problems. None of this was happening, which caused emotional response.

It is interesting to reflect on the interplay between individual persons and the group, how we leaders needed to understand where the emotional and "rational" parts of our work merge, and to "look more closely at those elusive unconscious mechanisms, both formal and informal, that we use when organizational life gets difficult" (Crawford, 2009, p. 80). Ideally, we want everyone understanding and having a shared perception of where the organization is headed and why, and have everyone pulling in the same direction, feeling involved, valued, cared about, respected, and feeling free to chip in with their ideas and observations—being committed intellectually but also emotionally.

In the case of the travel claim incident, we were not seeing the stress and tension that the reorganization processes were having on our colleagues, and a diversity of feelings influenced our leadership effectiveness. Many, including me, were "grieving the demise of collegiality, care and co-operation" (Blackmore & Sachs, 2007, p. 210) and felt less attachment to our organization. The loss of organizational commitment was producing a crisis of self-identity that led to disengagement on some people's parts. Our district was struggling with collective and individual alienation.

My purpose in telling this story, although emphasizing negative aspects, is to foster reflection that might point leaders in the direction of attending more carefully to feelings and emotions in particularly trying situations. I thought I knew enough and picked up on the vibes but it was still not enough to adequately handle this situation. Although everyone needed affirmation and recognition, we rarely received it in this work context; there was little support offered to anyone in our turbulent atmosphere. In the midst of unexpected circumstances, it is important to be able to count on our colleagues; however, at that time, you never knew where you stood with some people.

Our dilemma was that we were focused on performance and accountability rather than on our values and what we were working for in education. Our real work was being undermined and tested. We were distracted from our mission to provide enhancing learning opportunities for all and faced this crisis of trust and loss of commitment. A culture of blame and accountability that had emerged was not shared and the sense of contradiction impacted on our professional and personal selves. I felt tension and dissonance between the demands for organizational loyalty and my capacity as educational leader to make professional judgments with integrity.

I learned first-hand that the soft "feminine" skills of people management were as critical to good leadership and management as the hard "masculine" skills of financial management. I believe increased interdependence was the key. More than telling us a great deal about the effects of resource cuts, the incident is also instructive about the general psyche of a workplace when other demoralizations spill over into other situations. This story shows that structures have great power and that the milieu or atmosphere of an organization does as well. It appears to me that even with the best practice, in this situation it may still have been impossible to make everyone happy.

Little care was taken in managing all the radical changes; indeed, the culture produced more toxic, mistrustful, greedy organizations where people felt taken for granted, and more emphasis and importance were given to facts, budgets, numbers, and bottom lines. Some people did manage to make their mark, but their colleagues lost morale, institutional knowledge, relationships, power, and position. Consequently, many of us felt alienated, causing some to lose interest in the good things that were happening.

I learned many valuable lessons, besides how to survive, during that period of reform: that I was personally committed to public education, that it was crucial not to lose sight of what is important, and that there are many ways to settle differences. Leaders need to appreciate the difficult paradox or inconsistency when they meet it and then know how to deal with it in ways that are not purely managerial in nature but instead are morally sound (Shapiro & Gross, 2008). I believe that in order to repair the damaged relationships at that time, we needed to focus on re-establishing caring relations. The incident is a powerful account of the complexities, nuances, and contradictions experienced by decision makers and leaders.

One of the more interesting and unintended outcomes of this increased emphasis on staying within the policy is that it gave me a closer look into what was really in the hearts and minds of my colleague administrators. The incident had "the potential of creating opportunities for meaningful interaction but also the negative possibility of allowing both entities to observe the other under circumstances that were not flattering" (Shapiro & Gross, 2008, p. 154). It is important for leaders to be aware of their own emotions as well as other people's reactions, and to know how to channel them appropriately (Sergiovanni, 1992). "In most educational organizations leaders are continually dealing with difficult emotions and knowledge of emotion can be used to predict, control, direct and interpret what is going on in any given situation and many of these effects have profound social consequences" (Shaver, Schwartz, Kirson, & O'Connor, 2001, p. 171).

The difficulty for those in leadership positions is to acknowledge the personal in ways that enhance personal effectiveness and help manage any inner anxiety. "Although the experience of work is drenched with emotion, it is often viewed as tangential rather than fundamental to leadership, but leadership cannot function without emotion" (Crawford, 2009, p. 10). One program specialist in particular felt "a lack of positive expression of respect and recognition" (Sennett, 2004, p. xiv) and commented about never being told he did a good job and feeling taken for granted. This was all difficult to watch, be part of, and affect positively. The situation was exacerbated by structural and cultural divisions forcing competitive relations and social fragmentation rather than cohesion. We desperately needed more caring leadership that managed people respectfully, realized the importance of keeping calm and heading things off whenever possible, and used a "measured tone" (Crawford, 2009, p. 91). The places we work are part of a leader's emotional context, and in some difficult situations management of emotion may be a significant part of what leaders need to do.

Managing anxiety within the school system serves to emphasize leaders' vulnerability and how they manage these emotions is crucial not only to the success of their leadership but also to their personal well-being (Crawford, 2009). As a leader I had to think about:

- How do I work and interact?
- What situations do I avoid?
- Which ideas and issues do I emphasize?
- What was absent from my discourse?
- What messages did I convey knowingly and unknowingly regarding what and who I value?
- Whose voices and views were absent?
- Whose perspectives were we not considering?
- Am I truly an agent of change or am I really an agent of the bureaucracy?

Being from a "privileged" position as a successful female in a senior administrative position, I had to work through some harsh realities that affected me deeply. Many of the day-to-day decisions of educational leaders may cause emotional fallout, and we have to learn what to do about it. A leader's understanding of how someone's inner world may have a profound impact on the school setting is a key skill. At the same time, leaders have to allow room for self-understanding.

The manner in which people choose to communicate in both personal relationships and in organizational settings is significant. "Leadership is being all about responding to other people's feelings and situations" (Crawford, 2009, p. 81). Our programs division had built up a status within our district and we valued it. Our reputation was important to most because it offered security, connection, and understanding. After this incident, members felt threatened and diminished. Through reflection on this incident, I learned that it is human nature to be concerned about something that has gone wrong, but I believe it is also important to concentrate on how to prevent it from recurring. Greater effort is needed to focus on things working well rather than on mistakes.

The extent of ourselves that we disclose influences our relationships with others, how people regard us, and whether they can trust us.

> The new "emotion" valued in organizations is not so much about care and connection as it is about an objective determination about how to "perform" appropriate emotion and to express it in such a way as to deliver results: the competence of emotion. (Hatcher, 2008, p. 164)

I believe that school leaders who do their work well, emphasize "care and connection" with their values and are able to develop or foster that in others. "Care and connection can lead to high performance but may not be sustainable in the longer term" (Crawford, 2009, p. 102). The admin team members in our district were able to "perform" but to the detriment of our own values—we did not support others and we were not supported ourselves. We found ourselves altered by events, and even the most capable of us lost our ability to work well with others. Leaders need knowledge of both emotional labor and emotional wounding. This critical incident provides access to some of the deep emotional epiphanies and emotional wounds that were experienced. Other helpful, positive ways of handling key critical incidents with an emotional component could be shared, for example personal leadership narratives (Crawford, 2009), so that the cognitive and emotional aspects of leadership could be examined.

Our "disciplinary technologies of accountability had universalizing and normalizing effects that valued quantity over quality, image over substance, and money over intellectual work" (Shapiro & Gross, 2008, p. 217). The travel claim incident appears on the surface to require management tasks to make the organization run more efficiently in our neoliberal times. It was made apparent to me, however, that what might be interpreted as mundane tasks would only have worked well if the emotional context were conducive to it. If employees had felt valued, listened to, respected, involved in the decisions that affected them, then likely the reactions from the program specialists to the task of reimbursing travel claims consistent with policy would not have been as traumatic. Analysis and retrospection on this incident have confirmed for me the importance of the interrelationship between the person and the social context. In this case the emotional context hampered our leadership.

"In this complex and chaotic era, to educate leaders and not just managers it is important that morality and ethics are at the center of educating leaders" (Shapiro & Gross, 2008, p. 172). No matter if male or female, experienced or inexperienced, in large or small districts, the relationship between the rational and the emotional is complex but significant; yet, the notion that leaders can be emotional in pursuit of rational goals has not received much focus in the leadership literature (Crawford, 2009). As leaders we need to attend to the ways we look, sound, and act because how we are perceived, or are really, is key in the collective functioning of our organizations. The "ideal 'professional' behavior is rational and carefully emotionally controlled" (Crawford, 2009, p. 96). All of us who were educational leaders at the time struggled with the personal and ethical impacts of the consolidation as well as the emotions of our staff. I think it legitimate to ask whether too much was expected of district personnel at the time.

Historic procedures, such as rules related to travel claims, and established work habits and routines were all being changed with little interaction or forewarning. As discussed, some contested, others did not. These changing conditions caused significant discord and unsettlement among the group members about deep-seated core values of our work. When "rules change *radically*, there may be dispositional dissonances in which it is difficult for many to make the sort of internal accommodations" (Zipin & Brennan, 2003, p. 358) required. A deep underlying sense that their work was not valued caused "acting out"—some with tears, some with anger, others with frustration, and still others with disconnection.

Through this critical incident, I explored how apprehending another's reality and feeling might work within a bureaucratic organization. I explored how an individual or a group steps out of their personal frame of reference into that of others to consider different points of view, needs, and expectations. The meanings of care vary from one society to another and from one group to another; all humans need to be cared for, but the degree of care that others provide depends upon culturally constructed differences. My study of the perceptions of caring within a school district revealed differences of opinion within and among groups about the degree of care that was expected and realistic. Understandably, good care requires both human and material resources and generally there is less of both than those caring would like. It is always a struggle to determine which needs receive which resources, and in the school district there was conflict about what constituted adequate or good care versus the scarcity of resources. It is important to determine whether in our organization we had the capacity to deliver good care.

Instead of focusing on budgets, efficiency, accountability, and control, educational leaders will need to think of what is good for all people involved. This incident has taught me that the money allocated for meal expenses was not only a symbol of resources of value but also of autonomy.

It was viewed as a small perk for what was felt by some to be important but often unappreciated work. Changing the rules caused unsettled conditions, financial burden, and a shift in values. Several ways that I attempted to learn and demonstrate an ethic of caring were by listening to others, sharing responsibility for our efforts, and guarding/respecting individuals and their identities. However, the pressures of work environments now distance us from seeing how we treat others. At the time, we often only saw what needed to be done; the impact of our words and actions garnered little attention other than consideration of how they affected the budget or impacted on the long-term strategic plan. The "emergency" meeting called on short notice was an attempt by those of us with power to minimize negative fallout, clear up misunderstanding, and bring about compliance to the new rules. The political and financial implications of our work were attended to, but the social, cultural, inter- and intrapersonal implications were ignored.

The emphasis of a conservative educational politic, in conjunction with radical restructuring and reform, alongside a more "lean and mean" administrative structure impacted on our work. The "corporate managerialism" (Apple, Kenway, & Singh, 2005; Apple, 2005; Barlow & Robertson, 1994) and "neo-conservativism" (Apple, 2000) of the provincial government's mandates and of our local politics made our work contradictory. To complicate matters, the inconsistency of some leaders' behavior and my inability to count on them to follow through on agreed upon directions and decisions was very unsettling and constraining for me.

Reflection

Both incidents discussed in this chapter are representative of cutbacks, fiscal restraint, belt tightening, efficiency—what the literature describes as "corporate managerialism" (Blackmore, 1999, 2000; Seymour, 2004; Wrigley, Thomson, & Lingard, 2012). They are evidence of the government- and business-driven "new managerialism" that has impacted on school districts and schools. The incidents illustrate tensions between caring dispositions and the normative forces of the "rationalist economy." The new managerial rules and procedures are disruptive and troubling to many who sense a lack of care and respect for their work and perspectives. Through analysis of the incidents, I have been reflexively critical to illustrate the serious frustrations many of us working in education felt at the time.

Although there were numerous occasions set aside in our district for meetings and consultation to produce goal consensus, they were dominated by top-down one-way communications in which principals, program specialists, and others were informed of, and not informing of, the priorities. I am sure that often in these situations where there was a "manufacturing of consent" (Ferguson, 1984, p. 103), I was viewed by others as complying with the "old boys' club."

> Paradoxically, state bureaucracies, in seeking certainty in an era of uncertainty, have produced highly modernist responses (hierarchical, individualized, fragmented, technical, impersonal, instrumental, nonreflexive, unilateral) to postmodernist demands (flexibility, change, emotional management, teamwork, listening, nurturing, interpersonal competence, coping with value conflicts, gaining self-knowledge, embracing error), the former leading to conformity to bureaucratic norms rather than innovative bureaucratic leadership. (Blackmore, 1999, p. 114)

As illustrated in both critical incidents, I was concerned that in times of turbulence and rapid change, when taking care of the rights of others is a leadership responsibility, I might bring aspects of the organization into disrepute or misrepresent our goals and intentions.

The critical incidents I have articulated are powerful accounts of the complexities, nuances, and contradictions experienced by decision makers and leaders. They also illustrate how little forgiveness people are capable of—perhaps due to working under long-term stress. No doubt each of the district administrators, like me, could tell similar stories of sometimes futile attempts to be fair and caring while attempting to achieve change. These personal stories are representative of the work conditions of our current professional practice and illustrative of the experiences others can describe. Unfortunately, there are too many such incidents, and rarely are they the focus of sustained research and analysis.

Our education system was undergoing radical "restructuring" and reform, which came into play in these critical incidents. Power struggles and intrusion into the norms and values of individuals, groups, and communities were most disruptive and off-putting. The positions of individuals and groups in these situations are important to understanding our actions in terms of caring and power. I perceived power as capable of protecting my colleagues from outside sources and pressures that influenced our work.

There is need for caring to become a valued part of the social/public world with a balance among rules, principles, and moral judgments. Relationships with staff, pupils, and parents are quite literally at the heart of education (Crawford, 2009; Sergiovanni, 2003). There is need for dialogue to determine the just rules and regulations that are to serve as guides for making moral decisions. Through attempts to uphold the rules of the district without dialogue (for example, our travel claim incident), I directed my actions away from a climate in which we could nurture each other. My intent was interpreted as use of power to maintain the hierarchy and bureaucracy rather than care for individuals. I exercised control rather than practiced care.

For the organization to become more humane and less oppressive, an ethic of caring has to accompany the focus on principles, rules, and duty. Caring, justice, and power need to be working together. As educational leaders we must understand that the particular needs of individuals serve as guidelines for equitable and moral treatment for members of the larger school district. Power of position, of authority, provides the space in which moral debate of fairness and justice can take place. To facilitate this kind of dialogue and debate, leaders need to be driven by moral purpose (Sergiovanni, 1992) to incorporate caring into institutions currently dominated by justice, reasoning, and power-over ways of operating.

An ethic of caring requires organizational structure and leadership that support thinking and doing (Green, 2008). It demands appropriate resources, skills, and knowledge. What remains to be seen is whether educational organizations will be willing to give enough to change the system that has been entrenched with competition, autonomy, control, and independence in order to cultivate interdependence, connection, and community.

Everyone has a story to share about feeling excluded or denigrated at some point in life. Our challenge is to become critically reflective and aware practitioners working to engage and empower in emancipatory educational experiences. As a start, we can decide whether we are for or against greater standardization and accountability.

Although I thought I understood what those around me were going through, I truly did not understand the depth to which my actions affected their daily lives. This difference created a gap and affected my relationship building with people within the program division at district office, community leaders, school personnel, some school board members, and other district administrators. They believed I could not relate to them, and I felt they did not relate to me. The suggestions I gave were sometimes regarded with suspicion, not because they were unreasonable or impractical but because they were coming from the position of a powerful district administrator. This caused a great deal of concern for me and difficult situations for me to work through.

I took a long, hard look at my life and my part in what was happening in the lives of so many others. I realized that I came to these experiences at work with a determined agenda, and it was not realistic for me to expect to create democratic, inclusive relationships given our district and provincial context and legislated mandate to implement a radical reform of the system. I was aware that the people I worked with needed time to think and opportunities to express themselves, find solutions and a way forward together. They deserved to be valued and listened to but the reform machine, driven by standardization and cost-efficient mechanisms, afforded no care for the people in its path. For me to be successful in my assigned roles, I had to set aside my preferred ways of working and my beliefs about how people should be treated to get the job done. It dawned on me and shook me up that I was perceived by many whom I respected as "one of them."

In the midst of hurried timelines, long days, and strained relationships, miscommunications resulted and mistakes occurred. Some people were left out of meetings they should have attended and there was little time to offer meaningful background information and rationale for some decisions that were made. District policies and practices were inconsistent, contradictory, and even unpredictable. Many of us felt we were "flying by the seat of our pants" and struggling to keep some semblances of order for ourselves and others as we attempted to disassemble one system and recreate another. I wanted to care for people, accept their challenges and differences of opinion, and achieve as much "success" together as we could, but achieving that goal was impossible. My perceptions of myself and my priorities were transforming as much as our school system was. I realized back then that I was working in a position and in ways that conflicted with my personal beliefs and values. I was so absorbed in the turmoil that it dominated the direction of my doctoral studies.

I realized that I needed to do some soul-searching, self-analysis, as well as analysis of our education system. I investigated the research literature in the areas of conceptions and practices of care in workplace contexts as a way to discover more humane and socially just approaches to accomplish education reform. This was my way to engage in critical reflection and learn how I might apply more democratic and inclusive strategies in my work following completion of my studies. I found a meaningful purpose and was extremely motivated. I openly engaged in interrogating and analyzing myself, my practice, the reform movement in Newfoundland and Labrador, and the larger global trends in education. I was fortunate to be granted a year-long educational leave from my work to give focused attention to conducting my research. I viewed this then, and now, as a significant act of caring for me.

My bias was belief that the practice of caring in particular, and more humane approaches to reform generally, would not only improve the morale of everyone in the district and province but also help us to better meet our reform goals. I believed then, and still do, that when employees feel cared about (involved in making the decisions that affect them, have opportunities to work and learn together, have flexible time to think critically and dialogue about different solutions and options) then everyone, as well as the education system itself, will benefit.

I have learned many lessons—both academic and experiential—that I can apply in my work life: I prefer a great deal of teamwork and collaboration, and trusted relationships with scholars and practitioners. Consequently, I aim to create respect for difference and appreciation for building more inclusive communities and attitudes in families, workplaces, neighborhoods, and classrooms.

We need to gather other local and concrete stories about organizational life, the intricacies of everyday muddles related to managing organizations, and subject them to abstract and metaphorical interpretation (Czarniawska, 1997). Studying the drama of bureaucratic life and uncovering the hidden workings of organizations by confronting paradoxes will bring crisis to existing organizations and enable them to change. We cannot understand human conduct if we ignore its intentions, and we cannot understand human intentions if we ignore the settings in which they make sense.

6

"Insiders" Experience Turbulence

Too often we underestimate the power of a touch, a smile, a kind word,
a listening ear, an honest compliment, or the smallest act of caring,
all of which have the potential to turn a life around.

—Leo Buscaglia

This chapter investigates the extent to which the school district's espoused values of caring were actually understood and experienced from the perspectives of individuals in the district. "What constitutes knowledge depends on the consensus and ethos of the community in which it is grounded" (Dillard, 2003, p. 132). A conscious struggle in our attempts to lead, care, and do our work in education is articulated here to illustrate how we were often ambiguous about how we treated people. I believe the shared stories of experiences working in school districts during processes of education reform in Canada are applicable in planning and implementing policies and strategies in other contexts.

> Even an untold story, existing for years in the silence of a life, can come to be told, in words, to someone who enters a life and who may come to be trusted to listen and to care in ways that make its telling, with words, possible. But such telling is never easy. (Neumann, 1997, p. 109)

Caring Leadership in Turbulent Times, pages 167–198
Copyright © 2014 by Information Age Publishing
167

Gunter (2001) proposes that "engaging theory and theorizing with practice is essential to knowledge production within and about educational experiences, and positioning is central to this" (p. 65). The challenge in representing personal experiences lies in finding the theoretical tools as researchers to give voice to silenced people (Richardson, 1990) and contribute to the knowledge that informs practice in the future. In this chapter I share insiders' perspectives and experiences of attempting to work in caring ways as we strived to implement the policies and practices of education reform. This chapter offers unique insights into the personal, professional, and organizational perspectives of practitioners involved in all levels of education. I interpreted our story through analysis of interview transcripts and through the stories told by colleagues as they spoke through their day-to-day work. The data I analyzed included transcripts of individual interviews (teacher, director, administrative assistant, vice-principal, program specialist, and assistant director), and a focus group interview, with staff representatives (teacher, school administrator, support staff, associate assistant director, program specialist, and executive assistant). These were complemented with personal interactions, observations, and journal entries as well as data from archival records such as the minutes of school board meetings, memos, newsletters, and strategic plans. I reviewed these records to validate or extend upon the statements made by the participants.

Each of the participants had unique insights into the workings of the organization and acted in leadership and innovative roles connected with the intent and direction of the district. All held positions of influence within the organization and several were respected leaders in the provincial education system. Including myself, there were a total of 13 participants (referred to by pseudonyms): six females, in addition to myself, and six males. I provide a balance in the way women and men are presented, as it is important to hear the stories of those who are underrepresented to help establish a balance in the literature and expand options for us all. I share stories of our experiences to open up dialogue (Clandinin & Connelly, 2000) about issues that have been difficult to discuss in many of our educational work contexts. The cultural, organizational, historical, patriarchal, and contradictory stories that are sometimes invisible or considered inappropriate to talk about on a daily basis (Blackmore & Sachs, 2007; Blackmore, 1999, 2006) are illuminated. I explore how people, including myself, are being treated and how we create, perpetuate, or challenge the culture in which we live and work through our daily routines, conversations, encounters, and words and deeds.

I purposely chose participants who I believed had positive attitudes and experiences to share and who would speak knowingly about the caring initiatives undertaken by the district. The interview data represented the perspectives of many district employees whom I did not interview. I believe that the participants built on the positive commentaries of each other (Stewart & Shamdasani, 1990), and since my topic related to "caring" in our workplace it led them to attend mainly to the positive aspects of our work together in the district. Although I explained that the information they provided would not be used in any way related to rewards, promotions, or reassignments, I believe the participants, almost without exception, did not want to be perceived by me or their colleagues as anything but supportive of the district, its administration, and our directions. I have endeavored to frame quoted excerpts from participants with the utmost respect, while honoring a balance between accurate representation and critique.

First in this chapter, I provide introductory information about each participant. Secondly, I address their perspectives and expectations of care in their workplace. Thirdly, I include the participants' descriptions of the effects and impacts of the education reform process legislated by the provincial government. The fourth subsection addresses how the district's philosophy of organizational learning connects with participants' conceptions of care. Fifthly, I explain how various enactments of caring as well as uncaring behaviors were experienced or witnessed. The sixth subsection addresses the barriers and obstacles impeding the practice of care and includes discussion of the suggestions participants offered as ways the district could enhance caring in our workplace. The chapter concludes with reflection and a final analysis discerned from the input I received.

I talked individually with six district professionals. Paul, a program specialist responsible for elementary and intermediate programming, had served in several positions, including working with another school board as school development specialist, assistant superintendent, principal, corrective reading teacher, and high school English teacher. At the time of our interview Paul had 30 years' experience working in the K–12 education system. Having first-hand experience, he had a big-picture understanding of turbulence and change. He reluctantly retired in June 2004. Eloise, an experienced executive assistant, previously supported the work of senior district administrations in three school boards. She had knowledge about most of the functions within the district office. Nathan, one of three assistant directors in the district, had a PhD and approximately 30 years' experience as teacher, school administrator, university professor, and district administrator. In our district he administered three collective agreements, oversaw the work of schools, was responsible for employee wellness and occupational health and safety programs, staffing, and all personnel functions of human resource management. Ben, the director of education and district CEO, had a PhD and approximately 30 years' experience as classroom teacher, school administrator, university professor, and district administrator. Sharon, a classroom teacher, also worked part time as high school administrator. She was midcareer, having come to teaching late after working with local media. She was involved as a leader in many school, district, and provincial initiatives. Doris, a classroom teacher, was recognized as a lead teacher in the district, especially in the areas of literacy, technology, and learning resources, and was involved in a variety of school, district, and provincial initiatives.

In addition to the individual interviews, I met with a group of six district employees one afternoon for a focus group session. Gloria, the executive assistant to the director of education, had a broad understanding of the structures and various groups and levels within the board. Harold, the Human Resources Administrator, former teacher, vice-principal, and principal, worked with the teachers' association, and served on various district and provincial committees. Andrew, the curriculum consultant for Senior High School Mathematics, also a former teacher and vice-principal, had extensive experience working on curriculum projects at both the district and provincial levels. Peggy, a primary/elementary school teacher, was respected for her leadership in teaching and learning and worked on various district projects related to curriculum development and implementation. Brian, an experienced teacher and high school principal, worked through several school consolidation processes. Christine worked in technological support in a variety of situations with a variety of personnel across all divisions and levels within the district. When I conducted this research, I was one of the four district administrators.

Conceptions of Care and Caring

Nel Noddings explained succinctly that "without having care at the center of our lives, I think life becomes superficial, hectic, a continual pursuit of an elusive something in which people's lives lose meaning" (Seymour, 2004, p. 90). Through my study in the school district, being cared about meant colleagues were concerned for each other, not only in the workplace but also in life outside of work. When colleagues feel empathy, an "engrossment" (Noddings, 1984), a personal connection among colleagues and an acknowledgement of the need for a balance between time for work and time for a personal life makes employees feel comfortable and cared about. Throughout the interviews, a strong sense of the significance and importance of care and caring in the workplace was expressed. Each participant was aware that if the organization were to be effective and efficient all the people who comprise it and who make it work need to feel cared for and to care for others. They expressed a sense of personal as well as group responsibility for that within the district.

In essence, the transcript data indicated that *each* participant believed care had to be linked with justice, respect, trust/honesty, and equity. Each believed that caring promoted trust and vice versa. They sought to cultivate personal relationships with colleagues and believed policies and programs can help to create such relationships. All felt some degree of tension between their professional roles and personal commitments to care and believed that part of their own practice of care required them to promote care in and among their colleagues. The perspectives of the participants, reflecting their conceptions of care, have been organized under a number of subheadings.

Gender and Care

I sought to discover whether participants believed that gender made a difference in the practice of care within our workplace, and varying perspectives became evident.

Nathan, assistant director of personnel, drew on awareness of research literature. "One of the things that ha[s] been shown is that caring and nurturing are more characteristic of the feminine gender than the masculine gender." But Ben, also referring to the research literature, indicated that not surprisingly it "talks about feminine leadership characteristics . . . they're simply the characteristics of good leadership that are focused on developing professional learning. I don't think it's specific to any gender or any age." He explained that in the most current administrator preparation programs, there is recognition of and value given to a new paradigm where a re-conception of the role of education administration is defined, which advocates different leadership approaches, including caring. Ben described what he believed to be the situation in our district:

> You can look around and see all ages and genders in this district and find caring and uncaring people. I don't think it's specific to age groups or gender—it's experiences and perhaps it's simply personality in some cases. Caring is also something that can be developed through learning and that's what we need to do.

The traditional models we use in organizations have been the bureaucratic models, and all the CEOs have been male.

> The traditional models have been those who have had anything but caring approaches to organizational leadership. The women that succeeded—the pioneers, if I might say—who succeeded in those organizations weren't caring either because they didn't survive if they were caring or they had to hide their caring approaches.

Paul expressed satisfaction with the gender balance at the office in terms of the overall numbers of males and females in various positions, but he felt the atmosphere and culture of our workplace was dominated by the traditionally male leadership approaches, which he found less than desirable.

> We have a very good balance of gender here but I think "female think" is not often evident. I think there's got to be females'... sensitivity; people should be sensitive to each other in the way we do things. The other model, the opposite of that is "male think." ... I think the world of organizations would be a better place if we had a balance. You know, no concept of men winning for winning's sake should enter into children's lives, and we're dealing with children's lives... to win at all cost in this office just doesn't belong here.

He commented on corporate influences in education and how in that environment "female think" was especially important and relevant for organizational success.

> Caring has been seen as a feminine characteristic and has been equated with weakness. I work with other administrators who've seen it [caring] as a weakness. In fact I've even had one person say to me, "You're too nice."

Sharon added, "I still think that glass ceiling is there.... We're not allowed sometimes to care, because it's looked at as being a negative ability." Sharon appreciated that any leader needs to be able to use a variety of approaches in a variety of situations. She referenced the relationship she had as a vice-principal working with her male principal and talked about the difference between their approaches: "Sometimes he's more, 'Let's just get the job done and this... is the way it's got to be,' and I'm the other extreme; I will sometimes go that extra inning to stop the controversy or to work through the conflict. It's worked really well."

Caring and Conflict

Having to deal with conflict is inevitable in any organization; doing it in caring ways is possible but sometimes challenging. One of our colleagues, "Joe," was labelled a troublemaker. He had a temper, intimidated others, and felt challenged to answer to anyone in authority over him. He often issued verbal threats; many avoided him and viewed him as an untrusting and untrustworthy person. However, he was bright; he was a whiz with computer technology and had innovative and creative processes and skills that were assets but that also landed him in trouble.

He attempted to set high standards for himself and others but was intolerant of anyone who did not abide by set timelines—yet he could not abide by them himself! It was perplexing that what he did not accept from others, he was himself: tardy with meeting deadlines and he wiggled out of responsibilities. When given warnings with the best of intent, rather than respond in positive ways he became upset and despondent. He used frustration to work against his superiors and caused suspicion and mistrust. He appeared to delight in blaming others—it was always someone else's fault—which caused anxiety for himself and others. Joe kept his work to himself, would not share draft documents electronically or provide access to them. Most who worked with him felt he had power and aimed to control issues. Rather than represent the work of the district committee who helped create policy documents, he sought to take personal credit and often felt he was denied promotion or frozen out.

Critical questions: How do we deal with issues and people like this? What opportunity for caring leadership does it present? What might be some alternative measures to deal with frustrations? What personal and professional ethical codes clashed? Whose voices are silenced? Why? What rights does Joe have? How can we handle situations like this to lower the level of turbulence and demonstrate care?

Educators working in complicated organizations such as our school district frequently think and work through questions such as these. While some of us rely on the prescription of rules and guidelines defined through policies and procedures to determine our actions, others are receptive to less rule-bound approaches, preferring more individualistic approaches to resolving difficult situations.

Participants provided a number of examples of how they felt cared about even in difficult situations. Eloise appreciated that she was made to feel comfortable when she had to speak to the director on an issue that was bothersome. "I came out of it feeling really good, that I did have [legitimate] concerns, and I was listened to, and I felt very much supported." With respect to feeling free to offer her ideas and input she said, "With all the various people I've worked, I feel very comfortable in sharing how I see something," and that was important to her.

Gloria, the executive assistant for the director, was politically astute and explained how sensitive she and the director were to people and their concerns. "It's very important when people reach our office... you have to put them at ease." Gloria believed that the district demonstrated care by responding to calls of concern. When problems are brought forward, people are treated respectfully; they are not judged poorly because they are complaining or do not know something. Parents would tell Gloria that they felt their views were listened to and that district personnel returned calls and attended to concerns in a timely manner. These were features and practices that conveyed care for others as well as organizational effectiveness.

Eloise conveyed an awareness of the importance of care in the context of conflict:

> There are going to be conflicts in an organization. There are going to be differences of opinion. But you need to be strong enough professionally to address those up front as part of a relationship of care.

It is clear that participants had views about what care required. They believed honesty, forthrightness, and having courage to stand up for what one believes are important in a caring relationship. Such a relationship also requires mutual respect and concern for how *the other* is treated, spoken to, and responded to. Their comments relating to how job actions taken by striking employees (support staff workers) were dealt with further illustrated their thinking.

We had a second strike by our support staff at the same time that the newly consolidated school board was settling itself. Management personnel spent our mornings escorting school buses and teachers across picket lines, afternoons carrying on the educational work of the district, and nights cleaning schools to make them ready for students and teachers to work and learn the next morning. Most staff were uncomfortable and conflicted about having to cross the picket lines of colleagues they respected, and some strikers who worked respectfully alongside administration for years now found themselves on the "opposite side of the fence." Emotions ran high and some unfortunate action resulted, but after the initial turmoil and confusion had settled, a more sensitive and reasoned atmosphere was established. This was a second time around for most of the management team in dealing with striking support staff workers, and it was noted that the mood and atmosphere were markedly improved now compared to the previous strike.

> It's not "us" and "them." It's "we," we're in this together... we're respecting the people who are on strike, but they're also respecting the fact that we've gotta get kids in school.... [I]t wasn't animosity between or among people... there was more understanding.

The participants observed that caring does not mean always being nice or avoiding unpleasant issues. Gloria explained:

> If somebody cares about me and I do something wrong or they need to correct it or they need to give me constructive criticism, that's important in caring for me so that I will be able to perform better. To me, caring about people . . . is like the way you care about your children, you correct them, you help them, you teach . . . and that is being fair with me.

Another participant gave an example of how caring and trust work in difficult times:

> You and I have had professional disagreements, right? Tough ones but we have always managed—a day later, or a week—we've always managed to ask how are you with this now, and give each other a hug, or a hand shake, or a note. That's why you and I have been able to stay intact over the last number of years, right?

Clearly, care in an organization also takes resilience as well as good will. After a difference of opinion, it was important to put energy into keeping relationships intact and lines of communication open. Paul explained how he and I could have honest conversations to let each other know why we felt the way we did, how our behavior contributed to the situations we found ourselves in, and then we moved on. He felt our example could be a model for others seeking to solve problems in difficult situations, where mutual trust and respect are required. Each of us had to regulate our emotions, work closely together, have some tough conversations and make sure we each felt secure.

Caring and Respect

Participants expected to be cared about by being involved in decisions, having input, feeling listened to, and knowing their work was respected. They expected their achievements and accomplishments to be recognized and celebrated. They wanted to be respected and valued for the experience they brought and for what they could do. Caring meant to many that they would be involved in making decisions that affect them and others. They saw themselves as valuable professionals with extensive experience whose opinions should be sought by district administrators.

From the participants' points of view caring should include professional development. They expected opportunities to develop leadership skills and to gain credibility in the school district and province. They wanted possibilities to network with colleagues and felt cared about when this, and chances to work collaboratively, were enabled. Caring in the workplace demonstrated with recognition that people work and learn differently. Some interviewees believed the work environment was collaborative, especially considering the geography of the district and number of its employees. They cited opportunities for groups of educators to meet, determine their own learning needs, and enable one another's professional development. Employees appreciated opportunities to take risks and try new things without being blamed for failure.

There was discussion of the significance of the professional development program for teachers and how it enabled them, within some parameters, to establish the agenda for their learning, which was perceived as a way of valuing and respecting the professionalism of teachers. When educators were treated as professionals—encouraged to make judgments and decisions about their practices and priorities as opposed to being dictated to by others—they considered the work environment to be caring and nurturing.

Paul described how important it was for employees to be affirmed when they did good work, and he pointed out a perceived weakness in the district's approaches:

> Administration [District] wasn't big on affirmation. . . . For some reason or other, affirmation never got across to the program specialists very often and everybody needs a pat on the back; that never came through in my honest opinion.

While talking about a project he had undertaken, and clearly felt pride about, Paul described receiving calls from other directors from across the province asking about his project and telling him it was valuable. He had visited other districts to explain his initiatives, "but, there was none of that here. They say that's part of your job. You do what you're supposed to do." He elaborated on what he thought were the important characteristics of care and caring: "First and foremost is trust and respect."

The former principal spoke about the importance of feeling valued and how it motivated not only the individual but others as well. In recent years the board had taken specific measures to demonstrate that deserving teachers were valued. New teachers, in particular, who had been doing exceptional work had been acknowledged and granted tenure (job security) one year earlier than was required through their contract. This had quite an effect on many teachers, not only on those who were directly impacted. Everyone was encouraged by the recognition given to the deserving individuals, and it illustrated how professionals should indeed be treated within an organization.

Caring and Fairness

Some participants expected that in an organization where care is practiced everyone should be treated alike in terms of discipline, benefits, and opportunities. Others stated that there definitely should be different treatment for different people, depending upon the circumstance and history of individuals and their position within the organization.

Ben, the director of education, argued that employees who have a long history of having volunteered through involvement in extracurricular and cocurricular activities should be afforded special consideration and allowance, for example, when requesting a day to be away from work to attend a family event or celebration. At particular points during a career, an individual might be confronted with a unique challenge or family crisis; those employees should receive differentiated treatment at such times. The director argued that it was just and proper to sometimes step outside prescribed policies and regulations to do what was "right" for a person. This has been described as *the one caring* acting in nonrule-bound ways on behalf of *the one being cared for*, and the approach is advocated as necessary and desirable (Noddings, 1992, 2005).

Two of the interviewees argued to the contrary, that providing different treatment for different people as opposed to treating everyone the same was a problem in an organization. Some employees perceived "special treatments" as displays of favoritism rather than caring. They perceived that some people received "perks" while other deserving colleagues were unnoticed or their requests were denied. Questions were raised about the fairness and equity of such practices. These individuals believed that in a caring organization consistent practices regarding opportunities, acknowledgement, and rewards available to one employee should be available to all.

In a large organization with hundreds of employees it was difficult, and sometimes inappropriate, for the details of certain instances to be shared; mistrust and confusion resulted. Greater explanation and promotion of the board's policies were required and safeguards were needed so that powerful individuals were not able to secretly grant privileges without explanation. This was an instance when the "accountability from within" that was advocated through the district's espoused philosophy of organizational learning should have been better implemented. When working in a relation of care, the focus is less on rules and regulations, or fairness and justice, and more on attention to the particulars of situations and what is needed or required at that particular time for a particular person (Noddings, 1984, 1992). However, within an organizational context it is important that there be transparency in the actions taken and honest and forthright explanation made available in defense of why an individual or group was given "special consideration." Otherwise perceptions of unfairness and suspicions of favoritism cause more harm than good.

District personnel made efforts to recognize life outside of employment that demonstrated caring for the person as well as for the professional. Participants cited several examples of how district administrators acted in nonrule-bound ways to care for employees as people. Some loyal employees, who did not abuse sick leave or other leaves, enjoyed "special treatment." The assistant director of personnel stated that he believed "it will be more positive as years go by if our pattern of human resource management continues." He added, "If it reverts back to being restrictive and policy driven without the human interpretation, we could be back with increasing levels of [sick leave] usages quite quickly."

Effects of Education Reform

The participants at the time of my interviews were struggling to deal with the fallout of a decree from the provincial government mandating a second consolidation of school boards. Everyone was aware of the turmoil, confusion, and disruption this would cause in their personal and professional lives because they had all lived through a similar process only three years earlier. The dust was only just settling after that round of change when they had to prepare themselves for another. The following paragraphs represent their thoughts, fears, and observations about what they expected work to be like in the upcoming months.

A Morale Problem

Change involved building trust, redesigning the governance structure of the district, and re-visioning teaching and learning. These were concerns for everyone, but some who had been working in the education system for years received this second wave of reform less enthusiastically. Weariness among veteran employees fuelled talk about past efforts to make changes; they viewed current concerns for change as just another round of flurry that would settle back down eventually.

The staff had all participated in educational reforms and either directed and or were impacted by school closures and district consolidations.

Each of them had experienced uncertainty and stress related to job losses or reassignments, which affected them personally as well as professionally. Many problems and dilemmas accompanied each downsizing, reconfiguration, and restructuring effort. At the same time, staff members were also dealing with personal or family illnesses, deaths of parents, reduced energy, and approaching retirement.

The director described the effect of the legislation on the people of the district. He recognized the fact that the entire district was about to undergo radical change. Indeed, he did not know what his own future employment would be; yet, he voiced a desire to attend to employees' need for information and job security.

> It certainly negatively impacts the people who are directly affected, because they're stressed. But if we have a genuine message of caring, at least they feel supported and valued *here*, and we will do everything that we can, as an organization, even though this organization will change shape.

The school board consolidation process was on the minds of everyone, and it was discussed in various ways during the interviews. Some of the comments actually reflected empathy for district administrators and a sense of "being in relation" (Noddings, 2002) with them. Andrew noted: "Everybody is totally stressed but you hear someone else say, 'Well, you know, how can they [District Administrators] tell us—they're stressed themselves.' [Laughter] Everybody's in the same situation . . . just as stressed as we are."

While admitting that the stress affected her, Doris also expressed empathy with the district personnel, although she said she preferred not to know about some changes she was hearing about. There were too many stories circulating and it was difficult to discern fact from fiction; many of the reports were disruptive and unsettling.

There was some positive thinking and commentary on the topic of reform though. Paul believed that the past reform had not been all bad and that educators from the previous denominationally segregated system were now learning and benefiting from the opportunity to work together.

> Even though we've had some rough times, just because we went through different systems that operated two different ways [from denominational to nondenominational], you and I have always been able to talk about it. I think we're a lot richer too, for having come together. I think we've learned a lot from each other.

Eloise was trying to stay positive, too, but acknowledged that the uncertainty of the situation brought out the worst in particular individuals. "Some people are seeing the comfort level they've always had disrupted and they can't handle that and are fearing the new system. They're starting to suspect everybody, and thinking, 'Who is honest?' and 'Who knows what?'"

Distrust became an extension of the uneasiness with the processes and choices that had been made concerning job postings and the political nature of the school board's decisions. Some people seemed to always land on their feet, while other, equally competent and perhaps more diligent, employees received pay cuts and demotions. Social relationships within the staff were strained with only some having access to privileged information. "People who are guarded in the information they share provoke suspicion because people wonder what is being hidden and why. Just as openness breeds trust, suspiciousness breeds distrust" (Tschannen-Moran, 2004, p. 26). Some felt devalued and left "out of the loop"; others seemed to revel in the new power and position that the reforms made possible. Variations in positions of power brought discomfort, apprehension, and disillusionment. People did not engage in discourse; evaded confronting their own fears, anxieties, and biases; and the lack of communication surfaced in various ways. Some felt not listened to and isolated into groups and divisions. Failing to deal with those feelings damaged the potential for collaboration among the staff and between divisions; many employees, in one way or another, voiced the need for more caring.

The assistant director of personnel admitted there was a morale problem but believed that how we treated one another during this whole upheaval would determine whether people came through "with a good taste in their mouth or with bitterness that would last a long time." Paul used strong words to describe the morale issue:

> Is it caring what they've done with the four districts—the way they've ripped them apart? Now it's "dog-eat-dog" here! I mean you can tell that tensions and morale are low and I don't know how organizations can do this. . . . [I]t's certainly going to affect how caring we are to each other. [We] are competing with each other. . . . [W]e're moving into the process of people trying to find other positions and wondering who will get back with the new board and who won't. That whole cloud of ambiguity is hanging over everybody.

All these events and processes of life compounded the need for caring—the need for staff to be understood and accepted for what they were able to give to change. They participated in deconstructing a district they had strived to create and that tore them apart, severed relationships, and caused divisions between groups to deepen. Now they endured public protests, negative media reports, picket lines, demonstrations, and long work hours. People felt they could not openly speak about the positives of the past church-controlled denominational system because of a variety of sensitivities.

Educators did not oppose the efforts to build shared decision-making processes but struggled with the amount of time and energy required to accomplish the needed changes. Past experience and knowledge of the hierarchical organization in which they worked determined the degree to which they involved themselves in the current innovations and reorganization. Some staff members were skeptical and did not want to commit themselves to work that theoretically was sound but was ill-funded and lacked sufficient human and material resources.

Connection in the Midst of Workplace Politics

The confusion, ambiguity, and uncertainty surrounding the reform process were not confined to the district office. School personnel were aware that the turmoil affecting the office staff would trickle out to the schools and affect teachers as well. They acknowledged that communications would be disrupted, known networks and channels to take action would become disjointed. School personnel believed they should prepare themselves to handle situations and issues on their own because of the dysfunction expected at the district office. Paul commented, "We're definitely not going to see people from district office and have the support that we've been used to . . . now with a district the size of the new one—that's a concern of ours."

There was some comfort though when Doris learned that the current director, who had only recently had the opportunity to get to know her, secured the position of director in the new board. "Our new director is *our* director so I'm glad about that because at least he knows our school. But if we had gotten a director from one of the other districts, we would probably be lost in the shuffle."

Sharon, a teacher and vice-principal, expressed concern about the new district configuration.

> It's going to be so huge, how are we going to be able to adequately care for 44,000 students? . . . It's going to be quite a challenge for somebody to be able to infuse caring into such a large organization.

However, Eloise observed that reform is not all bad: "We get things done, like we're moving along at a faster pace this past few years, like we're more driven, and I like that."

There were references to the internal politics of the organization and questions about the manner in which decisions to fill positions would be determined. Some were skeptical about the fairness of the process and wondered if friends might look after friends rather than consider qualifications and experience as the key determinants of who would be the best candidates. There were many positions that had to be filled quickly in order to get the fast approaching new school year underway in a settled and organized manner. There likely were going to be shortcuts in the recruitment and staffing process. There was going to be a lot of fast and furious decision making, and employees had concerns about the fairness and openness of upcoming competitions.

Shared Decision Making as Caring

Sharon saw the term *organizational learning* as "a community of learners and a community of people—with feelings and thoughts and ideas." For Doris, a teacher, organizational learning meant:

> The school(s) and the district learn from their results in order to improve their success, improve the achievement of the students in the district, and as well, enable the teachers to learn so that they can better focus on the outcomes and achievements of the students.

Andrew described the organizational learning philosophy as "essentially a very collaborative approach" and went on to add, "I think we're very good at that, including all people, getting all people to believe that they do belong." He reiterated, "Since the inception of our new roles related to supporting organizational learning, I find the collaboration process has improved tremendously." Paul believed that "to create organizational learning you need to get decisions shared, and it is very easy to say, 'Let's share decision making' but people do not understand what it means."

At the GAC—a group consisting of principals, program specialists, and district administrators—there were many diverse interests and the director employed a new way to arrive at consensus. Developing shared decision making matrices was an ambitious undertaking intended to give everyone in the organization understanding and a degree of comfort with how decisions were made and where they fit in the process (for further detail refer to Chapter 4). The matrices had many iterations and ultimately reached a point of development where there was significant buy-in from all those participating, despite the fact that some felt the process was unnatural and contrived. From an organizational perspective, the process was consistent with what the research literature describes as building a learning community. The director, Ben, elaborated:

We talked about dialogue so that people felt free to express their views and their values. Genuine dialogue is about creating together an idea and not feeling ownership of the idea. We take an idea and build it together. Then we have a go at it—to see if it withstands scrutiny. I think we've made significant strides. People tell me, and I see that things are changing. We're not going to have environments that are genuinely caring until we get genuine dialogue in an organization.

Participants of this study discussed evidence of efforts to share decision making and they offered assessments of our progress. We had made a conscientious effort to include principals and teachers in a collaborative framework to deal with issues confronting us all. The strategic plan, the vision for teaching and learning, and the shared decision-making matrices were all developed collaboratively. As well, a conscious effort had been made to include the teachers, the administrators, the school council, the general public, and students. We aimed to be inclusive and were beginning to experience some positive results.

There were some challenges yet to work through in the transition from top-down decision making to the new model. Some administrators explained that if people were caring then they should be aware of the impact of their actions on others. Interviewees also remarked that individuals needed to appreciate and be more cognizant of the pressures they bring to bear on others through words and actions; we were all interdependent. If people in the system had respect and appreciation for the various roles and responsibilities of individuals and groups, it would be considered a demonstration of care. Ben in particular explained that he needed to feel trusted, valued, and respected just as others in the organization did, but he seemed to minimize care in the workplace, as he added his "perspective of care in an organization was much deeper than receiving 'warm fuzzy hugs.'"

Not everyone was satisfied with the district's efforts. One participant expressed strong views about not feeling a part of important decisions related to the reconfiguration of schooling in the district. His views were representative of others at the district office and throughout the schools. He was upset that he had not been consulted on things affecting his life and work and believed that too often decisions were made without consultation. He referenced the process used to close schools and was displeased that some of the professional staff at the district office were uninvolved in the redesign of school configurations. He said, "That blew me apart—blew me away!" In the former school board under the previous director's leadership, program specialists were integrated in the process. They were asked what they thought, why options would work, and why they would not work. This program specialist was especially disgruntled that, "The only times we were asked to do something under the current director's administration was when he felt he needed more information to give to the public." He felt program specialists' "opinions were not valued and that in itself can show that there's a lack of caring. Only getting information on a need-to-know basis—that's what the program specialists were relegated to in my opinion."

Sharon recognized the problem, which she saw as compounded by communication issues. Traditional top-down directions continued and implementing a district-wide initiative to share decision making was difficult.

> Well, part of it is logistics when you've got a staff of people who are in a classroom for five hours a day...and you've got to fit in committee meetings, staff meetings and school improvement meetings and other meetings and whatever,...it's not that they don't see the things as important; it's because it's not a part of the day that they are in...We need to be better at communicating—at every level.

Others were less positive. Paul was disgruntled with the district's efforts and spoke about an undercurrent of contradiction in directions. "The matrix that we have for sharing power and authority never really quite worked the way I would like to have seen it." The complex processes undertaken needed more time and support so that setbacks and challenges could be addressed. Unfortunately, yet another round of school board consolidations had been announced that left everyone wondering about the purpose of all the effort.

> I think that if we had a bit longer we would have been able to work on that...but they are big issues...and we were getting there but now, with the restructuring, a lot is thrown in the way.

Enactments of Care

When I asked Ben, the director, about his assessment of the practice of care in the district, he began with an honest reference to himself and his challenge to care, particularly in arbitration cases in which care had not traditionally been a feature of the negotiation process.

> I think we've made some progress...sometimes I'm an impatient person. I would like for us to make much more headway. That could only cause you to be less caring so there's a balance. I think the question of people feeling valued, on some fronts we've made a lot of progress, and I could show examples of that. Four years ago, we did have 62 grievances on the books. Now we have none that are active.

All participants gave examples of how they felt cared about in their workplace: individuals or groups sent cards, messages, called, or visited when there was a difficult personal event, such as an illness or death in their family. They felt a genuine expression of concern and interest in their well-being, which was greatly appreciated and helped them to successfully return to work. The director, assistant directors, and various individuals throughout the organization counselled colleagues/staff members who experienced personal crises. Many listened to and attempted to understand the others' realities and offered care that was appropriate to individuals. Webs of relationships (Gilligan, 1982; Gilligan et al., 1988; Noddings, 2002) developed; care was extended to others, accepted, and returned. The administration of the district often extended warmth and concern and encouraged it among others. As well, through official policy cards, letters, flowers, phone calls, and fruit baskets were provided to individuals to recognize key occasions in their personal as well as professional lives.

Generally, participants believed efforts to care were recognized and appreciated, but some were frustrated and disappointed when others rejected what was being done for them. Some efforts to care were viewed with suspicion, criticism, or distrust by others. It was also frustrating for everyone that there were never enough resources to adequately support the professional development program. There was good intent, but often the follow-through was insufficient. As administrators, we felt that no matter how much we did to collaborate, we were criticized when we made decisions without consulting or we caused confusion about who should actually be involved in making decisions on particular issues.

Caring as Opportunities for Collaboration

In our workplace, dialogue and collaboration were recommended and encouraged as tools to foster organizational learning (Senge, Scharmer, Jaworski, & Flowers, 2004; Senge, 1990, 2000). These occurred in a variety of ways and forums—formal meetings, one-on-one interactions, over lunch, and through emails. Support for and involvement with university partnerships and other community groups were also encouraged. One of the important ways to enhance caring practices for others, as well as organizational development, was to enable these formal and informal opportunities for colleagues to share their experience and understanding. These were vehicles to foster caring relationships and connection within the workplace and beyond.

There were significant investments in professional development, and educators were treated as professionals who determined for themselves what they needed to learn rather than be dictated to by others. Choice was offered, in professional development activities and programs, insisting that it not be a prescription that treated everyone the same. All office workers were urged to deal promptly and politely with all concerns brought to them, and we tried to establish a mentality of service and care for others. In keeping with organizational learning theory, we aimed for each to support the work of others and to see ourselves as linked, viewing our effectiveness (or ineffectiveness) as interrelated. Through the district's professional development program teachers were asked to identify for themselves what it was they needed to learn, from a personal as well as a professional perspective, in order to better do their work.

Those I interviewed used the word *support* to imply their need for caring from their colleagues, administrators, and others. Often staff felt supported and cared for when others agreed with them as individuals or small groups. They did not see support as the opportunity to explore ideas and issues, challenge each other, or work together in relation to their parts of the whole.

District administrators attempted to be visible and accessible to staff, aimed to talk, and have personal contact with them through an open door policy and frequent attendance at school meetings. We wanted to change the adversarial relations—between school with district, parents and community with district, Department of Education with district—and move from antagonism to co-operation and collaboration. We attended meetings with school staffs, the program division, and various other groups and attempted to flatten the hierarchy by establishing the GAC with whom we aimed to share decision making. Policies and practices were developed to determine who was to have what powers, rights, and responsibilities on various issues.

Efforts to establish trust, connection, and community through the lens of the bureaucratic rules and regulations of a hierarchical organization were challenging. Despite our good intent, acquiring, sharing, and utilizing knowledge through professional development were more difficult to accomplish than imagined. We were less visible than we wanted to be: demands outside the district and involvements at the provincial level took us away. There was little time for even our closest colleagues to catch us in our offices. We were unaware of the way things were being set up to reinforce rather than flatten the hierarchy.

Caring: Valuing, Supporting, and Respecting Others

Sometimes the removal of a physical barrier can be a demonstration of care because it enables needed communication and respects teacher professionalism. Sharon told a story from her school of the difference made to communications and rapport among teachers and school administration when a door between the staff room and the principal's offices was opened up. "Stuff was piled against it on both sides. It was never opened." She explained that staff felt listened to, respected, and cared about when the door opened. "The day I walked into the staff room and saw that door open was [laughter] ... you know, like in one of those old movies where the prisoner comes out of the dungeon and can barely see for the light!"

Teachers feel valued and cared about when they ask for something simple, such as basic supplies to do their work, and they are provided. It is sometimes challenging in large hierarchical organizations to get simple things attended to, and as Sharon said, "Even though one person asking for one thing doesn't sound like a lot, it is when you multiply that by hundreds and hundreds of people.... [B]ut sometimes you've just got to find that thing!"

We must learn to open our minds, break habits that confine us to work in isolation and deprive us of the supports we need to be the best educators possible. As individuals, we can reach out, listen with respect to our colleagues, and ask for help when we need it. Within our system of education, we need to recognize how we work and treat others so that we can consider accommodations that are supportive and sustaining of its professionals.

The interviewees were able to cite numerous examples of how individuals, and the district on an organizational level, acted to take care of teachers' well-being. For example, in the last two or three years, efforts were made to transfer people to positions they wanted. This may explain why the number of sick leave days had been reduced by about 100 per month on average.

Participants felt that care was taken in response to their needs for compassionate leave or to manage their sick leave requirements. Andrew commented on the support he felt when his father passed away: "It was overwhelming—the support for my family—overwhelming. It's something that'll never, ever leave me—the cards, the flowers, the visits, the support—it was unbelievable."

Overall, participants reported that physical well-being was supported with an understanding that it contributed to productivity and happiness at work. This also led to comments that balance was important. Within the district office, most felt that successes were celebrated as were birthdays and other significant moments.

Uncaring Behaviors and Practices

A caring rapport gets established through informal communications and the sharing of positive encounters. Word spread when the administration was approachable and supportive of employees. Communication, collaboration, openness, and networking were identified by most participants as fundamental features of a caring organization.

Unfortunately, not all the encounters and exchanges between and among personnel were perceived as caring. Incidents were reported when some felt unappreciated, unacknowledged, and misunderstood. The director cited an example of a janitor, actually referred to as a school "caretaker," who had been refused access to the staff room to eat his lunch. He was obliged to eat in his supplies room. The teachers believed that he should not be privy to the "professional" discussions and conversations ongoing in the staff room. Ironically, teachers urge administration to value them and their work, but they did not perceive their actions to be undervaluing the work of another of their own colleagues.

Acting in haste to implement school board decisions and to take measures to bring operational costs in line with budget allocations caused uncaring behavior from administrators. Paul noted a case in point occurred during the reassignment of itinerant teachers from district office to placements in schools.

> They went in their offices, took out their stuff, threw it in boxes outside the doors and when the itinerants came back from summer vacation they discovered that they were reassigned to schools. I mean, nobody consulted with them, no one allowed them to come in and take their books off the wall in an orderly fashion and certain itinerants came back and found other people in their office—moved in. I mean, what does that say about caring?

This incident left those directly involved feeling unappreciated and undervalued. Their personal effects as well as professional materials and supplies were unceremoniously packaged with little regard for how the process might affect either those directly involved or others working within the district office who believed they could be next to be expended. A much less than "people first" mentality was evident.

It was strongly felt that professionals should not be criticized or reprimanded in a public meeting and that for the leadership to do so was threatening, insensitive, and uncaring. Contradictory treatment also caused concern, especially when only some received perks, or when administrators reverted to heavy-handed behaviors typical of the authoritative and controlling strategies we aimed to change. The example from Nathan illustrates "how a hammer had been used to 'swat' the fly."

> We had one job that we expected one person to do that had four components. Now all four components are being done by about three different people. So it's an unrealistic set of expectations we had for him. He was

terminated and his position with us disappeared. He was given a severance package but perhaps ought to have been accommodated more caringly in our system.

Obstacles to Caring and Ways to Enhance Care

This section elaborates on what participants believed they received in the practice of care in our workplace and their suggestions for enhancements to the practice of care. Participants' reflections on the problems also led to suggestions and ideas for improving the likelihood of organizational caring.

Bureaucratic and Hierarchical Structures

Even within the framework of organizational learning, we worked in the context of a bureaucracy where there was hierarchy. Ben remarked, "we ha[d] to do what we ha[d] to do," which made it challenging to create true dialogue. People sometimes debated whether actions were precipitated from the perspective of an ethic of caring or from bureaucratic principles and compliance with rules. Hierarchical bureaucracies prevented us from building trust, and we were caught up concentrating on positional power. Using a bureaucratic approach, policies and rules were often interpreted strictly within a bureaucratic context instead of within an organizational learning environment. In a bureaucracy human relations are often not approached in caring ways.

We had organizational learning models, but individuals in the organization were willing to tolerate bureaucratic dysfunction and autocratic behavior. Then the messages of caring and true organizational learning were not fully implemented because "a bureaucratic hierarchy is a learning disability." Doris saw that "the empire is growing" and believed, "the top now will be a higher top."

Not being able to take a risk, fear of making a mistake, and the reprimands or punishment that might come from mistakes were understood to be significant barriers to creating a caring work environment for employees. One participant explained that "we're working with compliance—in a restrictive environment—compliance to government." Trust and respect should start from the top down; however, it appeared to some that we were unable to integrate sincere attitudes of mutual respect and care for others into our hierarchical and bureaucratic organization.

The GAC needed to consider ways of building trust among the staff. Caring required that the administration recognize the lingering effects of past consolidations and reconfiguration processes on the staff members who lived through the process, as well as the continued distrust among them as a result of unspoken and denied tension. Ignoring these aspects had the potential to sabotage efforts to build trusting relationships among the staff. Paul articulated what was at risk: "If you don't really take a look at how you are with other people, systemically, then I don't think your organization is going to go forward meaningfully." Sharon underscored the value of a trusting environment: "Trust is big! To create an atmosphere of caring—you have to feel it." Andrew, among others, saw they had a role as individuals regardless of their "place" in the organization: "My role is to be an advocate, being very positive, upbeat, trying to knock down some barriers... take the younger employees under my wing... give them a bit of advice."

The district's attempts to institute shared decision-making matrices required the existence of trust. One veteran educator expressed a plea for understanding. He appealed for value in what he did accomplish and was able to do, rather than blame and criticism for what he could not.

Eloise had respect for positional authority and much experience working in hierarchical educational institutions. Her comfortable ways of working had been defined by understanding the limits and parameters of positions and being able to successfully work within them. Her comments revealed the challenge the district would have breaking free of old paradigms and organizational theories while also working within them. The district was encouraging everyone to become involved in decision making, to collaborate, and to share relevant information for everyone's betterment. Eloise frowned upon those who stepped outside their "bounds": "People take on a level of responsibility that doesn't really fit into their job and they cross that line."

It is debatable whether it is important to start at the top to build the culture that is desired throughout an organization, or whether everyone is responsible to care in a caring organization. Eloise remarked, "I think caring has to come from your top—from your senior administration," but she also felt responsible to help create caring relationships at work. She aimed to help get answers and convey the feeling that each question, problem, and situation mattered. In these ways Eloise felt she was supporting administration's efforts and contributing to an ethos of care:

> I think if we could build the kind of thinking that everyone has some responsibility in an organization to build a culture of caring, we could move from where we are. So if we studied people's approaches and encouraged everyone to be leaders, we can set the tone for caring, where the approach is cool, calm, and collected, and no matter how high the ire gets, we stay calm.

Better communication was needed through structures as well as informal channels to enhance care. Paul reported how he asked the director to reinstate an organizational mechanism that he perceived was an effective communication tool in the former board structure, an Academic Council (a full-day monthly meeting of the director with program specialists and assistant directors).

> I asked the director when he destroyed that old organization, "You know, you believe in team building, right?" He said, "Yes." Well if you don't get together you can't build a team. The maintenance that we needed wasn't there and when we came together for that hour or two, you know, there would be 20 or 25 items on the agenda. Well, what time is that for team building?

Paul voiced the notion that people need time to talk about issues that are important to them. His remedy for the time shortage was to propose adding an additional structure. Paul indicated: "You were always left not finding out about things, and it hurt communications, and communication is basic in any organization." He also advocated for "more get-togethers—professionally and socially" to "initiate more dialogue." He thought it was necessary as a way to "balance the differences in the office between senior administration and program specialists...in terms of travel and material things." He emphasized the need for more team building and suggested that it could be done systemically if the director would nurture it. "I mean he [the director] talks about nurturing dialogue. He talks about critical friends, but somehow we don't get there."

Politics

One participant viewed "caring for" in terms of the power and politics that were inherent parts of work in the district. He described himself as naïve because he used to think that ability and achievement were the bases for reward. He talked about the hypocrisy of our work culture that emphasized goals, teamwork, and shared values; yet, there were differential treatments for different individuals and groups. Some received executive perks (such as travel benefits, expense claims, access to professional development opportunities and conferences) and enhanced benefits, but other educators had lost economic ground in recent years.

The district bureaucracy was known by some to slow down work accomplishment, and often politics interfered in the outcomes. Eloise observed:

> I suspect, sometimes it depends on who you go to, then it goes to somebody else, and it goes to somebody else, and by the time it gets to the director,

sometimes you know there's three or four or five people involved in it and sometimes, depending on who gets involved, it takes a different turn.

Other influences were impacting our work in the district. The director gave an example related to the imposition of political agendas while we attempted to implement our vision. We were sometimes stifled in our efforts due to the imposition of approaches and policies that were antithetical to ours. School administrator Brian voiced similar concerns about the political nature of our work, specifically about the continuing imposition of top-down direction: "I do believe there are people who have personal agendas to get done what they need to see done. And unfortunately, sometimes, you know, that kind of precludes everything else."

Lack of Resources

Resource issues, a key theme for the participants, affected the experience and interpretations people made of organizational caring. Because of the fragmentation of divisional structures and poor communication, there was a contradictory theme of isolation versus collaboration voiced by participants. Some expressed a feeling of being pulled back and forth. On the one hand there was focus on growth, learning, and risk taking, on the other, pressure to prove oneself, trim expenses, and raise standards. There was sometimes support but never enough, which caused individualization, isolation, loneliness. Sharon explained:

> The size is—the geography as well—is a major factor. I think that is our biggest barrier here ... the distance from district office—and not having a lot of personnel at district office who can work with the schools. You know, they're spread around—there's only a few of them there.

Interviewees felt tension among efforts to respond to top-down mandates from external forces and worked to enable grassroots decision making. The director actually discussed how he attempted to respond to the multitude of demands imposed. He expressed feeling challenged with limited resources and flexibility to lead in directions he believed were appropriate to assist local jurisdictions to chart their own course and meet their unique needs.

Paul, the program specialist, in particular expressed frustration with his lack of input into decisions and actions that impact directly on him, and he believed his work environment to be less than supportive because of it. Other interviewees, including the assistant director, administrative assistant, principal, and teacher, expressed satisfaction with the opportunities they had to affect the directions and priorities of the district. The program specialist believed the shared decision making processes were contrived and not truly open processes. Others expressed belief that the mechanisms in place to enable input from everyone in the education system were elaborate and genuine.

The need for more opportunities to network and learn from each other came through in most of the interviews. Paul implored, "There's got to be a way that we can get together more often as professionals." In that regard the director aimed to continue to implement the initiatives undertaken, and "be patient, and develop genuine professional learning communities." He expressed the need for additional resources to provide more support for schools as they developed as learning communities. We advocated for further investments of time and resources in the structure of Families of Schools as a way to work toward implementing an ethic of caring.

Contradiction and Inconsistency

As expected, the district struggled with mixed messages, inconsistent practices, and behaviors that posed major obstacles to overcome. Some were committed to moving forward with the new district visions and approaches, but many others struggled to understand them. They needed support and time to work through what the shifts in approach meant in their daily work. Some participants believed the talk about organizational learning and caring was more rhetoric than reality. There were people in the district who claimed they worked in the ways being advocated, when actually they did not. There were people who "played the game" but who were in fact sabotaging the effort, while others were riding out the change, thinking it would pass and things would revert to the way they used to be.

When I asked whether Eloise thought we had a caring work environment, she reiterated her response three times in our hour together: "It would depend on what day you asked." She referenced the changing nature of work in the district and how her perception of our success fluctuated.

> I find we try, and we very much have it to a point, but just as you think it's all in place, something is done to undo the good that you have felt over the last couple of months. Somebody does something to undo it.

Inconsistencies in our practices sent mixed messages that related to particular personalities and their varied approaches.

> I've often heard people saying, "Well if that was me, I would be called in about that—if that was me going through that, I would be quickly told about it." What's okay for some people is not for others.

Eloise saw consistency and fair treatment as desirable goals in an organization but accepted that in large organizations with many different personalities and approaches to working with people, inconsistency had to be tolerated.

Some ill feelings were evident about how the district worked and how it impacted on at least one person's role and functioning, which related to his loss of power, his wanting more, and feeling uncomfortable with where he fit in the hierarchy. Paul believed there was "chemistry between the director, or in some cases the assistant director, and a program specialist" and because of it, certain people received privileges and more "play, more committee work, and more leniency when it came to travel." He believed "the director was 'in with' some specialists more than others," and that bothered him. He described how he was "beginning to see program specialists' cliques" and did not appreciate feeling left out of the loop when a small group "always huddled in each other's offices." He resented that some program specialists seemed to have "a lot more opportunities to do things than others, and there was more control on behalf of the director towards some program specialists compared to others." He believed particular program specialists were "trusted to do things and were treated almost like an assistant director"; other program specialists were not "on the inside track." He observed there was "a lot more control exerted here (at district office) than the matrix makes it look like. . . . I found myself being controlled—my style being cramped in certain ways, especially when the director's agendas were brought forward." He articulated a clear struggle with how to balance personal and organizational priorities.

Having power does not mean you can change what is wrong. Ben discussed the challenges of trying to implement new philosophies and new approaches within well-established hierarchical cultures. He appreciated the difficulties for those who have embraced the organizational learning theory but have little experience in educational administration. They take on "the personal mastery concept and can lose themselves and not recognize that there is a bureaucratic reality." The director appreciated the challenge of working within an entrenched system to try to change it: "They don't have the experience to be able to put it in context and it gets them in trouble." Finding the balance between the ideal and the realistically possible, at a given point in time and in a particular context, takes skill and patience; he found himself in those frustrating circumstances himself. "An inhibitor is the bureaucracy that exists above the school system in the hierarchy. . . . The accountability model is one that's driven from the top. That gets really frustrating for me."

Participants suggested that the district administration ask for feedback throughout the district with respect to "how we are doing." Sharon acknowledged:

> There are some people who are never going to be happy no matter what you
> do for them.... [T]here [are] a lot of really good people in this district who,
> if they felt comfortable, could make a lot of very good suggestions at every
> level from the classroom on up.

There was a call from the participants for group meetings, committee meetings, and volunteer meetings to all become a part of a district-wide evaluation of effort. From various groups new initiatives and refinements to current ones could be suggested and worked out as a means to address contradictions and inconsistencies.

Personalities

The appointment of a new director in 2001 infused great hope and renewed enthusiasm. He was envisioned as leading staff, students, and our community into a new era for the school district and came to the district with considerable valuable preparation to take on our educational challenges. He had taught in schools and at the university and was well respected throughout the province. It was expected that his leadership would return us to a focus on classrooms and help flatten our hierarchical and bureaucratic structures. The director aimed to create a "learning organization" (Senge, 1990), but I do not believe he could comprehend the degree of change needed in order to establish the climate in which learning could grow and thrive. To establish a school district based on an organizational learning theory, an ethic of caring would be a complicated task as power relations drove our organizational structures. "School leaders attempting to nurture caring must recognize that it will be embedded within the power structure of a bureaucratic hierarchy" (Sernak, 1998, p. 45). More care was needed but many lacked depth of understanding about what it would take to accomplish it.

In a caring learning organization, all members assume aspects of leadership by taking part in decisions affecting them; leadership is distributed among many. Leaders, including directors of education, needed to reconsider their roles, which were shifting from being the primary decision maker and authority to one sharing decision making and management with others within, and possibly outside, the educational system. Accountability needed to be built from within rather than imposed from the top. In this process there was the assumption that the director's role would evolve and devolve. To that end, in ASD, groupings of schools, called Families of Schools, were established with the intent that administrators and teachers collaborate and co-operate to eventually change attitudes toward each other. We hoped to change the way staffs interacted and to create more open communication throughout the school community, trying to prepare us to work as a team and to be accountable to one another. We believed everyone was responsible with a part to play in changing the district.

There was tension between those with task-oriented versus people-oriented approaches to work. Some valued relationships with people and fostered a positive work environment as a first priority; others worked with a commitment and sense of urgency, duty, and responsibility to get "the job" done. There was undoubtedly an accountability theme at work in the district with expectations that student achievement indicators show improvement and tasks be completed in a timely and cost-efficient manner. Interviewees indicated there was impatience, and sometimes intolerance, for mistakes; all indicated they felt pressured to do more with less. Interviewees differed in their assessment with only some of them feeling that a message of caring was often voiced in policy documents and in various meetings but the concept was not lived out in the actions and practices of people throughout the district.

Reflection

As district administrators, we viewed ourselves as caring about people and knowing that everybody was important. We believed in respecting the dignity and worth of every individual. As a group we did not associate our efforts with feminism, but I believe we wanted to lead and be perceived as leaders very much within the realm of feminist theorists' exploration of organization and leadership emanating from an ethic of caring (Brunner, 2000; Grogan & VanDeman Blackmon, 1999; Grogan, 2003; Noddings, 1992; Tronto, 1989). We wanted to create a new order—a school district that was a learning organization operating in an atmosphere of care.

To many, our district administration represented relief and a symbol of change after a difficult history. We brought a readiness for change, a reputation of caring and concern, and we modeled hard work. We expected quality and pride in schools and in the people associated with them. We established high expectations, pride in work, and strived to build trust.

I found there were several notable commonalities among our voices. We had each experienced discontinuities and interruptions in our lives that required us to make choices about if and where we would continue to work. All of us felt pride in the work we had an opportunity to do throughout our careers, but some were embittered and frustrated with all the changes that had come too fast and with the ways we resorted to treating each other. Each of the educators whose voice is represented here was passionate about their work and career and self-confident in their ability to handle multiple tasks. We all believed a diversity of perspectives was needed. Ours were strong voices, all with keen interest in people; yet, we felt attempts had been made to silence and control us. We each identified supports crucial to our continuing efforts and well-being. It had been difficult to negotiate our way through various systems of beliefs that did not complement one another. Contradictions and moral dilemmas were prevalent.

We felt challenged by patriarchal boundaries that manifested in our workplaces and tried to confront the hierarchies we recognize were influenced by long-standing cultures and traditions. We had all experienced various methods of surveillance embedded throughout our district operations but worked to contest and resist these negative aspects and create new traditions. It was a struggle, though, to interpret and help construct environments more consistent with our democratic principles.

Differences were also evident between our perspectives and approaches. Some openly challenged and resisted new cultural norms that contradicted our personal values, and others worked within them. We each found our own ways to survive the reforms and to maneuver our more competitive and individualistic contexts. Nothing is impossible to a determined person: we can challenge patriarchal aspects of social and cultural constructions in educational organizations and encourage questioning and reasoning as well as feeling and intuition. We can learn to negotiate traditional boundaries if we develop necessary attitudes and skills.

I learned a great deal from the people who participated in my research. Their comments and perspectives offered provocative insights into our shared experiences during this time, and they showed how they viewed themselves as marked by cultural perception of their roles. They revealed our experiences as educational leaders and the ways we dealt with the turbulence faced at various times and in various work situations. Aspects of our experiences differed, but many of my long-standing common beliefs and experiences have been echoed.

The stories represented in this chapter give us all a better understanding of complex issues that have not been fully appreciated. My hope is that these perspectives about the practice and potential of more caring relationships will foster new and deeper understandings, and they may also "create bridges of appreciation" (Ali, 2000, p. 6) between men and women who have not worked in those roles with those who have. This chapter expresses hopes, strengths, challenges, and a sense of the complexities involved in our doing caring work in an organizational context. Readers can appreciate the creativity and complexity within educational leaders' lives. I trust our perspectives and experiences contribute to a fuller understanding of the issues relating to practicing an ethic of care in educational work and also help form new understandings of how educators perceive their roles, what they see as their opportunities and challenges, and whether there is potential for change within the world of work in large hierarchical educational organizations.

Unfortunately we struggled with conflicting discourses. On the one hand was "managed professionalism" (Blackmore & Sachs, 2007, p. 83) and the exploitation of democracy with an accompanying intensification of work, rising expectations, raised standards, more testing, and more prescriptive curriculum. On the other hand we advocated for democratic leadership with degrees of autonomy, innovation, creativity, teamwork, collegiality, higher order thinking, professional judgment, and problem-solving approaches to challenges.

> What I have found, wherever I have looked, is that ordinary people, when they are given, or when they take, the opportunity, are quite capable of making good decisions—in many ways more capable than those who have the official positions of decision makers. (Rebbick, 2009, p. 52)

The result was the controls outweighed any freedoms so that people felt disempowered. The second reform was economically driven. We lost sight of the well-rounded education our policies called for, and our focus narrowed back to the three *R*'s with other curricular areas becoming secondary. Strategic planning was the buzz phrase. Schools had to fit within the district plan and the districts had to fit within the provincial plan; we all had to be aligned. There were increased demands for recording and reporting, and the "new transparency" was "both paradoxical and disciplinary" (Blackmore & Sachs, 2007, p. 86). Lines were being drawn between those who performed according to the expectations (for example, on criterion-referenced tests and public examinations) and those who did not. Underperforming schools, districts, and teachers were identified, and competitive relationships between teachers, schools, and districts became the norm. The new accountability of professional management, together with outcome-based curriculum and assessment, reduced our capacity to focus on the individuals in our local situations (students, teachers, parents, colleagues), and there was less room to be innovative outside the prescribed priorities. Although schools and districts felt increased control over their initiatives and internal priorities, they felt decreased control over external factors.

PART **III**

Calming the Turbulence

7

From Enlightenment to Empowerment

*Change does not roll in on the wheels of inevitability, but comes
through continuous struggle. And so we must straighten our backs
and work for our freedom. A man can't ride you unless your back is bent.*
—Martin Luther King, Jr.

Politicians and the general public declare students to be our most precious resource, but Canada's educational leaders are in turmoil as they struggle to cope with funding cuts, school closures, board consolidations, cries of underachievement, job action, increased accountability through standardized testing, and the challenge to include an ever more diverse student population with an equally diverse array of needs. I have been reflecting on some of our past to discover that life does not have to remain as turbulent in the future.

My research focused on people who have been integral in a radical educational change process. I attempted to reconstruct our experiences in ways that will contribute to the reform literature from a humanistic perspective through the lens of those most affected. "Things and people and relationships are understood and structured, and remembered in narratives" (Friedl, 1994, p. 91), and in this research the stories told are of great

Caring Leadership in Turbulent Times, pages 201–227
Copyright © 2014 by Information Age Publishing
All rights of reproduction in any form reserved.

importance and significance. They provide insight into and a better understanding of the complex lives and work of educational leaders. My work helps form new understandings of how leaders perceive their roles, what they see as their opportunities and challenges, and whether there is potential for change within the world of work in large hierarchical educational organizations.

An important understanding that seems to be missed in our discussions about our work and how to qualitatively as well as quantitatively reform it is that taking a caring stance does not mean we are not held accountable. "Caring and commitment to students demand that you hold high expectations for teaching performance" (Tschannen-Moran, 2004, p. 84) and, indeed, for all our efforts in education.

This chapter has implications for how the next generation of leaders in educational administration might perceive their roles and how they might work. The stories of our shared experiences of work in the district are applicable in processes of planning and implementing change efforts in other contexts. I believe it important to hear the stories of those who are underrepresented, and I hope my and other feminist perspectives will provide more balance in the way work relationships generally, and education reform specifically, are enacted and represented. I explored possible common themes, similarities and differences in gender perceptions, experiences, and their impact on how educational organizations operate. I also included fragments of my personal stories. As hooks (1989) argues, sharing one's past and one's memories through narrative allows others to view these experiences from a different perspective, not as singular isolated events but as part of a continuum. The narratives offer provocative insights into complex meanings and life in general, and they show how we view ourselves as marked by cultural perception of our roles. The stories represented in this book give us all a better understanding of issues that have not been fully appreciated. Consequently, I perceive our stories as "a platform for empowerment" (Hamdan, 2009, p. 7).

Comprehending that subjectivity in social research is impossible to avoid (Walkerdine, 1994), I examined many of my assumptions and came to appreciate how my biographical, cultural, and historical lenses led to my understandings (or in some cases, lack of understandings). Often in my work, and frequently throughout my studies, I have felt uncomfortable with what I took for granted. It was in the discomfort, though, that I learned significant things about myself and the world around me. I examined my position of privilege as a white educated female working from a position of power within our Canadian education system and learned to disrupt some dominant views and ways of working that surrounded me and to which I was contributing. I explored the value of practice and its contribution to theory and certainly understand how theory guides much of what we do in education. I have learned to become comfortable with discomfort and believe it is both necessary and helpful.

Throughout this chapter I discuss a number of key issues:

- work in education is stressful but there are other more progressive ways of working;
- issues of power and politics are universal;
- people and relationships are what make organizations successful and effective, or not;
- leadership is critical to creating more socially just organizations; and
- there is need for more caring work by both men and women.

Neoliberalism and the New Managerialism

Being a district administrator during education reform was dangerous and often personally and professionally damaging work. "The lack of women in those positions is indicative of deeper organizational problems requiring a change" (Blackmore & Sachs, 2007, pp. 59, 248). Women are positioned within competing managerial discourses of "flexibility, diversity and the conversation of scarce resources on the one hand, and...productivity and accountability on the other" (Glazer-Raymo, 1999, p. 203). Seen as either too compliant or too resistant, I felt vulnerable and in an unenviable position.

> In globalized postindustrial service and knowledge-based economy, productivity gains are to be achieved through the managing of people better by getting more for less. Despite optimistic "new wave" management discourses in a "deregulated" autonomy and teamwork in flatter learning organizations, the educational reforms of the late 1990s, we argue, were characterized by increased regulation, both internal and external, of educational labor in organizations, regulation that was process and out-come driven, not learning centered. (Blackmore & Sachs, 2007, p. 174)

Greedy organizations demand more for less and undermine women's work as they intensify labor, practice increased surveillance, and demand compliance (Franzway, 2001). Little care was taken about how to manage all the radical changes, and indeed the culture produced toxic, mistrustful, greedy organizations. Few of us felt we could contribute valued institutional knowledge about relationships and how systems worked because everything and everyone was new. Some reveled in their power, and others felt alienated. Exercising survival techniques became normal.

Neoliberal, rational, rule-bound logic (Noddings, 2001) with performance embedded into this new managerialism became the norm. Achievement and growth were determined by external outcomes; standards with transparency and consistency were our preferred values. We managed limited resources, devolved daily management from the provincial government to districts to schools, competed for funds, and provided feedback through accountability processes focused on outcomes and test scores. New controls through strategic plans were implemented with increased surveillance of professionals in education.

Following numerous amalgamations and closures arising from demographic shifts, economic hardship, and claims of student underachievement, the effects were larger schools, fewer districts, the elimination of religious control of education, and restructured relations among central bureaucracies, regions, and schools. Many of us struggled and experienced a "professional identity crisis within the 'managerialized' structural realignment of lived practices, social relations and intersubjective dispositions (especially ethical dispositions)" (Zipin & Brennan, 2003, p. 352).

Others have aimed to change the current direction of educational leadership away from an overly corporate and controlling model toward the values of democratic and ethical behavior (Shapiro & Gross, 2008). With the goal to achieve a transformed community,

> the traditional leader is a functionary of a system that is becoming ever more centralized, corporate, and removed from the influence of students, families and communities. The new . . . vision promotes democratic life and ethical reasoning growing from the heart of the community toward the wide world. (Shapiro & Gross, 2008, p. 171)

Women in Educational Leadership

Corporate and governmental processes not only reconfigured organizations but also produced discourses that created opportunities for progressive practices traditionally considered women's ways of leading. Increased interdependence is essential and networking opportunities needed to be "nurtured through affiliation and cooperation rather than rationality, separation and manipulation" (Barrett, 1995, p. 1342). Women leaders, already seen to be the managers of the personal and the private in traditional gender relations, are now expected to do the emotional management work of organizations—a "natural extension" of their domestic work of caring and sharing associated with popular notions of women being good at teaching young children and women's ways of leading and managing (Belenky et al., 1997; Helgesen, 1995; Steinem, 1992). Management is thus "capitalizing on emotions"; yet, "success continues to be in the language of male-type behaviours and emotional expression, men and women abiding by the emotional rules of masculinist organizations" (Blackmore & Sachs, 2007, p. 19).

Some careers and workplaces are considered predominantly male and others predominantly female. The hegemonic perception that women are naturally suited to certain tasks gives men more control (Hamdan, 2009). Still, "people question a woman's ability to perform a task just because it is normalized as a male task" (Hamdan, 2009). Both men and women are as capable. A frustration for many women is that the private sphere is culturally constructed to be a woman's realm, and the public sphere is relegated to a man like a patriarchal extended family (Hamdan, 2009). "Gender discourses persistently reinforce patriarchy within various contexts. . . . [M]any women are subjected to these gender discourses in a variety of ways and in a variety of contexts, sometimes even indirectly" (Hamdan, 2009, p. 64).

The potential of identifying and exploring a hidden dimension of organizational life—that of emotions—is now being addressed in organizational and educational theory (Crawford, 2007; Fineman, 2000; Fullen, 2001; Sergiovanni, 2003). Shifts to the relational aspects of leadership (Brunner, 2000a; Gunter, 2001; Noddings, 1984; Wheatley, 2005) are occurring as well as focus on personal and professional identities. Emotions and motivation are understood as connected rewards leading to collegial relations, recognition, commitment.

Women leaders face extra challenge when we desire success because we work in predominantly masculinist discourses. A deeper analysis is required of administrative practices of care within contemporary education reform and the ways women negotiate opportunities to care for others as they are kept in check by the expectations, rules, and requirements that go along with these practices. It is interesting to note the skills that are valued: planning, organizing, coordinating, controlling, criticizing positively, taking responsibility, making yourself heard, learning to be sneaky, following unspoken rules, cleverness, collecting evidence, and conforming to standards. There is a frustrating mix of messages that conveys an attitude of service to others, using tact, grace, manners, and charm even when dealing with critical board members or colleagues. Women's roles need to be examined so that we do not perpetuate suppression by being passive (Brunner, 1999; Hamdan, 2009; Steinem, 1992).

Nothing is impossible. "Education opens up opportunities for women, and economic independence grants women freedoms that threaten patriarchy" (Hamdan, 2009, p. 57). Patriarchal aspects of social and cultural gender constructions in educational organizations can be challenged, questioning encouraged, and feeling and intuition valued as much as reasoning. Males and females both need ability to negotiate traditional boundaries, seize the freedoms available, foster personal motivations, and reward self-realizations. Cultural traditions and practices that have been imposed, justified, and carried on continue to prevail, due in large part to the hegemony of male power. Social patriarchy rewards decisive, firm, strong leaders rather than those considered compliant and "feminine." Women must seize their "power and authority to bring equitable social order within their communities as well as Canadian society, where they can discuss issues of all inequality"(Hamdan, 2009, p. 69) and exert and create "new social and cultural ideas for inclusion"(Hamdan, 2009, p. 69).

Unfortunately, negative publicity has been used to shift schools, educators, and districts to compliance with the accountability measures, and educators risk being labelled troublemakers (Blackmore, 1999) if they resist and resent these measures. We do not have the freedom to foster a progressive and transformational culture in education. Rapid changes have been forced upon reluctant communities, generating resistance and resentment instead of improved outcomes. It takes wisdom to patiently support and challenge order to lead individuals, schools, districts, and society toward positive and productive change.

From Economic Efficiency to Social Justice

The trend toward economic efficiency identified in this study is not unique to our district or province; it is at work in education regardless of the jurisdiction. Within the discourse of economic rationalism, policy makers believe that if smaller, less equipped districts and schools are closed with educators and children moving into larger, better equipped centers, money will be saved and improvements in student achievement and facilities will result. Staff within our district—and in other education institutions globally—have worked with the apprehension that they may lose their jobs or be reassigned, and public pressure has added further challenge. The work of school districts is mystifying to the general public, and the media only contribute to the mystery by ignoring accomplishments and emphasizing problems. Disputes with parent and community groups continue to be presented far more often than reports about improving student achievement results and other positive developments.

A positive trend in current school reform efforts focuses on building partnerships that require a balance of authority, control, and power through shared decision making and management. Decisions are to be shared among educators, administrators, students, parents, and various other government and community groups and fit the model of empowering leadership (Grogan & VanDeman Blackmon, 2001). The aim is to develop more people-oriented, relational, and collaborative ways of working in which people care about one another (Sernak, 1998).

I examined the attempts of the district to engage with social justice practices of progressive and transformative education. There certainly was good intent and significant action to establish a more caring and inclusive work environment with various structures and policies implemented as well as many individuals doing their best to work in caring and collaborative ways. There is much that can be learned from these experiences that can benefit other educational institutions and organizations attempting to practice care within hierarchical and bureaucratic environments.

"School has been expected to perform such miracles as single handedly [*sic*] putting an end to a nation's social ills or making it a leader in the global economy" (Martin, 2011, p. 183). One should expect that a successful process of education reform would be characterized by discernible positive changes in attitudes and actions regarding the delivery and experience of education (Solomon et al., 2011). What has been missing from our reform processes has been fairness and equity, social justice, inclusiveness, sensitivity to difference, and empathy to the needs and experiences of others (Solomon et al., 2011). We contradict our claim of commitment to caring when we move to formulas, standardized curriculum, testing, measuring, counting, and comparing. Having to do more with less, yet expecting to raise the level of student performance and overall system effectiveness has added a great deal of stress. Today there appears to be greater disconnection and less interdependence among educational partners.

We district administrators were preoccupied with avoiding court challenges and so stuck to following prescribed "fool-proof" procedures. "Standardization as a policy and as a practice was antithetical to issues of inclusive education" (Solomon et al., 2011, p. 72). Most of us felt that "standardization as an attempt to equalize the ways in which different people are treated, and the concept of equity, which denotes equal treatment as not necessarily equitable, were in conflict" (Solomon et al., 2011, p. 84). We were focused on uniformity and sameness as opposed to valuing diversity. The reform process became a mechanistic system that reduced educators to technicians, and our communities felt they were being taken through a legal process devoid of meaningful consultation. Most of us felt like we were being programmed.

Consequently, many good people are leaving the education profession because they feel they are being controlled, disrespected, and blamed.

What is missing from the business perspective in education is the importance of connection, contact, and care among and for all the partners in education (students, teachers, parents, and administrators). "The humanity of the education process and the people within it seem to be lost through the bureaucratization of education" (Solomon et al., 2011, p. 90). The standards-based movement has created a climate where following rules and a cookie-cutter approach to education are valued over critical thinking.

The troubling trend of neoliberal and neo-conservative forces is that they are ignoring established research for political and ideological ends (Solomon et al., 2011). Caring work is intangible. Some administrators seemingly (and in my study, apparently) give contradictory and inconsistent support to social justice initiatives. We say we care but our actions indicate otherwise.

> Burnout and the pressure to conform to rigid (and counterproductive) standards are leading teachers to search for alternative career options.... Concurrently, many who would have considered entering the field of education in the past are reconsidering their options, given the current reform climate. (Solomon et al., 2011, p. 108)

I have discovered that we need a deeper, more genuine understanding of others and more patience to understand the significant resistance to the imposition of a major change. As administrators we thought we were acting as caring, committed, and conscious professionals, when we actually were too rushed and pressured to properly implement the magnitude of the changes expected of us. Complex and deeply rooted systems and practices cannot be steamrollered through. Adequate time was not built in to plan for successful implementation of the reform process. We needed to be able to put ourselves in others' situations and facilitate respect for individuals, groups, and communities to see beyond our immediate context. We were so busy doing the reform, we did not critically examine all that was going on around us and what we were doing (or not doing).

Realities of Power and Politics in a Hierarchical Organization

The relationships that existed at the district developed as a result of the bureaucratic hierarchy, a type of domination exhibited through top-down authority. The hierarchical organization and accompanied role descriptions of district personnel were prescribed and funded by the provincial government. The organization used power to dominate, subordinate, or manipulate through enforcement of rules and regulations to maintain social and organizational divisions among the various groups in the district and throughout the province.

Through our focus on and intent to create an organizational learning environment, our district personnel pursued systems thinking (Senge, 1990) with overlapping layers and levels, each with varying degrees of authority, control, and interdependence. However, the structure of "divisions" and our clear role descriptions were barriers. Social stratification by position meant each level was accountable to the one above. Few decisions were made without approval from above, and there was reluctance to approve even routine, as well as the nonroutine, requests or activities without consulting immediate authorities.

Most people approve of and support the notion that educators create a system in which caring thrives. There is a misconception, though, that we all understand what "caring" means and how it works in our workplaces. It requires more than a feel-good approach to education. It is not only about enhancing self-concepts and creating a pleasant environment where people enjoy working and learning with each other.

From an organizational perspective, caring involves leaders responding not only to the particular needs of individuals but also the needs of the entire system. Leaders must make sense of all the talk and action in terms of what would benefit the entire district. They have to factor in the expectations of superiors and make decisions that sometimes anger, frustrate, and upset staff members. Caring between administration and staff is unequal, for position in the bureaucratic hierarchy situates administration as dominant and staff as subordinate. Administration makes final decisions for personnel as a whole. Decisions arise from positional power. As leaders we should understand that power in relation to those for whom we intend to care. There is no guarantee that leaders' decisions, despite their attentiveness and willingness to dialogue and listen, are appropriate for the whole community. Mistakes do happen and leaders do slip into paternalism, authoritativeness, and dogmatism (Jagger, 1995).

The district administration wanted to believe the development of shared decision-making matrices would bring a new way of working together that was more democratic and less top-down. We intended to build collaboration among all groups and flatten the traditional hierarchical, authoritative model of organization within the district. We needed caring as we dealt with the confusion and lack of clarity around our work and relationships. The director, along with others, facilitated the processes of matrix development, which was quite complicated to say nothing of how difficult it was to implement.

As the leader, the director was responsible for keeping the big picture in focus. He took a hands-on approach and was diligent and hard working in his efforts to build the necessary understanding and momentum to make the matrix work. He struggled to keep the group and the process focused and productive. He sought to involve others and shared facilitation of the process with those he hoped would take on a personal commitment to implementing it. He wanted efficient working sessions, open communication, and respectful relationships among staff, and he worked tirelessly to share his vision. But behind all this was suspicion by some that these efforts arose from the director's desire to enhance his own power. Sometimes in the struggle to share power (for example, to take control of the budget), educators requested information that was not forthcoming from district administration in ways they could understand. The shared decision-making process felt imposed, and our commitment to establish a caring community often became subsumed in the maintenance of the power positions.

This is an example of the district administration's intent to effect caring power, "to use power to free and enable people and give them capacity to work through shared decision making processes" (Kincheloe & McLaren, 2000, p. 284). Unfortunately, by pushing hard the director and assistant directors lost credibility among the staff; our intentions were not seen as caring for others but as self-serving. Some interpreted the development of the shared decision-making matrices as maintaining, and perhaps even increasing, administrative ability rather than demonstrating care for employees by involving them in the important decisions that affected them. Insistence on detailed plans and discussions of accountability and consequences caused staff to perceive the district administration as desiring more authority rather than sharing it. The director needed assurances that he would not be risking failure and damage to his reputation with the elected board and throughout the district and province. He did not want to weaken his power base, which caused questioning and uncertainty as to whether he really cared for others or used the rhetoric of care and shared decision making to promote himself.

Caring and Power

Caring and power are intertwined, and the relational webs of the two can intersect to form relationships of caring power. An ethic of care requires caregiving to be situational, suspending adherence to rules and regulations designed to ensure fairness via objectively judging the situation (Noddings, 1992). To accomplish that, emphasis is needed on relationship building and a community of learners, with connection, interdependence, and collaboration. An ethic of caring has been conceptualized as webs or circles of relationships that lead to connection between and among individuals that also build community (Gilligan, 1982; Noddings, 1984, 1992). Although the levels of the hierarchy were clearly separated, interconnections among the groups and individuals were necessary to accomplish our work. Caring is not simply a response to a moment of decision making that involves justification of moral choices. An ethic of care requires continuously working together to build and sustain affirmative relationships with others and requires reciprocity between the one who cares and the one receiving that care (Sernak, 1998).

Noddings (1984) drew attention to the ways we situate ourselves in relation to the persons with whom we work, to the ways in which we practice in a collaborative way, and to the ways all participants model in their practices, a valuing and confirmation of each other. An ethic of caring within an institutional setting requires discussion of reciprocity from a distance, acknowledging the need for caring to flow not only from leaders, but also to them and among them. Reciprocity in a hierarchically organized educational setting would likely not exist because of the dominant and subordinate roles. Caring likely would not flow both ways; rather, it is expected to flow from the top down. Because of our positions, administrators are expected to provide caring and are rarely considered to be in need of care ourselves. Justifiably, employees were focused during the reforms on their own interests and concerns, and were unable to empathize or support their administrators' need for care. Administrative emotional labor (Hochschild, 1983) for the staff was unreciprocated.

To establish a school district based on an ethic of caring is a complex task because power relations drive the organizational structures. In a relation of care the leadership role is distributed among many. Leaders, including directors and assistant directors of education, need to reconsider and shift their roles from being the primary decision makers to sharing that authority among those within the educational system.

Most participants thought positively: they looked for district leadership to establish trust among various groups and held learning and caring as goals for all. Most believed that the atmosphere at ASD seemed ripe for the development of an ethic of caring, but it needed more guidance in directing change that would lead to trust. They believed that trust in turn would serve as the basis for co-operation and collaboration.

Inadequate communication is a problem in efforts to build caring relationships. Adversarial relations result between administration and staff when a good communication system is lacking. In contexts such as at ASD, staff needed an increased exchange of information, and it would have been worth the effort to expend extra time and energy in that direction. Not knowing the reason(s) behind decisions contributed negatively to perceptions of staff relationships. Misunderstandings developed when there was a failure to communicate, and it put some in a position of feeling not cared for. Giving reasons for decisions would have demonstrated caring for others, evidenced trust in them, and opened doors for personal relations of caring to develop. Feeling pressure from community and from school reform to improve student learning, and having insufficient resources to support it, frustrated change agents in their efforts to care. The necessary supports and resources from government to accomplish the changes required were essential so that people felt cared for in the process.

In corporate models of education the establishment of the model becomes the goal rather than a means to accomplishing something worthwhile. This manifested itself in the work of educators in the school district. For example, budget and personnel cuts were made for efficiency rather than improvement; school closures were effected to reduce costs rather than improve education programs and services; and school district and board consolidations were carried out to downsize rather than better serve people's needs. Evident themes of disillusionment, disappointment, disengagement, and loss were worthy of exploration in terms of their connection to concepts of care. Critical incidents and interview transcripts describe insensitivities, misperceptions, misunderstandings, miscommunications, and a lack of time and other resources. A significant number of people had their positions declared redundant, respected professionals were let go with little attention or due recognition, and some left in conflict.

The incidents reported and discussed reflect turbulent times in education that give cause for reflection about the future and how we treat people. Through consideration of critical incidents we can assess the importance of relationships and the social aspects of our organizations. During these troubling times, there is need for much emotional labor (Hochschild, 1983) and concern for ourselves and others. It is a struggle for leaders to press on with the business of the organization and attend to the needs of others and of themselves.

The strategies and decisions of the province to mandate education reform and how to implement it left communities and local school districts to respond and manage their new conditions. While consolidating school boards and closing schools makes sense on rational and fiscal bases, it did not produce the expected rational outcome—a better education system—because the sufficient material and human resources needed to successfully implement the reform were not forthcoming until much later than they were needed.

There were many dichotomies and contradictions made evident through our district work. On some days, many of us spoke eloquently and convincingly about the need to be able to count on each other and know what the right thing to do was. On other days, hierarchical, authoritative, power-over voices demanded adherence to direction. We sought genuine dialogue but could not handle challenge to our positions or the school board's collective wisdom. At a time most employees lost economic ground, levels of executive compensations were rising. This exacerbated the hypocrisy of corporate cultures that emphasize common goals, teamwork, and shared values.

How can cynical employees, working with constraint and through reform, trust the powers that be to treat everyone fairly and be concerned about everyone's interests? As a whole, people in the district had a difficult time working together. Some wanted connections, and others feared it would cause them to lose their autonomy. Some wanted to build trust through work with their peers but did not trust those at other levels in the hierarchy. To gain legitimacy and trust, and lay the groundwork for caring, there is need for a willingness to remove obstacles which prevent people from being treated with fairness, respect, and professionalism. Being alert to the needs of staff, students, and community requires significant time and effort, and commitments from everyone throughout the system, often at the expense of self. We all struggled at times with how much we needed to disregard our own needs to satisfactorily attend to the needs of others, but there is only so much any individual can do when physically and emotionally exhausted at the end of the day.

The district leadership team attempted to change the paradigm, but getting there was slow and painful because a true transformation would affect everyone and take years to implement. In ASD, there were many suppressed feelings that required more sensitivity. "In an ethic of care, caring is not simply a response to a moment of decision making involving justification of moral choices. An ethic of care requires continuously working together to build and sustain affirmative relationships with others" (Sernak, 1998, pp. 123–124).

Contexts Undermining Care and Power Relations

Often there were hostile and challenging contexts, and it became difficult to balance power and practice care simultaneously. I found myself working in a difficult situation as a feminist employed by males in a male-dominated, hierarchical organization. My descriptions of critical incidents illustrate how I felt pressure to act politically to achieve desired goals, which conflicted with feelings of allegiance to care for people working within the bureaucracy and for other members of our school community. I experienced significant tension as I tried to do my job in fair and caring ways. My position in the organization as a district administrator entailed a relative degree of formal and institutional power, and my tensions had much to do with power and how to deal with it.

The district bureaucracy constructed and maintained order in the organization through decision-making matrices, organizational charts, structures, divisions, physical barriers, policies, and regulations. The bureaucracy defined the issues (strategic plans, visions, growth and development plans), and the mode to represent them (charts, forms, boxes, matrices), and thus designated what was important. The result was impersonal, detached, compartmentalized roles and responsibilities, and the options were to either engage with the bureaucracy (fit inside the box, system, or division) or work outside it. I tried to engage with it and do what I could to change it from the inside, but often I became assimilated into it. I believed, though, that I could work from inside to bring change and improve caring relations, soften the structure, and build collaborative solutions.

Near the end of the process a number of us felt tired confronting issues, and we wondered what difference our work would make. Some usurped the authority of the administration, causing the director to become agitated and territorial. He reverted to having to deal in unilateral and hierarchical ways on some issues and with some individuals. This response caused many not to see support for shared decision making and collaboration, but only as continued top-down authority and power. Despite the matrix, some staff sought the director's approval for change initiatives before taking action because they believed if they did not have his support, there was no point in proceeding.

Teachers and school administrators throughout the district also had difficulty understanding their changing roles. We all wavered in our thoughts about shared decision making, leadership, and care. Despite new policy development, the establishment of protocols and procedures, and significant dialogue, many worked in ways that maintained the current system and climate. Some of us believed we were merely voicing messages of empowerment and democracy, and placating others by allowing limited leadership and decision-making opportunities. Although many of us strongly desired to change bureaucratic structures, we were unable to imagine one in which power could be used to care for each other, and the community as a whole, and in which collaboration would be the norm. Even though the district was ambitious and attempted to stimulate fundamental debates about the purposes and approaches of schooling (teaching and learning), and sought to have wide input, the relationships between educators and their obligations to significant workloads and new demands limited our progress. Systemic change was undermined when leaders at the district and provincial levels attempted to simplify and proceduralize complex philosophies and ways of working in the interest of quick results.

I argue that existing power structures can be used to develop and practice caring in hierarchical organizations. They can be adapted to create an environment in which power can be used to sustain caring. However, the relationship between caring and power is complex: both are relational, reciprocal, contextual, and socially constructed (Sernak, 1998). The discussion of our administrative work in the district, while not perfect, is an example of my argument, which raises critical questions about the nature and function of power.

- Can power and caring successfully integrate and intertwine rather than exist as opposing poles?
- Is power needed to produce caring relationships?
- What do we say to those who are disillusioned or complacent, to those still enthusiastic and dedicated, and to those who are skeptical because of failed reforms and broken promises?
- Is it necessary to have "power over" (Brunner & Bjork, 2001; Brunner, 2000a) in order to achieve a cultural climate and organizational structure that support caring or is that notion an oxymoron?

Power relates to what can and cannot be said, who speaks with authority and who must listen, whose social constructions are valid and whose are erroneous and unimportant (Kincheloe & McLaren, 2000). I saw power linked to oppression. I wanted the ethic of care to get beyond issues of power, but I needed to understand the various and complex ways that it operates to dominate and shape consciousness.

> Power is a basic constituent of human existence that works to shape the oppressive and productive nature of human tradition. We are all empowered in that we all possess abilities and we are all limited in the attempt to use our abilities. (Kincheloe & McLaren, 2000, p. 283)

I have focused on the productive aspects of power, its ability to empower, ability to establish critical democracy, and ability to engage marginalized people in helping them to rethink their role(s).

Thinking of administration in relation to power that connotes author-ity or control is easier than seeing it in relation to caring. In our district, the defined hierarchy of power reinforced the aspect of control, even as the staff strived to create an atmosphere of caring for one another and for the whole school district. Sometimes the care that was offered was seen as power—power to control colleagues or to gain "perks" for themselves, or to move up the ladder. The lack of communication and fragmentation of effort turned attempts to care into power struggles. There were attempts to offer care, but there was little dialogue and practice or confirmation of the work. Most seemed not to know how to receive the care offered, and unfortunately, interpreted caring as control. Simply possessing an attitude of caring and being in relation with others was not enough.

It was difficult for the staff to consider the caring of the administration in the context of our roles in the institution. We wanted to be caring. We talked about it often, recognizing the importance of caring among staff and others and that it was crucial for good teaching, learning, and working to occur. However, power, authority, accountability, and responsibility were also directly addressed in conjunction with our role as district administra-tors/leaders. While we aimed to care for others, we also had to ensure the school board's needs were addressed and that government officials were responded to promptly and competently.

Our pace and striving for perfection were difficult for people. As ad-ministrators we tried to model the best. For example, in report details and work ethic we saw ourselves as organized and efficient, and we wanted the same of everyone else. We put forth maximum effort and expected it from others, whether it was cleaning floors, developing the schedule for classes, managing a professional development day or athletic event, or monitoring and tracking the budget. In the face of district and provincial pressures, authoritative direction was faster than building relationships that enabled collective and collaborative decisions. We sought to quickly bring positive change to the district, but it often happened at a cost to relationships.

We understood that giving up control was necessary to establish caring and straightforwardly talked about it, but the use of power-over manifested itself in unexpected and inconsistent ways. At times, we spoke and acted confidently as protectors and genuine caregivers; at other times, we were overtaken by the power of others (government, the elected school board). We tried to frame our use of power in the pursuit of what was best for others, seeing control and authority as ways to gain ground for students, do what was best, achieve high expectations, and to generally address the needs of others.

From the perspective of the director, who was the final authority, conflicting issues emerged. The school board reaffirmed his accountability and contradicted his efforts to share leadership and decision making. By being in charge he had power, control, and authority, but shared leadership connotes empowerment and caring for others. The administration was caught in the middle, between traditional beliefs and structures, and understandings of leadership as emerging and shared. Such ambiguity fostered misunderstandings and misconceptions.

From Traditional to Transformative Paradigm

I have come to appreciate our attempts to make the transition between the traditional concepts of leadership authority and control toward a vision of shared leadership and an ethic/practice of care while immersed in a structure of power. A significant reason why change was stalled was the bureaucracy of the organization itself. It was actually over-organized and had too many layers. Each change we considered, each problem we encountered, we attempted to solve using the tools of bureaucracy—committees, working groups, authority, and control. It was difficult to create a caring environment for the entire district as we continued to work within the established authority-based structures.

The work we were doing required time, resources, trust, and connection. The staff seemed to recognize and understand that; however, the history and turbulence of reform and demanding hurried nature of work in the current context stood in the way. The administration as well as staff required the creation and maintenance of relationships (giving and receiving care) in order to pursue an ethic of care. The district administrators were blamed for spending too much valuable time on developing the matrices and for not dealing with some of the other pressing and immediate issues that were on the minds of school principals and program specialists, in particular. Dialogue was welcomed but steered and directed to our perspectives, and consequently some people gave us what we wanted rather than risk having original thought be discredited or ignored. We often expected others to sacrifice important personal and family time that left them feeling uncared for.

As an administration we were "living contradictions" (McNiff & Whitehead, 2000) in many ways. We said we understood that change took time, yet we were very impatient. It was difficult to accept that we all make mistakes and there was a tendency to blame rather than support colleagues. Clear messages were sent regarding reprimands, punishment, consequences, and accountability. In a "learning organization" (Senge, 1990, 2000, 2006) people are expected to take responsibility, learn from mistakes, and thus increase knowledge and competence. This was not the atmosphere created. Rather surveillance and power over were the predominant sentiments.

We did attempt to meet the needs of others as a way to demonstrate care. We promised to systematically make available professional development opportunities geared to individual growth plans but had too few resources to follow through and sustain the supports needed. This led to skepticism, a lack of faith, and eventually to mistrust of individuals and the system to honor their commitments. We visited funeral homes, attended graduation ceremonies, sent cards and letters, making what we perceived were real attempts to personally care for others. As administrators we attempted to understand others in order to understand how to care for them and saw ourselves as caregivers to staff and students while also feeling the need for care ourselves. We did all we could to be nurturing and sensitive; however, we had difficulty making it work. Many of our actions were counterproductive to the vision and values we articulated. Mistakes, incompetence, and challenge disturbed us, and often our impatience and intolerance showed, conveying an uncaring and insensitive attitude that was not our intent.

Although many of us voiced messages of empowerment and democracy and strongly evidenced a desire to change bureaucratic structures, we were unable to actualize an environment in which power was used to care for each other and the community as a whole, and where collaboration was the norm. Even though we defined new mechanisms through which we aimed to work, there were few changes in our protocols between the district and schools, and among district office staff and the divisions. New roles and processes for working together were ambiguous. Everyone continued to view the director, and to a lesser extent the assistant directors, as ultimately responsible for the successful operation of the district. The administration struggled with what their roles as leaders in a shared power environment could be. There were no models to follow other than management by top-down authority. Essentially, the administration was offering to share power but determining when and how it would occur, which presented a dilemma as to how to care while simultaneously using positional power.

Although the administration advocated a team approach modeled on the merits of the five disciplines of organizational learning (Senge, 1990, 2000), we experienced many obstacles and barriers that limited opportunities to bring about and sustain meaningful change. There were staff who wanted but resisted leadership and some who wanted to be cared for but were used to controlling. Worthwhile partnerships existed among common groups; however, they each had their own interests and wanted to work with the district on their own agendas.

Promotion and engagement in reflection and critical self-awareness were necessary as a district office staff and as a school board. We had initiated critical dialogue and encouraged multiple perspectives regarding our anti-oppressive practices and exposed positions of privilege and could have learned other valuable lessons in the process. We needed to look at ourselves and one another with the aim of fostering equity, individual responsibility, social difference—qualities that are the best in all of us. This would not have been easy, especially when we were under constant pressure and scrutiny. Such a process might have forced us to assess the accuracy of and intentions behind our actions. We knew on one level that there were better ways of working. We verbalized new philosophies and pedagogies through policy and in meetings, but under pressure and time constraints our actions reverted to old approaches that had worked for us in the past.

Situations that entail placing something we care about in the control of another person are situations that require trust (as in the travel claim incident I described in Chapter 5). To some extent the outcomes depend upon, or are determined by, someone else so we have to feel confident that things will work out. As I discovered, sometimes they do not. Sometimes our expectations are not met and what was cared for gets harmed (as my relationship was with the program specialists) because someone was careless with trust. "Trust in relationships is dynamic, in that it can be altered instantaneously with a comment, a betrayed confidence, or a decision that violates the sense of care one has expected of another" (Tschannen-Moran, 2004, p. 63).

Through writing this book I have relearned how crucial it is to ensure staffing practices identify the individual people who will build the kind of culture we want and contribute to the kinds of perceptions, appreciations, and actions that are vital to improving workplace cultures, making them happy and productive. We need a change in language, focus, and action. "Strategy" and "strategic" are business words that figure prominently in contemporary talk in education. We need to move away from business models and use the language of education instead.

Administrators are expected to lead and at the same time learn a set of unspoken rules. We are required to position ourselves, schools, students, and staff in relation to fiscal bottom lines and where we fit on a comparison chart. We feel constrained and lack freedom to lead in ways we want. Amidst the school reforms, there was not much interest in what I was doing or what I considered important. Now I realize that was both a challenge and an opportunity. While it was difficult to build momentum and a critical mass to advance initiatives and directions I believed in, others were distracted away from my work, and it gave me some room within my parameters to maneuver, experiment, explore, and work beneath the radar of scrutiny.

Leadership for Social Justice

Even with the most idealistic leadership, as long as we have a hierarchical set-up, it is difficult for leaders to lead in the ways advocated through research. I have learned that when well-intentioned leaders fail to care about and earn the trust of their staff and larger educational community, their visions are doomed to frustration and failure.

To what extent does policy making rely on persuasion/coercion and regulation, or genuine dialogue and collaboration? In current care theory, caring refers not just to an agent who "cares" but also to relation, and we must consider the response of the cared for. Therefore, an organization might need to design multiple policies to navigate the maze of possibilities it encounters. It would be best not to use universal policies that require coercion, because coercion produces resistance and weakens the relation (Katz et al., 1999; Noddings, 2001).

> It is no secret that the success of educational reform in Canada depends upon inspired leadership. However ... despite the honest efforts and intentions of many school leaders, it is clear that strong leadership is not enough. The ways in which we envision and enact leadership must also change if we are to see our school system renewed and transformed. (Ryan, 2009)

Competent and caring leaders are concerned about relationships and balance high degrees of support with their high expectations. They demonstrate a considerable degree of commitment to and respect for people as well as the organization. As discussed, respecting others shows care, as does providing employees with the resources—human and material—they need in order to do the work expected of them.

Leaders who turn around turbulent, demanding, and demeaning organizations describe people and their workplace in positive terms and ensure people feel confident and competent to do their work. It takes significant time and interest—care—on the part of leaders to have the conversations and do the necessary networking. Effective leadership requires effort, courage, persistence, vulnerability, humility, and forgiveness. But everyone benefits when all members of a community work together and are willing to go beyond the basic requirements of their positions. Communication flows freely, there is a high degree of trust, the workplace is positive, and everyone learns and grows—open, healthy, and caring.

Creating Transformative Learning Communities

There are two basic underlying structures of organizations: bureaucratic and professional (Hoy & Miskel, 2001). Bureaucratic organizations rely on hierarchy of authority for coordination and control, whereas professional organizations rely on trust in the expertise of the professionals to exercise discretion in responding to the needs of clients. Education is both bureaucratic and professional. At times, bureaucratic structures, regulations, and rules impede productivity. In those cases, leaders need to help remove the barriers so that people can get on with solving problems. Those in formal roles are trusted to do what is expected of them so that others throughout the bureaucracy are able to confidently carry out their work. Expectations cannot be divergent.

It is critical that teachers feel confident that their leaders have their best interests at heart and will do whatever is possible to help them develop as professionals. Leaders in positions of trust must refrain from exploiting others to advance their own interests; demonstrate consideration and sensitivity for the needs and interests of others; communicate respect; be visible and accessible; demonstrate integrity in telling the truth; and keep their promises. We must find ways, both large and small, to communicate good will and caring toward each member of the school community. Small expressions of appreciation for extra effort—a kind word or a brief note—can go a long way toward fueling the motivation for more of the same. When colleagues can predict how others are likely to behave in a given situation, they are able to develop a sense of caring for one another and the relationship.

> The most important moral and performative facet of teaching is the ability to foster and maintain informed and respectful relationships among teachers, students, parents and administrators. These facets are complex dynamics born out of personalities, emotional intelligence, and educational philosophy. Such complexities cannot be easily quantified and needs [sic] to be understood and assessed over time in a variety of contexts by a number of people. (Solomon et al., 2011, p. 105)

"Professional learning communities share three important features: the adults in them act and are treated as professionals, there is a focus on learning, and there is a strong sense of community" (Tschannen-Moran, 2004, p. 107). They are characterized by the quality, tone, and content of dialogue among the professionals, and leaders set the example. "Cultural norms in a PLC [Professional Learning Community] can facilitate trust by encouraging a culture of cooperation rather than cutthroat competition"

(Tschnannen-Moran, 2004, p. 108). Leaders can create the structures that facilitate collaboration and shared decision making, openness, and constructive feedback (Senge, 2000).

Trust and Caring

The culture of a learning organization supports and sustains trust. The more innovative and effective an organization is, the more likely it is to have an atmosphere of trust. Tschannen-Moran (2004) found that a sense of caring or benevolence was the single most often mentioned dimension of trust in colleagues. The importance of taking a hot meal to a sick staff member, helping new personnel get started, sharing ideas, and "looking out" for one another cannot be overestimated. Accepting responsibility and not shifting blame for errors to others are significant. Another way that people help build and sustain a sense of trust in the collective is through "compensatory trust," whereby people cover for one another when they become aware that someone may have dropped the ball (Kamler, 1996). People make choices in how they respond to conflict: sometimes consciously and thoughtfully, other times reacting in the heat of the moment.

One of the primary causes of the disruption of trust is conflict that has been handled poorly. "How individuals respond to conflict can either foster trust or damage it" (Tschannen-Moran, 2004, p. 129). People respond to their environment. For example, when there is a lack of trust in our workplaces, people become guarded in their interactions, and "energy is diverted from common goals and channeled into self-protection" (Tschannen-Moran, 2004, p. 131).

An obstacle to collaboration is a strongly instilled sense of autonomy, which we are often reluctant to give up. Fear of losing autonomy is connected to reluctance to expose ourselves to scrutiny and criticism. Some gain status through talk but do nothing innovative. Some feel threatened when others collaborate.

Leaders set the tone for caring relations through their example and taking proactive strategies to make connections. Some leaders in our hurried and demanding workplaces today not only complain but also are disrespectful, frustrated, and doubtful of the ability of others around them to do competent work. Still others work to establish positive connections to motivate productive engagement in a problem-solving atmosphere. They demonstrate caring and competence themselves and are proactive in supporting others. They have a focus on success and earn respect by being fair and consistent. Humor goes a long way to helping make the workplace one where people want to be, and it shows when colleagues are trusting and willing to be vulnerable with each other. There is no place for sarcastic, demeaning, or inappropriate commentary in a caring workplace. Everyone wants to feel our professional competence is respected and our caring for others acknowledged. This is as true for the people leading as it is for those throughout an organization. Some anonymous advice I was given somewhere along the way comes to mind as trustworthy and wise: "Hold a tight rein over the three *T*s—thought, temper, and tongue—and you will have few regrets."

Leaders often find themselves caught seemingly having to play one individual, group, or community against another; it can feel as if, regardless of the course of action, it will hurt one group or another. This was the situation we found ourselves in when we were negotiating what would be fair and reasonable reimbursements for travel costs, and when we were consulting with the communities throughout our district as to the future of schooling in their areas.

I have experienced first-hand how the absence of care and trust impedes effectiveness and progress and how mistrust can spread like a disease that erodes performance. Hurt feelings from that time strained my relationship with my colleagues and other partners in education. Some believed they should not have to change the way things were for them, others felt we administrators were reasonable, and others felt we betrayed them. I learned that regardless of what you do for people, in some situations you will still be viewed and treated as a "cold," detached, and uncaring administrator. As much as I attempted to value others and make concessions, still I had to implement policy. It is difficult to be put in the position then of having to repair damaged trust and mend relationships. It would be wise at those times to engage in the four *A*s: "admit, apologize, ask forgiveness, and amend ways" (Tschannen-Moran, 2004, p. 155).

When conflicts result in hurt feelings, it is important to put mechanisms in place to help members of the community restore their broken relationships. It is the role and responsibility of educational leaders to make sure disputes do not get in the way of the group's ability to fulfill mutual goals and work together. Conflict is an inevitable element in the change process (Fullan, 1993); there will be differences of opinion as to how to achieve goals. Power dynamics get disrupted, some people feel loss, but still change might be the right way to go. Resisters are not bad people; what is important is that they be listened to and helped to move through their reactions. One valid way to do that is to demonstrate care for the individual, the organization, and its goals. "The willingness to engage in a constructive, albeit difficult, conversation is a concrete and powerful way to show you care" (Tschannen-Moran, 2004, p. 153).

While our newly established district took on many worthwhile and valid initiatives in an attempt to build a shared vision and collaborative environment, organizational structures, such as shared decision making that can bring the insights of more people to solving complex problems in education, required time and attention to nurture caring practices. Without it, in our case, communication became strained, making our problems more difficult to solve.

Too many rules cause resentment, so it is important to work to build a common vision that gives members confidence and motivation to give more than minimal effort. In order to cope with the turbulent changes and demands of accountability, we need demonstrations of care. Many of us were asked to change our fundamental beliefs about our education system, dismantle what we had given a career to build, and change practices to build a new system. In this environment, the degree of interdependence required high levels of sensitivity, trust, and care. Without it some of us focused our energies on protecting ourselves. "For schools to realize the kind of positive transformation envisioned by school reform efforts, attention must be paid to issues of trust" (Tschannen-Moran, 2004, p. 175). Finding ways to overcome the breakdown of trust is essential if we want schools and districts to reach the aspirations we hold for them.

Reflection

I believe people derive most of their happiness through relationships, the development of individual talents and abilities, and congenial work. "In pressing for professional status we sometimes fail to look carefully at the internal commitments and requirements of an occupation, and we may neglect the ways in which occupational life contributes to human flourishing" (Noddings, 2003, p. 215). From my perspective, the education given to education students should include information on the potentially emotional nature of practicing and living an ethic of care. (The topic warrants more attention in preparation programs than it has been given to date. See further discussion of this point in Chapter 8.) Unfortunately, the district's efforts to care were often turned into power struggles. There was little dialogue and practice, or confirmation, of the caring effort. The inability to collaborate and work together on priorities we professed to share severely limited what we could accomplish, and the history of reform and demanding, hurried nature of work in the current context stood in the way of establishing trust. The leaders and implementers of change might pursue ways to limit the number or extent of the demands being placed on people throughout the system. Perhaps, when possible, the most caring measure can be to refuse particular initiatives and requests and use protected time and resources to slow the rate of change, minimize its negative impact on people, and build the potential for successful implementation. Taking a stand to value people and their efforts, as well as understand limitations, would support the creation and maintenance of caring relationships.

Caring can and should become everyone's business, and not be viewed as a responsibility only for leaders. The earlier discussion of the ethic of caring as webs of relationships is anything but simple and straightforward to accomplish within organizations. For leaders in organizations to involve the appropriate people from the beginning, and honestly seek their advice as it pertains to decisions that affect them will be no small feat. As evidenced throughout this study, it was difficult to create a circle of care throughout the entire district community while continuing to work within the established authority-based structures. As district leaders, we may have had the skill required to care, but little time to exercise the capacity. We may have had the knowledge, but not enough resources. Some of the social constructs, such as hierarchical divisions and the decision-making matrices, actually created destructive patterns for our work. Everyone needed support, but we were unable to provide it to each other as a staff.

I have uncovered significant contradictions within the education system that employees are forced to face: The contradiction of internal policies with outside influences and pressures, and the predicament that identified needs cannot be addressed with the resources available. Bureaucrats are faced with multiple tasks, much conflict, and confining rules. They act to translate demands from all sides into purposeful outcomes, with procedures and politics limiting their scope of action. Despite messages of growth and development, learning and caring exist on the one hand, and on the other are consequences, blame, survival, accountability, and fiscal restraint. Work in education today is oppressive, contradictory, and prone to crisis.

> Current contradictions and paradoxes in education reflect the different social, political, and economic forces that are at work in the larger society. Perhaps if we identify and explore the contradictions, they will provide us with a foundation for questioning how education administration can be done differently, and thus lay the groundwork for more refreshing ways of redefining education administration. (Grogan, 2003, p. 22)

In the future, we will all have "to become comfortable with contradiction, work through others, appreciate dissent, develop a critical awareness of how children are being served, and adopt an ethic of care" (Grogan, 2003, p. 22).

Without caring relationships and networks of trust, education systems are likely to founder in their attempts to provide constructive educational environments and meet the lofty goals society has set for us because energy, needed to solve the complex problems of educating a diverse group of students, is diverted into self-protection. To be productive and to accomplish organizational goals, schools and districts (the whole education system) need cohesive and co-operative relationships. Care and competence are necessary to share the appropriate information with the people who need it.

To be a caring leader takes courage, sensitivity, and a willingness to deal with difficult situations and different people in a straightforward and forthright manner. A caring stance does not mean that we are unaccountable. On the contrary, caring and commitment to others demand that we hold high expectations for our performance, but our high expectations need to be supported with guidance to help others meet the standards. It is crucial to learn how to blend achieving goals with demonstrations of concern for those with whom we work. There is a fine line when balancing a task orientation with a focus on nurturing relationships, because in some situations, it is easy for one to dominate. Overall, caring leaders evidence both support and challenge in good measure.

Recent newspaper reports in Nova Scotia, Canada, confirm that the cycle of neoliberal education reform policy is far from having run its course:

> Shrinking budgets and declining rural populations have pitted boards against parents around Nova Scotia during recent years. Seeking to spend less money on mortar and heating fuel, boards have sought to centralize education by closing small schools. These schools, however, are often the last institution in communities that over the decades have seen their garages, grocery stores, legions, and Lions clubs close. So the battle, from the view of many parents' groups, has been fired by the knowledge that if they lose their school, they lose one of the last institutions holding their community together. Boards, meanwhile, have maintained that they are responsible for education and not economic development. The battles have been fierce. . . . Composed largely of lifelong educators who ran for seats out of a sense of duty to northern Nova Scotia's youth, the board [Strait Regional Board] is mandated with maintaining a balanced budget despite declining enrolment and multimillion-dollar budget cuts from the Department of Education in 2011 and 2012. (Beswick, 2012, pp. 12–13)

The Newfoundland and Labrador Government pressed forward with a third school board consolidation in September 2013, just as many other reform processes are ongoing in other jurisdictions. It all gives timely credence to this study's participants' beliefs that education organizations of the future will continue to be bureaucratic and hierarchical; they will be rules- and procedures-driven; and quite possibly, they will be less caring. Many of us expect to continue to be led by top-down management styles responsive to externally imposed change agendas. We caution that school districts are becoming bigger but not necessarily better; there is and will continue to be less effective communication, demands to do more with less, a rushed pace, loss of personal connections, and less collaborative and more competitive work environments. If this is to be so, what can be done to counter it? Approaches with potential to protect people's sanity and well-being and an alternate way forward for organizations and their leaders is the focus for this book's concluding chapter.

The bottom line is people, and when the people in education feel cared for—and are themselves caring—it will pay dividends in helping the entire system to succeed. Creating productive, transformative learning communities with a large infusion of caring people at various levels of the education system can make the world a better place.

8

Building Caring Bridges Toward More Socially Just Educational Communities

Never believe that a few caring people cannot change the world.
For, indeed, that's all who ever have.

—Margaret Mead

When one looks at struggling educational institutions—the effects of corporate managerialist agendas and the increases in apathy among some educators—one is often compelled to question what can be done about it. My work responds to the challenges of these global trends with a caring perspective on how to create change in the lives of disenfranchised educators. This book is a first step toward unlocking the secret to creating more caring work environments during times of tremendous challenge and complexity. The most powerful ingredient in any change is people in their organizational and community contexts.

Throughout my 30-year career in education, I have worked in various capacities and have a vested interest and passion in interpreting the lived reality of work in educational organizations and in studying caring leadership practices in action. Besides having served in leadership positions, I have an

Caring Leadership in Turbulent Times, pages 229–254
Copyright © 2014 by Information Age Publishing
All rights of reproduction in any form reserved.

in-depth understanding of how, despite good intentions, the pressures of day-to-day challenges implementing turbulent reform can overwhelm and push the ethic and practice of care into the background. I framed my doctoral research based on my work as a school district administrator. My interests allowed me to study and understand many challenges and obstacles while I searched for, and aimed to practice, an ethic of care—a concept that seems to be taken for granted and seldom questioned or explored, especially in the context of work in organizations.

My work helps to reposition a body of research about caring leadership and points to refreshing new possibilities related to leading to care and caring to lead. My research about the embodied practices of a group of district leaders who were treated in uncaring ways and the spaces that can be created for understanding and improving upon current reform processes endeavors to establish caring practices across the challenging reform terrain in education.

I offer my work in the spirit of hopeful educational change, "not stupid optimism" (Wrigley, Thomson, & Lingard, 2012, p. 12). As educators, it would be helpful for us to proudly re-embrace what draws us to the teaching profession—our love for people. There is good reason for hope and faith in care, and I think it necessary if we are to create a better system of future education for our young people and ourselves. I suggest we start with questioning our philosophies and reassess why schools and school districts exist, identify what we do well, what we can do better, and perhaps question what should not and cannot reasonably be expected.

I have geared my efforts toward self-awareness, self-analysis, and critical engagement with issues of school reform and how I, and others, have been treated in that process. At the outset, I was much less aware of the workings of privilege within the school district where I worked at that time, but through the exercise of thinking critically, I felt responsible to counter some of the uncaring ways we worked. I considered how my privileged position shaped my research and revealed how my personal experience has shaped my understanding of myself and others (Chapter 2). All of us working in the education system in Newfoundland and Labrador during the late 1990s and early years of the 2000s discovered first-hand that "moving beyond White privilege identity becomes more nuanced when the dynamics of religion and culture are added to the mix" (Solomon et al., 2011).

I have witnessed and experienced care that preserves dignity, supports a sense of community, and extends my knowledge and advocacy for caring leadership in the future. I have also suffered the hurt caused by uncaring words and behaviors from people I looked to for leadership and guidance. Caring is not the core "business" of education, even though education is considered a caring profession. I have critically examined what my colleagues and I contributed and failed to accomplish for others within a particular institutional setting and how we impacted the lives of people throughout our school district. I believe that if we are to do better, we need to understand the impacts of our policies and practices on the people affected by them as well as on the quality and effectiveness of our work in education.

Certain groups of educators, and others involved in the education system, are experiencing negative and unfair treatment that relegates them to the unenviable position of feeling uncared for, powerless, marginalized, dismissed, disenfranchised, undervalued, and/or unappreciated. Keeping this in mind, critical areas need to be addressed in order to help them and change how we "do" education. These critical areas can be summarized as philosophical perspectives, the process of reform, and the context of education, and they will need to be qualitatively addressed to make a difference. There is too much at stake not to rethink our approaches to working with people in contemporary educational organizations. This final chapter examines these broad areas from the perspective of providing direction for further action.

Confronting Assumptions and Philosophical Perspectives

Critical theorists can help educators rectify wrongs, identify key morals and values, and help us to consider tough questions, including who makes the decisions, who benefits from them, who has the power, who is silenced, and what can make a difference? Instead of accepting the decisions and values of those in authority, we can challenge the status quo to deal with inconsistencies, hard questions and debates, and challenges. Interrogating our values, rethinking and reframing our positions and conceptions (of privilege, power, culture, language, and even justice) can help make us realize how our morals and actions may need to be modified over time.

> Justice aims at a society and at personal relationships in which people are treated fairly, where they get what they are due, in which they are respected as equals, and where mutually agreeable conditions of cooperation are respected. Caring aims at a society and at personal relationships in which nurturance and relationships are highly valued. (Strike, 1999, p. 21)

For Noddings, "Caring is the very bedrock of all successful education ... contemporary schooling can be revitalized in its light" (1992, p. 27). Social justice is a pivotal concept associated with the ethic of care (Gross,

Shaw, & Shapiro, 2003) and although the ethic of care has been associated with feminists, men and women alike attest to its importance and relevance. Male ethicists and educators (Barth, 2003; Sergiovanni,1992; Solomon et al., 2011) have helped to develop this paradigm, but with recent trends— locally and globally—heavily influenced by efficiency and accountability frameworks that exert pressure on people at all levels within organizations, applying social justice perspectives and addressing humanistic needs are often neglected. Increasingly, economic rationalism is becoming the basis of education policy (Apple, 2004; Burbules & Torres, 2000).

To practice more care in work environments is difficult and resource-draining work. It may seem unrealistic to involve the appropriate people, for example, in making the decisions that affect them in these "new times," when more and more is expected and demanded, but it is a goal toward which we can work. It is incumbent upon us all, regardless of our positions, to use our own power to make a difference and seek to be involved.

On several occasions, groups and individuals throughout ASD were given opportunity to participate in policy development, react to drafts of documents, request the kinds of professional development opportunities they wanted, and voice opinions and concerns. Despite these demonstrations of care in our professional environment, few actually embraced the prospects. Often staff did not perceive what was being offered as demonstrations of care. Instead, they perceived our efforts as managerial attempts to "look good." Staff members were understandably more comfortable with what had been the "normal" ways of working. They worried about job security, and how the changes working their way through the system would affect them and their employment. There was so much going on that it caused us all to make choices that minimized additional risk for ourselves. As administrators with the best of caring intentions, we were perceived as more uncaring than caring. Administration and staff together were caught in a hierarchical system being encouraged to think and act in new and challenging ways, and without adequate time and necessary resources to ensure the initiatives could be successfully implemented. To recommend that organizations demonstrate concern for employees' personal lives and their families and recognize the home and work connection appears to be an ideal that goes against the grain of externally mandated reform processes.

Proactive reform approaches, including the development of democratic leadership and the promotion of a value for difference, seem inconsistent with current organizational realities. As district administrators, we found ourselves caught in an impossible bind. We were committed to acting in the interest of the public good, and to doing what was good for education, but struggled to accomplish our work within the confines of neoliberal politics and policies. Having an attitude of care is not enough, but it is an important incremental step toward having more open, honest, public debates about education and less closed-door decision making. In ASD, despite having many prerequisites for care in place, the pressures of imposed agendas from above, hurried time frames, and insecurities related to employment complicated the district's efforts to care; consequently, some within the organization perceived their efforts as inadequate.

I have taken on the responsibility of "giving voice to silenced people," and presented "them as historical actors by telling their collective stories" (Richardson, 1990, p. 64). The collective story I have told of ASD educators working to implement education reform highlights the turbulence associated with top-down, mandated policy direction. Consistent with the literature, there are themes of misuse and abuse of power, the chaos inherent in radical change, personal and family challenges that were felt—especially from a gender perspective—and the undesirable pressures associated with uncertainty and insecurity. Remembering and reconsidering these experiences helps to challenge our assumptions about them and ourselves.

Through concerted effort by all of us in education we can interrogate and interrupt dominance and power and choose to work and teach for social justice in the Canadian school system. This is difficult to do without administrators assuming dynamic leadership roles to counter uncaring and inconsiderate practices that serve only the elite interests and promote social injustice. Although there are competing models of effective leadership, current scholarship on socially just educational practices emphasizes the importance of educational leaders in implementing and sustaining inclusive practices that empower others (Ryan, 2006). For example, Shields (2004) advocates transformative and dialogic leadership, and proposes a transformative agenda through leadership for social justice and equity. Both propose shifting our focus from protecting self, positions, structures, and traditions to taking care to increase the potential of others to learn and make positive contributions. I use the word *transformative* to refer to a profound change in consciousness, in the sense used by Freire (1970, 2000). Such a change involves critical reflection and questioning, in shifting perspectives that contribute to social change. Leadership involves the ability to influence others and shape their decisions and actions that affect organizational goals. Leaders with a caring orientation use that power in positive ways and ensure everyone in the school community has a voice in decision-making processes. This requires moving beyond orthodox ideologies that sustain existing power structures by interrogating assumptions and realigning perspectives.

Changing Direction

I have been critical of current leadership and management theories and practices, and in this concluding chapter I make recommendations to inform policy direction and workplace practices for the future. I explored the subjective, personal, and relational nature of work, as well as the detached, objectified, and impersonal elements of work environments. What I found were feelings of neglect and disenfranchisement among people within organizations and negative consequences of policies that are counterproductive in terms of meeting both the organization's needs and the aims of education. Particularly in Newfoundland and Labrador, the organizational and personal impacts of three rounds of massive restructuring processes between 1997 and extending into 2014 require analysis and reflection within the context of the conditions because of the impacts on the people who carry out the policy directives.

While policies reflect the social, political, and economic conditions from local and global perspectives, there is much evidence that top-down, bureaucratically and economically driven agendas disrupt people's lives and have questionable success in implementation. From the voices represented through my research, it is clear that the human toll does not justify the means. Unfortunately, due to increased legislation, financial restraint, demands for accountability, and disconnection from a hierarchical and over-regulated bureaucracy, education continues to be susceptible to each swing of the political pendulum. I argue that the product of education should not be measured by formulas but rather by individual and collective achievement.

Even in the face of challenging reform, leaders can implement a caring vision that holds genuine promise to change education in socially just ways and toward a wider democratic citizenship.

> Most assuredly there is growing momentum for reclaiming educational reform from neo-conservative and neoliberal political agendas, and committed teachers' concomitant desire to move education in a more critical, democratic direction where socially just understanding of the true purpose of teaching and learning extends beyond reductionist, stilted, and expedient business-oriented measures of learners' abilities. (Solomon et al., 2011, p. 110)

Through consideration we can assess the importance of relationships and the social aspects of our organizations. I return to the fundamental belief taught by my parents that no one is better than anyone else and that everyone is deserving of respect. "Do unto others as you would have them do unto you" (*The Holy Bible*, 1946, Matthew 7;12) is a principle that applies equally to students, teachers, parents, trustees, district administrators, support staff, community representatives, and government personnel.

In our district, our intentions and some of our practices were indeed good. We developed shared beliefs about the need to be happy, safe, respected, cared for, and valued. We wanted a positive environment to promote learning and support all with community involvement, engaging projects that were creative, joyful, exciting, surprising, challenging, and that took learning seriously. We wanted everyone to talk to each other, work hard together and independently, make mistakes and ultimately succeed. Promoting positive learning and achievement were our expressed shared responsibilities.

Each person and our various contributions deserve to be valued and to accomplish that requires us to be open, approachable, and never too busy for anyone, which is difficult in today's work climate. Current change efforts based on neoliberal goals produce powerful conflicts for everyone involved in public education; from leaders and staff to students and community, all are confronted by the contradictions between goals of economic efficiency (rather, the reduction of public resources) and processes of caring. School boards would be wise to debate and consider the ways they can connect more closely with teachers, principals, community groups, and other key stakeholders in education.

In essence, our work in ASD aimed to care for employees, and others, but due to a combination of factors (some within the district's control and some beyond it) people were not satisfied and did not feel cared for. Although we were exhausted, still there were flickers of positive energy and hope intermingled amongst the skepticism and cynicism. Some people believed they could change, and help the system to change, in positive ways. Our caring experiences and attitudes evidenced that reformers need to allow time to build trust, connection, and community; moving forward in this new direction is not something individuals acting in isolation can accomplish.

Some leaders do in fact care that global policy agendas are driving our local priorities in education; that managerialist agendas are having as much influence in education as educational philosophies; schools are becoming more competitive than caring; our colleagues are stressed and dysfunctional; politics is more important than learning; public education is viewed as a business; leadership is about more than power, control, and position; and collaboration and building relationships are strengths needed by (both male and female) leaders. However, for organizations to become more humane and less oppressive, an ethic of caring has to accompany the focus on principles, rules, duty, and accountability. "We need to stretch our imaginations so that we discover new visions of society in which caring is a central value and institutions truly facilitate caring" (Fisher & Tronto, 1990, p. 56). Caring, justice, and power need to be working together. As educational leaders we must understand that the particular needs of individuals serve as guidelines for equitable and moral treatment for members of the larger institution. To facilitate dialogue and debate of fairness and justice, leaders need to be driven by moral purpose (Barth, 2001, 2003; Sergiovanni, 1992) and incorporate caring into our institutions that are currently dominated by justice reasoning and power-over ways of operating.

An ethic of caring requires organizational structure and leadership that support thinking and doing. It demands appropriate resources, skills, and knowledge, but the question remains: Are there educational organizations with leaders willing to give enough to change the system that has been entrenched with competition, autonomy, control, and independence in order to cultivate interdependence, connection, and community?

The organizational model for schools for much of their existence has been a bureaucratic one (Brien & Williams, 2009). Fullan (2005) argued that it was unreasonable to expect schools to change their leadership culture significantly and to sustain that change within the confines of a larger district system that continued to operate according to the principles of a traditional bureaucracy. The best hope to change the current situation in public education lies in replacing the normalized view of the hierarchical and bureaucratic organization with perspectives that view the maintenance of relationships as crucial. It will be necessary to find ways to extend our networks both inside and outside school systems to provide productive courses of action for people interested in creating a better life for students and educators in schools and beyond.

When considering educational reform, "policy makers will want to examine the current power relationships, for creating a climate of caring in schools will take place within those already established links" (Sernak, 1998, p. 128). It is necessary to understand the various and complex ways power operates to dominate and shape consciousness (Chapters 4, 5, and 6). "We are all empowered, in that we all possess abilities and we are all limited in the attempt to use our abilities" (Kincheloe & McLaren, 2000, p. 283). Our challenge as educators and staff members (some of whom feel more empowered than others) is to seize the windows of opportunity that open to us, to value and demonstrate an ethic of care, and to use our own power. If we focus on the productive aspects of power, the ability to empower, and the ability to establish critical democracy we can engage people in rethinking their roles and come to see power as working back and forth between ourselves and others. A sense of interdependence can be cultivated, with all individuals feeling ownership and group connection.

Creating Space to See Differently

Although the dominant discourse in educational policy is driven by economic rationalism, educators have a responsibility to resist policies that are inconsistent with more humanistic ways of working. The knowledge and power to make substantial change resides with those who work with the people who perform meaningful work on a daily basis. Despite the restrictions of policy-driven agendas, the spaces that exist between theory, policy, and practice create opportunities for local possibilities and interventions that need further exploration. The current economic crises and the expectant calls to reform that will surely follow as a response to new fiscal realities will foreground the challenge to cope with reform movements with more humane practices. The voices of those who have been at the core of educational change must be heard among the new calls for reform efforts in order to meet the challenges of the new order.

An examination of the ideological basis of economic rationalism as a basis for education reform must be questioned, just as it is questioned as the sole rationale for economic reform. The current economic crises raised questions globally about the wisdom of the ideological underpinnings informing the direction of economic policy. This economic rationalist approach that has shaped the direction of education policy over the past 30 years now needs a reflexive analysis. Theorists like Apple (2000), Burbules & Torres (2000), and numerous others have railed against the neoliberal and far right leanings shaping the direction of education and warned of the perils inherent in this direction. Given the failure of these policies in economics, it is imperative that their influence on education policy be examined in a new light. The organizational and personal impact, as evidenced by the experiences of those interviewed, raises serious questions about the merit of reform at any cost and the long-term disruption of people and organizations for the public good.

Crossing Toward Ethical and Social Responsibility

The effects of corporate managerialist policies and the strategies employed to mandate and implement education reform in Newfoundland and Labrador left communities and local school districts in upheaval, struggling to respond to and manage their new conditions. We must necessarily move away from imposing decisions to a more "dialogic process of reform"

(Blackmore & Sachs, 2007, p. 14), in order to refocus on the purpose of education and therefore on educational leadership and management. "This requires us to reopen debate about educational governance, inequality, and social justice that addresses long-term issues of education inequality but with different manifestations than those confronted in the twentieth century" (Blackmore & Sachs, 2007, p. 268). A more democratic and person-centered philosophy is needed. Caring organizations must cultivate personal relationships, especially by listening and responding to those who are critical. By honouring opposing perspectives people feel respected, listened to, and involved, which all foster commitment and care. Educational leaders of today need to be knowledgeable about their diverse communities and demonstrate compassion and care for their intellectual and emotional needs (Noddings, 2001; Sernak, 1998; Shapiro & Gross, 2008). This will take us a long way toward creating a more democratic and moral world.

How can we achieve renewed optimism with so much turmoil ongoing about organizational and institutional change? Employees want to believe that a better future is possible. Canadians have indicated that they want more from their working lives: not only economic security and a decent standard of living, but also opportunities for personal development and the fulfillment that comes with making a contribution (Lowe, 2000). The spaces that exist at the intersection of theory, policy, and practice can provide opportunities for intervention, engagement, and agency among educators rather than passive compliance to outside forces. If people really are our greatest resource, and if the global economy really is moving from an industrial/capital base to a knowledge base, we need to make commitment to people central in our workplaces.

Corporate and governmental processes to reconfigure organizations have paradoxically made clear that we need more culturally diverse societies. At the same time, there are new discourses about styles of leadership offering a positive way forward for the future of management. We are shifting to "relational rather than competitive values" (Barrett, 1995, p. 1342). There are ongoing efforts to change the direction of educational leadership from an overly corporate and controlling model toward the values of democratic and ethical behavior. Our leadership goal must be to achieve a transformed community, to practice democratic and ethical educational leadership through a sustained process of open dialogue, a right to voice, community inclusion, and responsible participation toward the common good. This is a daunting project, especially for those living and working through the turbulence of education reform. Studying educational leadership is far from easy at the best of times, and it is especially challenging during turbulent times. "No matter what the requirements or configurations of schools, educational leaders in the public sector will likely face greater stresses and increased demands for the successful performance of all students and for outcomes established by governmental and community groups" (Kochan & Reed, 2005, pp. 71–72).

In these "new times" it is important for organizations to become more ethically and socially responsible in order to attract the best employees and be successful in today's competitive environments. I advocate that administrators, and other leaders in education, would be wise to conduct critical self-analysis, which will involve examining their philosophical orientations. It will be helpful to re-evaluate our basic beliefs about people and how we treat them. Those who want to make a difference can either continue to reinforce orthodox thinking or embrace transformative thinking. This book's premise is that educators cannot continue to think and work in ways that treat people unfairly, unjustly, or hurtfully to silence and marginalize them. We need to problematize educational knowledge and practice by asking:

- In whose interests are we working?
- Whose ways of knowing are privileged and whose are devalued?
- To what extent do our educational policies and practices promote care, equity, and justice?
- How can we challenge the status quo?

To address these questions, we can start by educating ourselves about what care, justice, and equity mean and what these should look like in our various educational contexts and organizations. Once we understand social justice principles, we must also implement them and reject top-down imposed priorities that have not included meaningful consultation with input from the people who will be impacted by them. We can change our communication and interaction patterns related to what and how reforms will take place. Traditional decision-making processes are no longer justifiable given our understanding of democratic leadership.

Pathways to Educating Leaders for an Ethic of Care

If the ethic of care is used to help resolve dilemmas, then there is need to revise how educational leaders are prepared. In addition to being taught the importance of hierarchy, an ethic of care will require leaders to consider multiple voices in their decision-making processes. Caring leadership is essential, and more stories of leaders who are working to be authentic in their dealings with people would be helpful in providing some refreshing and hopeful guidance for others in the field of educational administration.

It is the responsibility of preparatory programs at university to provide leaders with the appropriate skills for transformative leadership practices; thus, strategies are needed to infuse these programs with the necessary theoretical constructs, practical applications, and examples of caring from the local context. Leadership preparation and development programs need to explore and "confront the contrivance of a de-emotionalized educational administration culture" (Beatty, 2009, p. 157).

Preparation programs for teachers, administrators, and management personnel need to stress the importance of going beyond an idealistic focus on caring to equipping people with practical strategies to practice care in today's complex work environments. These skills would include learning to listen with openness to what is heard; learning to challenge the thinking and conclusions of others in constructive and respectful ways; learning to differentiate approaches to people in ways that meet their needs; raising awareness of differences and equipping employees to respond to differences in constructive ways; creating environments that foster learning and development—not control; seeking to understand all perspectives in a situation and support approaches that encourage others. All educators could benefit by learning self-care strategies (as well as ways to care for others).

Connecting Leadership With our Hearts and our Heads

Sound leadership acknowledges and involves both the head and the heart. It is important to know how to make informed ethical decisions, taking into account both the rational and the emotional contexts—especially during turbulent times. This age in education is rife with inconsistencies, complexities, paradoxes, and turbulence. It is imperative that we who are educational leaders maintain a dialogue to advance democratic and caring leadership so that we can begin to appreciate our differences and work toward common understandings.

Individuals can focus on development of inner strength, courage, the ability to receive and absorb criticism. We need to develop inner strength to withstand inevitable criticism and to be able to continue with a commitment to care, even when it is unpopular. Worthwhile learning can come from criticism, so we must not be afraid of confrontation. Instead we should engage in dissenting dialogue through meaningful debate and allow suppressed criticisms to surface in order to work through them. We must not allow frustration and impatience to shake our resolve or push us to a state of anger or defensiveness. Administrators must learn to deal differently with conflict, negotiate better, take time before acting, exercise patience with themselves and others, and enable a greater involvement of women.

Leaders must "walk their talk" and carry the banner for care by being personally involved in action plans and change but avoid micromanaging. Believing we are the only ones who can do a job infers a lack of confidence in those to whom we say we trust. Leaders will be wise to monitor progress but let others make it happen.

Leaders need to spend time with the naysayers in an organization, to seek their support and draw them in because they do want to be associated with success. It is important to analyze the competition with understanding and respect, and then bring along rather than force an issue. By accepting differences and looking for others to help provide a wider and richer perspective, problems can be defined and potential solutions found. It will require discipline and patience to present a low threat to new ideas and promote the concept of team through meaningful collaboration. Responsibility must be the goal as opposed to assigning blame, reprimands, or punishment. If people are to be treated as professionals, then the administration has to believe in their expertise and expect the best from them. This is possible only in relationships and it is indispensable to success.

Leaders must find out what is important to others, then make it important to themselves, and remain calm and focused even when things are happening quickly around them. Leaders today are expected to model excellence and understand the extraordinary potential of each of their colleagues, the tentative nature of knowledge, the necessity of continuous growth and renewal as a professional. They are expected as well to reject hierarchy and value others' abilities and contributions, celebrate creativity and exhibit energy (intellectually, emotionally, and physically), nurture others and self, and on top of all that feel dignity and know they make a difference (Barth, 2003). Rewards and incentives are triggers for change and help employees to recognize there is something in it for them.

As leaders we need to know ourselves and keep in touch with our core, to make mistakes, fail and succeed, give and forgive, follow our heart and soul (Barth, 2003). We need to care for ourselves as well as for others and build ourselves and others up by associating with positive people. We need inspiration and caring, too: from colleagues, books, conferences, seminars, observations, and collaboration. Skillful leaders learn the strengths and weaknesses of each individual and develop strategies to change the old system of doing things.

Little else in our lives consumes as much of our time and thought as our work. We need dialogue to determine the just and caring rules and regulations that are to serve as guides for making moral decisions in our workplaces. It takes skill to instill a sense of urgency rather than stress, pressure, and impatience. A positive working relationship with individuals and groups is essential for change to be a success. When change is initiated based on identified need through compassion and integrity, employees will recognize the genuine leadership and feel motivated to support change.

Work is personal despite the many warnings, "Don't take it personally!" Our relationships with others are at the heart of all of us, and we should choose words and actions carefully, recognizing we are leaders of people. "In times good and bad, our efforts are really measured by the heart, by how in the years to come, people remember how they were treated in the tough times" (Zimbalist, 2005, p. 141). We all should examine our values and how we feel about the way we treat others to determine how we contribute either positively or negatively to our world. It is helpful to consider how we view others who think differently than us, what our beliefs are about those with whom we work and interact, how we react to others who hold views that differ from our own. Do we silence them? In what ways do we validate or negate their identities and perspectives?

I hope the need for more care will gain a higher profile in the educational community as a priority for effective learning communities, and I want to stress that caring work is as suitable to men as to women. Today our schools are moving towards a more collegial, co-operative, transformative, service approach in a learning community with important shifts occurring in roles, relationships, and responsibilities. Traditional patterns of relationships are altered: authority flows are less hierarchical, role definitions are both more general and more flexible, leadership is connected to competence for needed tasks rather than to formal positions, and independence and isolation are replaced by co-operative and interdependent work (Murphy & Seashore Louis, 1999).

Forging Links Between Caring and Empowerment

By modeling caring behavior we energize and empower others. Colleagues who see us care for others and who feel cared for themselves have courage to take risks to confront orthodoxy. They are confident to resist and speak up, prepared to develop critical awareness, and trusting to engage in transformative learning and action because there is no shame in making mistakes. There will be no blame. When we model self-respect, equity, fairness, democracy, collaboration, others are likely to embrace these values, which in turn can lead to mutual respect and acceptance. Conversely, those who are prone to making derogatory remarks about others are modeling behavior that sustains prejudice, stereotyping, and discrimination. "Modeling behavior not only involves overt actions, it also includes nonverbal behaviours, which contain cryptic, unintended messages that others notice all the same" (Egbo, 2009, p. 177). Functions of leaders that offer significant guidance to others intent on creating trusting and caring work environments include: visioning, modeling, coaching, managing, and mediating (Tschannen-Moran, 2004).

Often our intentions and visions are admirable but our methods to realize them are not. I have experienced first-hand that negative and cynical attitudes do not inspire but rather sow discord and distrust. For example, people detect hidden agendas and when they do, they get the sense they are being controlled and maneuvered. Our energy would be better invested in being open and developing positive attitudes and approaches that inspire and motivate others. We need to develop our emotional intelligence (Goleman, Boyatzis, & McKee, 2002) so we can "walk our talk."

Modeling personal humility and being "soft" on people but tough on projects allows leaders to balance a strong work ethic with care for people. It is significant when employees see their leader(s) model norms of conduct that promote the well-being of everyone in an educational community. When the leader defends, acknowledges, rewards, and promotes the ideas and efforts of others it sets a tone and precedent that others want to emulate. The whole organization benefits when colleagues see that everyone's contribution is necessary to the success of the organization. To become the "lead learner" (Barth, 2003) by regularly reflecting on our words and actions, stepping back and thinking before we respond, and even apologizing when necessary would bring about a radical change of an encouraging sort and positively affect the climate in our workplaces.

Coaching others involves finding the balance of pressure and support. Leaders are responsible to pinpoint progress and ensure accountability, but in the process it is important to differentiate our treatment of people based on their different needs. Some may need more supervision, guidance, and formal evaluation processes, others may need less or even none. Leaders in organizations must be good managers who are efficient and keep control but realize they do not do it all themselves. Delegating responsibility and sharing decision making are key elements in democratic cultures. Fewer rules and less rigid procedures are necessary in a professional organization because people know what they are supposed to do and engage in productive tasks to accomplish it. The environment is not manipulative, demanding, pushy, or quick to assign blame.

Every organization attempting to accomplish change has to deal with conflict from time to time, so it is essential for leaders to intervene, be strong in mediation, repair relationships and build trust, use conflict management strategies, and find productive ways to deal with broken trust, misunderstanding, hurt feelings, and disappointment. They get everyone working together and get people the help they need to build a collective sense of efficacy.

Educational leaders in addition to being professionals have personal lives. Unfortunately, "the headteacher as an emotional being is neglected in a target-driven accountability culture" (Crawford, 2009, p. 106). The discourse of accountability constructs teaching as a deficit profession (Shields, 2004), and administrators and teachers resent "the political and ideological forces denigrating their sense of professionalism" (Solomon et al., 2011, p. 27). They feel "disempowered by a top-down, externally defined, and driven obsession with measurement" (Solomon et al., 2011, p.27).

Some practical suggestions to help support educators both as people as well as professionals include establishing a safe place to openly discuss concerns, collaborate, communicate, and work out crisis situations. We can establish mentorships with a confidential support person to reflect on things without any danger of being judged as inadequate. Mentors are people with whom we can share the difficulties of our work. Time and space for professional development can be provided to discuss and reflect on the personal and emotional aspects of our work in education. It is useful to have others in a similar situation to network with as members of a school—whether pupils or teachers—need to feel they belong to at least one *sentient* group, or a group of people working together who are able to respond to each other emotionally as well as intellectually (Richardson, 1973). Provision of professional development opportunities to evolve personal leadership narratives is a useful tool. It would allow educators to examine how they are shaping their own story of leadership and how they might affect others in the process. Relationships in the workplace are crucial in inspiring the best from people and healing past difficulties. Organizational work is relational and interdependent (Senge, 2006): we have to work closely together (Brunner, 2000; Lucas, 1999) and emotion is unavoidable (Crawford, 2009; Lucas, 1999).

The work of reconnecting must become a central purpose. Right now we teach isolated subjects without establishing their relevance to the world and we teach students subjects without relevance to their lives. We have the power to choose and stop being worn down by our dividedness.

Sharing the Responsibilities of Democratic Education

Power, whether enacted by governments or exerted in classrooms, saturates educational practice, research, and theory. Education can enable empowerment, but it is also implicit in the reproduction of social inequalities. Those who are disempowered may be complicit in their circumstances because they see no alternative or because they subscribe to a different value system that does not recognize dominant conceptions of educational worth. How, then, should the relationships between power and education be addressed? Because of the hierarchical nature of the relationships within education, it is the responsibility of the person with greater power to take the initiative to build and sustain trusting relationships (Tschannen-Moran, 2004).

> As innovation and creativity become the driving forces for successful organizations, the hierarchical patterns of leadership flatten. Survival in the global economy requires companies to become learning organizations that can respond quickly and creatively to shifts in the international marketplace.... Consequently leadership is redefined from being a characteristic exhibited by relatively few individuals at the top to a capacity for improvement that permeated every level of the organization. (Brien & Williams, 2009, p. 8)

Beairstro (1999) proposed an organizational model for school that builds upon the professional bureaucracy—the adhocracy. This model has a less rigid leadership approach that provides for shifting of leadership responsibility according to varying levels of expertise. The adhocracy is not an entirely new concept, and we are most comfortable with its most common form—the community. The community model recognizes both the commonality and diversity that exist among a group of interdependent individuals. It balances the stability of collectively established norms with the provision of opportunities for change. The move toward the community model for schools is closely aligned with the development of learning organizations.

"In a democratic society, it is vital that students learn to think reflectively, function at high stages of moral reasoning, and be autonomous decision makers" (Glickman, Gordon, & Ross Gordon, 2005). This is happening in some places and gives us reason for optimism. I believe that if this is what we are aiming for, then it is time we begin to expect the same of ourselves and our colleagues by examining:

- Where are we now?
- Within our local context do we see evidence of caring relationships?
- What is our legacy to our students, teachers, and communities?
- Are our students served effectively?
- What do we stand for?
- What are the strengths and challenges of taking a caring approach to work and leading?

New Modes of Operation

In order to achieve long-term sustainability of the educational agenda, new ways of conceptualizing leadership within organizations are needed. The use and abuse of power to dominate, subordinate, or manipulate through enforcement of rules and regulations has questionable long-term value in motivating employees to be committed to the organizations' goals and objectives. Wheatley (2005) challenges Western cultural views of leadership as being contrary to what life teaches and counterproductive both locally and globally:

> If we are to develop organizations of greater and enduring capacity, we have to turn to the people of our organization. We have to learn how to encourage the creativity and commitment they wanted to express when they first joined the organization. (p. 72)

Educational leaders will continue to face many problems because of increasing accountability. We must return to our true purpose in public education, "to prepare students to be thoughtful, caring and even critical citizens who are able to make wise ethical decisions" (Shapiro & Gross, 2008, p. 175). Educational leaders should act with integrity, fairness, and in an ethical manner, thus exemplifying commitment to bringing ethical principles to the decision-making process in developing a caring school community (Noddings, 2001; Sernak, 1998; Shapiro & Gross, 2008). Those aspiring to become educational leaders should take advantage of any opportunity to create a personal code of ethics and ethic of care based on their own life experiences and critical incidents because it is helpful to reflect on our own moral compasses and professional behaviors as we engage in decision-making processes.

Educational leaders have been challenged to move from solo management decisions and toward community involvement in the decision-making process, a participatory process (Furman & Gruenewald, 2004; Wheatley & Frieze, 2011; Wheatley, 2002). The distributed leadership model is one in which the work and the decisions of the educational leader are shared with appropriate others (Elmore, 2000; Spillane, Halverson, & Diamond, 2001).

We cannot ignore the reality of the impact of rapid change on social norms nor can we diminish the value of learning from all that was best from our past. "Changing purposes and contexts call for a new organizational paradigm, a redefinition of educational leadership, and a reconsideration of the education of teacher leaders" (Brien & Williams, 2009, p. 19). This book offers opportunity to rethink what it means to be an educational leader and provides leadership for more socially just policy and practice. We need the kinds of leadership that ask us to address hard questions. I offer these for consideration and reflection by leaders of today and tomorrow:

- How should I treat the other professionals who are working with me to implement decisions, mandates, and priorities?
- Are there laws, policies, guidelines, and approaches that are appropriate and should be followed when working through the turbulent times of education reform?
- Who should develop the policies and guidelines and decide on the approaches that might be appropriate in changing situations?
- What concepts should be considered beyond laws, rights, policies, and guidelines?
- Will the decisions and actions taken make a difference in the lives of students, teachers, or the local community?
- What course of action is in the best interest of the people involved? Why this action or inaction?
- Who gets hurt? Who is helped?
- How can the current turbulence be escalated or lowered?
- What is it about a given story that makes it a valuable learning experience?
- Can caring for people help to refocus and re-energize individuals, the school, the district, the community?

I have discussed care as both an ethic and action that grows out of a willingness to adopt an "other-centered" perspective and to take action on behalf of others. The opportunity to work and study in ASD, especially during stressful and demanding times, was energizing and encouraging, as well as challenging. All the participants sought to understand the perspective of others and were committed to respecting and acting on behalf of others— often on behalf of others who opposed them.

In recent years there has been a flurry of professional development sessions, books, and university courses related to democratic schools, professional learning communities, educational leadership, and the development of safe and caring school cultures. They all center on relationships and behavior and moral ways of working for the common good.

A sense of relation, connection, and community is crucial to the work we do. Indeed, I believe our world would benefit by understanding how the practice of care can both strengthen relationships and enhance our work effectiveness. On the other hand, if caring relations are ignored then our effectiveness and sense of well-being will be weakened. Care is basic to what it means to be human. It remains to be seen whether the education system will be provided with some much needed support and relief to enable the seeds of positivity to flourish and overtake the negativities of the past. Powerful learning is taking place in some educational organizations as vision and policy blend to form partnerships committed to caring as well as improvement and change. I believe successful districts will continue to emulate caring and learning and improvement will spread.

There is a popular perception among leaders in education that caring is a "soft," feminine, and perhaps even desirable goal, but in tough, competitive work environments it may not be valued (Sennett, 1998). Caring does not seem to square very well with financial restraint, cutbacks, job losses, school closures, and school board consolidations. Sharon, a school administrator in ASD said, "We're not allowed sometimes to care because it's looked at as being a negative ability." This belief and understanding was articulated with some urgency by Paul, a program specialist who pointed out, "Caring and nurturing are more characteristic of the feminine gender than the masculine gender."

Caring has different meanings under different conditions, and the positive effects of caring are limited in particular environments and within certain structures such as those at work in hierarchical and bureaucratic organizations. In a caring organization employees will know what is expected of them and have opportunity to do what they do best. They will be able to demonstrate their strengths, feel good about their work, and make a contribution. They will feel their administrators and others at work are concerned about them as people, believe their opinions count, and that their work is valued. They will have ongoing opportunities to learn and work independently and collaboratively with others. Caring for employees means their basic needs are attended to: there are fair expectations of them, they have the materials and supplies they need to do their work, and they have others to talk to and work with who are willing to listen with respect to their colleagues.

Caring in education is about understanding and applying the principles of human nature in the change process. Effective leaders need to be intellectuals who understand people and relate to the feelings of those around them. Through caring interactions, individuals and organizations can transform the ethos of workplaces and create new ways of addressing the problems associated with globalized, neoliberal trends and reform processes. Caring policies and practices can be incorporated in ways that not only foster better work relationships, but also contribute to the accomplishment of organizational goals. I have explored how caring interactions between public sectors, and among individuals and groups within organizations, affect the design and implementation of policies and the delivery of services, and I argue that in terms of their objectives, educational organizations and conceptions of care are not worlds apart.

Looking Down the Road

Broader changes in society, and specifically reform in education, have led to the emergence of new topics for study—care and caring in organizational contexts. Nel Noddings's and Joan Tronto's concepts and processes of care offer significant resources for further studies of caring in leadership, other educational institutions, and organizations generally. Employees' perceptions of feeling cared about define in large measure the success of organizations and affect their performance. It is worthy of investigation to determine how organizations are affected when employees feel cared for. As well, research is needed to build understanding of the relationship between employees feeling that they are taken care of at work and their engagement with and accomplishment of assigned work. Theory needs to describe what constitutes good caring in the context of work in organizations and the public domain. We need to rethink how particular circumstances are socially constructed (for example, how policies get developed) and explore opportunities to make new interpretations of situations. More study is needed in the area of top-down and bottom-up relationships to examine the connections between emotion and leadership among groups of principals and district leaders.

The way society views men and women in terms of behavior requires further examination. There has been a gendered rational/emotional dichotomy, where rationality has been assumed as "typically masculine" and emotionality as "typically feminine" (Crawford, 2009, p. 143), and rationality has been judged as the only appropriate behavior in school leadership. These dichotomies are far too simplistic. Both men and women have been constrained by the educational leadership literature's focus on rationality to the detriment of understandings and expressions of emotion as important for effective leadership. "Feelings are necessary to make good decisions" (Crawford 2009, p. 145). Indeed, we must acknowledge the power of emotion to sustain and drive educational leadership and influence learning. Many relevant issues and questions for further research emanate from my work here.

- What happens in a caring organization/group that helps create a community of learners, and what are the various roles of leaders and others in sustaining this community?

- What might educators do to practice care as a way of surviving education reform, restructuring, and life in a hierarchical, bureaucratic organization?
- How can we balance justice and caring and find ways to have them work together in a manner that nurtures growth and learning?
- How do people in other organizations understand and interpret caring in their workplaces? Is there reciprocity in terms of caring among them?
- Is power needed to produce caring relationships?
- Is it possible for caring and power to be integrated within the work of a bureaucratic and hierarchical organization so that reciprocal relationships can develop?

Some schools and teachers have significantly influenced teaching practice through acts of caring leadership and organization, not by being legislated, mandated, regulated, or coerced. We need to think beyond our presumptuous idea of caring for others and doing what is good and make those ideas the objects of serious inquiry that can help to make life better for people. We need to consider the appropriate forms caring can take in organizations. A good question is how can policy enable more of this? Consideration of the kinds of policy that could promote caring practices, as well as what happens to those who experience the consequences of decisions, are other areas deserving of further study.

Although this research examines one point of view and provides a unique lens from the perspective of one group of players who were intimately involved in this radical restructuring process, it leaves unexamined multiple perspectives from classroom teachers, students, community leaders, and school boards, who each have unique stories to contribute to the analysis and interpretation of policy direction and its impact on individual lives and organizations.

Reflection

This research represents a new way of looking at caring in the context of neoliberal managerialist agendas and philosophies and is presented from a practitioner researcher perspective. I argue that more caring can actually contribute to higher functioning and more productivity (which should be appealing to those adhering to the dominant discourses in education today); however, my interest is in having people respected more, feeling fulfillment and personal satisfaction with themselves and their work. I argue that if organizations contribute to having happier, motivated, and engaged employees who are willing to learn new things, then that will lead to greater success, achievement, and accomplishment for the organization as well. How to accomplish it in the context of resource cuts and demands to do more with less is a challenge. Caring, in the organization where I worked, had been shaped substantially by good intention and initiated by particular individuals, but it was limited by external pressures as well as prevailing patriarchal bureaucratic beliefs and practices of individuals and groups within the organization.

In general, the matter of education is complex and multifaceted because of the presence of competing ideologies and approaches. This issue becomes intense in the context of education reform. The practical work of reconciling the goals and purposes while validating everyone's perspective is challenging, especially when we layer onto the work significant limitations of time and resources.

This chapter argues that educators are able to make a difference through the policies and practices they adopt, beginning with critical self-analysis. I believe educators are wise to analyze the questions of who they are and how their biographies and personal narratives affect the choices they make. In order to create more socially just schools and education systems it will be helpful for educators to also engage in institutional analysis. It is essential to know ourselves if we are going to know and understand others with whom we work and interact. We can do this by gaining knowledge of others' personal and professional strengths and their life outside of work. Educators who aim to work for change must develop dynamic caring relationships with the communities within which they work.

This book explores how the restructuring of an education system in one province of Canada worked out "on the ground" and shows how difficult it was and how it was complicated by hierarchical structures and a mix of individuals and groups that included the broader community. Until now the significance of and implications for care in educational, as well as other, institutions and organizations has for the most part been unexplored. One of the strengths that makes this study a worthwhile research contribution is that it brings together policy development and implementation with the research literature on caring. It helps fill a gap by documenting a clash between discourses of care and discourses of new managerialism referred to in various ways through the identification of contradictions, inconsistencies, and miscommunications. My stories and reflections on everyday incidents inform us about larger themes, trends, directions, manipulations—work that pushes and disrupts social conventions in organizations. In this case my situation is local but the application is global.

My work contributes to a broader understanding and knowledge of women's work and their social positions within it. I have tried to illuminate the different social experiences of men and women and expect that my struggles will resonate with the experiences of others. Few attempts have been made to write a book about women's work from the perspective of those working within senior leadership roles in education—others have written about it but not experienced it first-hand. This book sheds light on controversial issues concerning the similarities and differences between women's and men's approaches and perspectives to work in education and challenges assumptions about equality and the caring nature of education. It reveals various standpoints of women within gender discourses regarding their roles, responsibilities, and potential and contributes to a growing body of literature on women in educational leadership, offering a glimpse into our lives.

We each can we take our critical narratives and move them to action to create change. Narratives of insider knowledge, written from marginalized perspectives, can help us to (re)act in different ways to people in various work contexts and a critical analysis of ourselves and our contexts can provide much needed "talk back" and consciousness. This book is my attempt to stimulate some critical tension to help create change within patriarchal and bureaucratic organizations.

History will not go away but new stories of pain, fear, caring, and hope can help to create new systems. I do not aim to force change; rather, I hope to inspire it. Through the stories shared in this book I hope readers will discover something about the complexity and potential of caring in organizational work places and discover how to inspire themselves and others when work seems difficult and discouraging. We must believe that positive change is possible and we each can be contributors to it.

Through the interest and support of colleagues, family, university supervisors, and friends, I have come to see emerging patterns in my life, found my voice, and now I see my career as an educator from the perspective of one who is caring. I am still the person who grew up in a rural fishing village in eastern Canada where caring was prevalent, but now I bring more than 30 years of teaching and leadership experience to my themes of caring and education reform to make my work personal, powerful, and political. I have examined some of the twists, turns, and complications to understand my work world more fully and acknowledge that there are no easy answers or quick fixes. I have honestly and sincerely examined painful aspects of working in a large organization during the turbulence of education reform. Mine is an alternative to the dominant stories with a balance between objective and intimate analysis. My ethno-autobiographical writing presents an approach to contentious educational, social, and interpersonal issues rarely addressed in research literature with the expectation that readers will connect to and understand the importance of a feminist sociological perspective as a lens for examining work experiences. I hope I have helped create spaces where women's stories and experiences can be valued and combined with social justice activism.

The work reported here stands as an example of practitioner research that contributes to the construction of new understandings related to educational change, organizational theory, and leadership. Reflecting on turbulent times with people affected by policies and practices of imposed education reform, this book serves as an example of the potential for caring in practice. It does not offer linear and simplistic solutions but instead delves deeply into the complexities of the turbulent times accompanying the everyday work of leading and implementing education reform. It illustrates that caring in an organizational setting is difficult and complex work. This book integrates personal and professional learning and gives voice to some perspectives, positions, and people who have been silenced. Subordinate voices and voices of experience come together to present everyday experiences as a source of credible and powerful knowledge. I focused on a topic for which, as district administrator and university academic, I could help initiate change. I identified contextual influences and explored the value, potential, and challenges of caring in order to promote organizational improvement and more meaningful and rewarding relationships. This work builds on good educational theory and practice and enhances our ability to comprehend key issues that help us apply knowledge in practice.

We need to challenge the principle that people and how they are treated is one of the least significant factors for consideration in schools (Whitaker, 1997). This certainly applies to district leaders, and particularly women, and is a factor in why so few women are currently offering themselves for top leadership positions in education. I have witnessed too many careers end without regard for the person. No wonder so many smart young people do not want leadership positions in education. External accountability is valued above people, even though we know the harm this inflicts. Especially during troubling times, there is need for much emotional labor with concern for ourselves and others.

With respect to the potential to change caring practices in organizations, it is realized that the very nature of organizations themselves needs to change. Organizations will have to become less hierarchical and allow for more bottom-up decision making and influence. A more democratic and person-centered philosophy is needed. The entire community must be leveraged to build ownership for new visions and to build trust by delegating responsibility. To build respectful relationships in the process of collective decision making, people need time to assess and evaluate their progress and to afford them increased flexibility to make adjustments throughout the process of their work. In order to be more caring, organizations must cultivate personal relationships, especially by listening and responding. We have to find ways to demonstrate to people that we value their knowledge and creativity by publicly recognizing their efforts and rewarding them as well. It is time to determine the extent to which people believe organizational goals come before caring about people and whether there are interventions that would make a difference. In rising to this challenge, caregivers will have to be able to tolerate ambiguity and instability, as well as adapt to changing needs and foster learning for all.

I have gained a deeper understanding of care and caring in practice. My study and work confirm that caring within hierarchical, bureaucratic organizations is complex—it requires attention, commitment, courage, and collective action. It also affirms the importance of seeking ways to promote it for teachers, administrators, students, and their families, and for the general betterment of the educational enterprise itself.

I conclude with the inspiring words of Jack Layton (2011), former Leader of the New Democratic Party of Canada, who passed away on August 22, 2011. Jack led the party to official Opposition status for the first time in history in the 2011 Canadian federal election. In his final correspondence to the nation he implored,

> *My friends, love is better than anger.*
> *Hope is better than fear.*
> *Optimism is better than despair.*
> *So let us be loving, hopeful and optimistic.*
> *And we'll change the world.*
>
> —Jack Layton 1950–2011

References

Abel, E. K., Nelson, M. K., & Nelson, M. K. (1990). *Circles of care work and identity in women's lives.* J. Smith (Ed.). New York, NY: State University of New York Press.

Acker, J. (1990). Hierarchies, jobs, bodies: A theory of gendered organizations. *Gender and Society, 4*(2), 139–158.

Acker, S. (1999). Caring as work for women educators. In E. A. Smyth (Ed.), *Caring professions historical and contemporary perspectives on women's professional work* (pp. 277–295). Toronto: Toronto University Press.

Ali, S. (2000). Gender and human rights in Islam and international law: Equal before Allah, unequal before man? Boston, MA: Kluwer law International.

Anderson, G. (1990). Toward a critical constructivist approach to school administration: Invisibility, legitimation and the study of nonevents. *Educational Administration Quarterly, 26*(1), 38–59.

Anderson, G. (2001). Disciplining leaders: A critical discourse analysis of the ISLLC National Examination and Performance Standards in educational administration. *International Journal of Leadership in Education, 4*(3), 199–216.

Andrews, R. L. (1985). *Integration and other developments in Newfoundland education 1915–1949.* St. John's, NL: Harry Cuff Publications Limited.

Antle, R. (2013, March 26). NL chopping 1200 positions to rein in deficit: Projected $1.6B shortfall drops to $563.8M, mostly due to oil. *CBC News.* St. John's, NL: CBC. Retrieved from http://www.cbc.ca/news/newfoundland-labrador/story/2013/03/26nl-budget-live

Apple, M. (2000). Between neoliberalism and neoconservativatism: Education and conservatism in a global context. In N. Burbules & C. Torres (Eds.), *Globalization and education, critical perspectives* (pp. 57–77). New York, NY: Routledge.

Caring Leadership in Turbulent Times, pages 255–272
Copyright © 2014 by Information Age Publishing
All rights of reproduction in any form reserved.

Apple, M. (2001). Markets, standards, teaching, and teacher education. *Journal of Teacher Education, 52*(3), 182–196.

Apple, M. (2005). Are markets in education democratic? Neoliberal globalism, vouchers, and the politics of choice. In M. Apple, J. Kenway, & M. Singh (Eds.), *Globalizing education* (pp. 209–230). New York, NY: Peter Lang.

Apple, M. (2010). *Global crises, social justice, and education.* New York and London: Routledge.

Apple, M., Kenway, J., & Singh, M. (2005). *Globalizing education policies, pedagogies, and politics.* J. L. Kincheloe & S. R. Steinberg (Eds.), (Vol. 280). New York, NY: Peter Lang.

Apple, M. W. (2004). Creating difference: Neo-liberalism, neo-conservatism and the politics of educational reform. *Educational Policy, 18*(1), 12.

Argyris, C., & Schon, D. A. (1974). *Theory in practice.* San Francisco, CA: Jossey-Bass.

Ball, S. (1997). Good school/bad school: Paradox and fabrication. *British Journal of Sociology of Education, 18*(3), 317–336.

Ball, S. (2000). Performativities and fabrications in the education economy: Towards a performative society. *Australian Educational Researcher, 27*(2), 1–25.

Ball, S. (2003). The teacher's soul and the terrors of performativity. *Journal of Education Policy, 18*(2), 215–228.

Ball, S. (2008). *The education debate.* Bristol: Policy Press.

Ball, S., Dworkin, G., & Vryonides, M. (2010). Globalization and education: Introduction. *Current Sociology, 58*(4), 523.

Ball, S., & Reay, D. (2000). Essentials of female management: Women's ways of working in the education market place? *Educational Management Administration and Leadership, 28,* 145.

Barlow, M., & Robertson, H.-J. (1994). *Class warfare: The assault on Canada's schools.* Toronto: Key Porter Books.

Barrett, F. (1995). Leadership for the 21st century. *Enterprising Nation: Renewing Australia's Managers to meet the Challenges of the Asia-Pacific Century, 2,* 1289–1342.

Barth, R. S. (2001). *Learning by heart.* San Francisco, CA: Jossey-Bass.

Barth, R. S. (2003). *Lessons learned shaping relationships and the culture of the workplace.* Thousand Oaks, California: Corwin Press Inc.

Bateson, M. C. (1990). *Composing a life.* New York, NY: Plume.

Beairstro, B. (1999). Learning to balance bureaucracy and community as an educational administrator. In *The education of educators: Enabling professional growth for teachers and administrators.* Tampere, Finland: University of Tampere.

Beatty, B. (2009). Developing school administrators who lead with the emotions in mind: Making the commitment to connectedness. In *Canadian educational leadership.* Calgary, Alberta: Detselig Enterprises Ltd.

Beck, L. G. (1994). *Reclaiming educational administration as a caring profession.* J. Murphy (Ed.). New York and London: Teachers College Press.

Behar, R. (1996). *The vulnerable observer: Anthropology that breaks your heart.* Boston, MA: Beacon Books.

Belenky, M. F., Clinchy, B. M., Goldberger, N. R., & Tarule, J. M. (1997). *Women's ways of knowing: The development of self, voice, and mind.* New York, NY: Basic Books.

Bennis, W., & Nanus, B. (1985). *Leaders: The strategies for taking charge.* New York, NY: Harper and Row.

Beswick, A. (2012). It's more than just a building. *Herald Magazine, 1*(3), 12–13.

Biesta, G. (2004). "Mind the gap!" Communication and the educational relation. In C. Bingham & A. M. Sidorkin (Eds.), *No education without relation* (Vol. 259, pp. 11–22). New York, NY: Peter Lang.

Bingham, C., & Sidorkin, A. M. (2004). The pedagogy of relation: An introduction. In C. Bingham & A. M. Sidorkin (Eds.), *No education without relation* (Vol. 259, pp. 1–7). New York, NY: Peter Lang Publishing Inc.

Blackmore, J. (1999). *Troubling women feminism, leadership and educational change.* Buckingham, Philadelphia: Open University Press.

Blackmore, J. (2000). Globalization: A useful concept for feminist rethinking theory and strategies in education. In N. C. Burbules & C. A. Torres (Eds.), *Globalization and education, critical perspectives* (pp. 133–156). New York, NY: Routledge.

Blackmore, J. (2006). Social justice and the study and practice of leadership in education: A feminist history. *Journal of Educational Administration and History, 38*(2), 16.

Blackmore, J. (2007). Equity and social justice in Australian education systems: Retrospect and prospect. *International handbook of urban education, 249–264.*

Blackmore, J. (2011). Achieving more in education but earning less in work: Girls, boys and gender equality in schooling. *Discourse: Studies in the Cultural Politics of Education, 22*(1), 123–129.

Blackmore, J., & Sachs, J. (2007). *Performing and reforming leaders: Gender, educational restructuring, and organizational change.* Albany: State University of New York Press.

Booth, D. (1999). Telling stories: Our own and others. *Orbit: Story Matters, 30*(3), 3.

Boyd, W. (1997). Competing models of schools and communities: The struggle to reframe and reinvent their relationships. *Leading and Managing, 3*(3), 188–207.

Brady, J. F., & Hammett, R. F. (1999). Reconceptualizing leadership from a feminist postmodern perspective. *Overseas Publishers' Association, 21*(1), 41–61.

Brien, K., & Williams, R. (2009). Redefining educational leadership for the twenty-first century. In T. G. Ryan, *Canadian educational leadership.* Calgary, Alberta: Delselig Enterprises Ltd.

Brody, C., & Witherall, C. (1991). Story and voice in the education of professionals. In C. Witherall & N. Noddings (Eds.), *Stories lives tell* (pp. 257–278). New York, NY: Teachers College Press.

Brunner, C. C. (1998). The new superintendency: Power and decision-making. In *American educational research association.* San Diego: AERA.

Brunner, C. C. (1999). *Sacred dreams: Women and the superintendency.* New York, NY: State University of New York Press Brunner.

Brunner, C. C. (2000a). *Principles of power: Women superintendents and the riddle of the heart.* New York, NY: State University of New York Press.

Brunner, C. C. (2000b). Unsettled moments in settled discourse: Women superintendents' experiences of inequality. *Educational Administration Quarterly, 36*(1), 76–116.

Brunner, C. C., & Bjork, L. G. (2001) (Eds.). *The New Superintendency.* G. M. Crow (Ed.), (Vol. 6). London: Elsevier Science Ltd.

Bubeck, D. E. (1995). *Care, gender, and justice.* Oxford: Clarendon Press.

Burbules, N., & Torres, C. (2000). *Globalization and education, critical perspectives.* New York, NY: Routledge.

Buzzanell, P. M. (2000). *Rethinking organizational & managerial communication from feminist perspectives.* Thousand Oaks: Sage Publications, Inc. Buzzanell, P. M.

Canadian Broadcasting Corporation. (2013, April 17). Nova Central School Board Trustees Speak Out. *Central Morning Show.* Gander, NL: Canadian Broadcasting Corporation. Retrieved from http://www.cbc.ca/central-morning/episodes/2013/04/17/nova-central-school-board-trustees-speak-out/

Card, C. (1990). Gender and moral luck. In V. Held (Ed.), *Justice and care essential readings in feminist ethics* (pp. 79–98). Boulder, Colorado: Westview Press.

Carib, I. (1992). *Modern social theory.* New York, NY: St. Martin's Press.

Chodorow, N. (1978). *The reproduction of mothering: Psychoanalysis and the sociology of gender.* Berkeley: University of California Press.

Clandinin, D. J. (2001). Lives in school. *Among Teachers: Experience and Inquiry, 30,* 2–5.

Clandinin, D. J., & Connelly, F. M. (2000). *Narrative inquiry experience and story in qualitative research.* San Francisco, CA: Jossey-Bass Publishers.

Clandinin, D. J., & Connelly, M. (1998). Stories to live by: Narrative understandings of school reform. *Curriculum Inquiry, 28*(2), 149–164.

Clandinin, D. J., Pushor, D., & Orr, A. M. (2007). Navigating sites for narrative inquiry. *Journal of Teacher Education, 58*(1), 21–35.

Collard, J., & Reynolds, C. (2005). *Leadership, gender and culture in education.* New York, NY: Open University Press.

Corbett, M., Wright, A., & Monette, M. (2007). Policy narrative for Nova Scotia. In *The evolution of professionalism: Education policy in the provinces and territories of Canada* (pp. 149–167). Vancouver, BC: University of British Columbia, Centre for Policy Studies in Higher Education and Training.

Coser, L. A. (1974). *Greedy institutions: Patterns of undivided commitment.* New York, NY: The Free Press.

Court, M., & O'Neill, J. (2011). Tomorrow's schools in New Zealand: From social democracy to market managerialism. *Journal of Educational Administion and History, 43*(2), 119–140.

Crawford, M. (2007). Emotional coherence in primary school headship. *Educational Management Leadership and Administration, 35*(4), 521–534.

Crawford, M. (2009). *Getting to the heart of leadership: Emotion and educational leadership.* London and Thousand Oaks: SAGE Publications.

Czarniawska, B. (1997). *Narrating the organization: Dramas of institutional identity.* Chicago and London: The University of Chicago Press.

Daly, M. (2002). Care as a good for social policy. *Journal of Social Policy, 31*(2), 251–270.

Daniel, Y. (2009). The quest for equity and excellence in public schools: A portrait of transformational leadership. T. G. Ryan (Ed.), In *Canadian Educational Leadership* (pp. 45–64). Calgary, Alberta: Detselig Enterprises Ltd.

Das Dores, G., Abrantes, P., & Pereira, I. (2004). Transitions case studies executive summary for the EU Framework 5 Study "Gender, parenthood and the changing European workplace." Retrieved from http://hdl,handle.net2173/75014, Manchester Metropolitan University: 10D Research Group

Day, C. (2004). The passion of successful leadership. *School Leadership and Management, 24*(4), 425–438.

Delong, J. (2002). *How can I improve my practice as a superintendent of schools and create my own living educational theory?* University of Bath, UK: PhD thesis. Retrieved from www.bath.ac.uk/~edsajw/delong.shtml

Delpit, L. (1995). *Other people's children.* New York, NY: New Press.

Denzin, N. (1984). On Understanding Emotion. San Francisco: Jossey-Bass.

Denzin, N. (1989). *Interpretive interactionism.* Newbury Park, CA: Sage.

Dibbon, D. (2012). The impact of education reform on school board governance. In G. Galway & D. Dibbon (Eds.), *Education reform: From rhetoric to reality* (pp. 217–251). London, Ontario: The Althouse Press.

Dillard, C. B. (2003). The substance of things hoped for, the evidence of things not seen: Examining an endarkened feminist epistemology in educational research and leadership. In M. D. Young & L. Skrla (Eds.), *Reconsidering feminist research in educational leadership* (pp. 131–159). New York, NY: State University of New York Press.

District, A. W. S. (2003a). *Our vision for teaching and learning.* Bay Roberts, NL: Author.

District, A. W. S. (2003b). *Teachers' personal and professional growth and development.* Bay Roberts, NL: Author.

District, A. W. S. (2003c). *Teaching and learning decision making matrix.* Bay Roberts, NL: Author.

Du Gay, P. (1996). *Consumption and identity at work.* London and Thousand Oaks: SAGE Publications.

Dufour, R., & Eaker, R. (1992). *Creating the new American school: A principal's guide to school improvement.* Bloomington, IN: National Educational Service.

Dunning, B., P. (1997). *Education in Canada: An overview.* Toronto, Ontario: Canadian Education Association.

Egbo, B. (2009). *Teaching diversity in Canadian schools.* Toronto, Ontario: Pearson-Prentice Hall.

Elangovan, A. R., & Shapiro, D. L. (1998). Betrayal of trust in organizations. *Academy of Management Review, 23,* 547–566.

Elmore, R. F. (2000). *Building a new structure for school leadership.* Washington, DC: Albert Shanker Institute.

Enomoto, E. (1997). Negotiating the ethics of care and justice. *Educational Administration Quarterly, 33*(3), 351–370.

Evans, R. (1996). *The human side of school change—reform, resistance, and the real-life problems of innovation.* San Francisco, CA: Jossey-Bass.

Fagan, B. (2012). The abolition of denominational governance in Newfoundland—unnecessary, unwarrented. In G. Galway & D. Dibbon (Eds.), *Education reform: From rhetoric to reality* (pp. 119–135). London, Ontario: The Althouse Press.

Fairclough, N. (1992). *Discourse and social change.* Cambridge: Polity Press.

Fairclough, N. (2003). *Analysing discourse: Textual analysis for social research.* London: Routledge.

Fairclough, N., & Kress, G. (1993). *Critical discourse analysis.* Unpublished manuscript.

Ferguson, K. E. (1984). *The feminist case against bureaucracy.* R. J. A. Steinberg (Ed.). Philadelphia: Temple University Press.

Fineman, S. (2000). *Emotions and organizations.* New York, NY: Sage.

Fineman, S. (2003). *Understanding emotion at work.* London: Sage.

Fisher, B., & Tronto, J. C. (1990). Toward a feminist theory of caring. In E. Abel & E. K. Abel (Eds.), *Circles of care* (pp. 35–62). New York, NY: State University of New York Press.

Flade, P. (2003). Great Britain's workforce lacks inspiration. Retrieved from http://lifework.arizona.edu/ea/supv/great_brit.php

Folbre, N. (2001). *The invisible heart: Economics and family values.* New York, NY: The New Press.

Foucault, M. (1980). Two lectures. In C. Gordon (Ed.), *Power/knowledge: Selected interviews and other writings 1972–1977* (pp. 78–108). New York, NY: Pantheon.

Foucault, M. (1984). The order of discourse. In M. Shapiro (Ed.), *Language and politics.* Oxford: Basil Blackwell.

Franzway, S. (2001). *Sexual politics and greedy institutions.* Annandale, Australia: Pluto Press Australia.

Franzway, S. (2005). Making progressive educational politics in the current globalization crisis. In M. Apple, J. Kenway, & M. Singh (Eds.), *Globalizing education* (Vol. 280, pp. 265–279). New York, NY: Peter Lang.

Franzway, S., Court, D., & Connell, R. W. (1989). *Staking a claim: Feminism, bureaucracy and the state.* Cambridge: Polity Press.

Freire, P. (1970). *Pedagogy of the oppressed.* New York, NY: Seabury.

Freire, P. (2000). *Pedagogy of the oppressed.* New York, NY: Continuum.

Friedl, E. (1994). Notes from the village: On the ethnographic construction of women in Iran. In F. Muge & S. Balaghi (Eds.), *Reconstructing gender in the Middle East: Tradition, identity, and power* (pp. 85–99). New York, NY: Columbia University Press.

Friedman, M. (1995). Beyond caring: The de-moralization of gender. In V. Held (Ed.), *Justice and care* (pp. 61–77). Boulder, Colorado: Perseus Books Group.

Fullan, M. (1993). *Change forces probing the depths of educational reform.* London, England: The Falmer Press.

Fullan, M. (2005). *Leadership and sustainability system thinkers in action.* Thousand Oaks: Corwin Press and Ontario Principals' Council.

Fullan, M., & Steigelbauer, S. (1991). *The new meaning of educational change.* Toronto: OISE Press.

Fullen, M. (2001). *Leading in a culture of change.* San Francisco, CA: Jossey-Bass.

Furman, G. C., & Gruenewald, D. (2004). Expanding the landscape of social justice: A critical ecological analysis. *Educational Administration Quarterly, 40*(1), 47–76.

Galway, G. (2011). The economics of educational reform: Discourses of efficiency and effectiveness. In G. Galway & D. Dibbon (Eds.), *Understanding educational reform: Religious-social, humanistic, political and economic dimensions* (pp. 95–116). London: The Althouse Press.

Galway, G. (2012). The economics of educational reform. In G. Galway & D. Dibbon (Eds.), *Educational reform: From rhetoric to reality* (pp. 95–116). London, Ontario: The Althouse Press.

Galway, G., & Dibbon, D. (2012a). Introduction. In G. Galway & D. Dibbon (Eds.), *Education reform: From rhetoric to reality* (pp. 1–9). London, Ontario: The Althouse Press.

Galway, G., & Dibbon, D. (2012b). Lessons for the policy community. In G. Galway & D. Dibbon (Eds.), *Education reform: From rhetoric to reality* (pp. 275–284). London, Ontario: The Althouse Press.

Gee, J. P., Hull, G., & Lankshear, C. (1996). *The new work order behind the language of the new capitalism.* Boulder, Colorado: Westview Press Inc.

George, J. M. (2000). Emotions and leadership: The role of emotional intelligence. *Human Relations, 53*(8), 1027–1055.

Gergen, K. (2004). Self-narration in social life. In M. Wetherell, M. Taylor, & S. Yates (Eds.), *Discourse theory and practice* (pp. 247–260). London, England: SAGE Publications.

Gidney, R. (1999). *From hope to Harris: The reshaping of Ontario schools.* Toronto, Ontario: University of Toronto Press.

Gilligan, C. (1982). *In a different voice: Psychological theory and women's development.* Cambridge, MA: Harvard University Press.

Gilligan, C. (1995). Moral orientation and moral development. In V. Held (Ed.), *Justice and care: Essential readings in feminist ethics* (pp. 31–46). New York, NY: Westview Press.

Gilligan, C., Ward, J. V., McLean Taylor, J., Bardige, B., Ward, J. V., McLean Taylor, J., & Bardige, B. (1988). *Mapping the moral domain: A contribution of women's thinking to psychological theory and education* (Vol. 2). Cambridge, MA: Harvard University Press.

Glazer-Raymo, J. (1999). *Shattering the myths: Women in academe.* Baltimore: Johns Hopkins University Press.

Glickman, C., Gordon, S., & Ross Gordon, J. (2005). *The basic guide to supervision and instructional leadership.* Toronto, Ontario: Pearson Education Limited.

Goleman, D. (1995). *Emotional intelligence: Why it can matter more than IQ.* New York, NY: Bantam Books.

Goleman, D., Boyatzis, R., & McKee, A. (2002). *Primal leadership: Realizing the power of emotional intelligence.* Boston, MA: Harvard Business School Press.

Government of Newfoundland. (1933). *Memorandum on Education in Newfoundland for the Royal Commission* (Royal Commission No. CNS-B0614) (p. 47). St. John's, Newfoundland: Author. Government of Newfoundland and Labrador. (2011). *Education statistics.* St. John's, NL.

Green, M. G. (2008). *Caring relations at work: A case study of one Canadian school district* (Doctoral thesis, University of South Australia, Adelaide).

Green, M. G., & Tucker, J. (2011). Tumultuous times of education reform: A critical reflection of "caring" in policy and practice. *International Journal of Leadership in Education.* 14,(1), 1–19.

Greene, M. (1995). *Releasing the imagination: Essays on education, the arts, and social change.* San Francisco, CA: Jossey-Bass.

Grogan, M. (1996). *Voices of women aspiring to the superintendency.* Albany: State University of New York Press.

Grogan, M. (2003). Laying the Groundwork for a reconception of the superintendency from feminist postmodern perspectives. In L. Skrla & M. D. Young (Eds.), *Reconsidering feminist research in educational leadership* (pp. 9–34). Albany: State University of New York Press.

Grogan, M., & VanDeman Blackmon, M. (1999). A feminist poststructuralist account of collaboration: A model for the superintendency. In C. C. Brunner (Ed.), *Sacred dreams: Women and the superintendency* (pp. 95–113). New York, NY: SUNY Press.

Grogan, M., & VanDeman Blackmon, M. (2001). A superintendent's approach to coalition building: Working with diversity to garner support for educational initiatives. In C. C. Brunner & L. G. Bjork (Eds.), *The new superintendency* (Vol. 6, pp. 95–113). Amsterdam: Elsevier Sci. Ltd.

Gronn, P. (2003). *The new work of new educational leaders: Changing leadership practice in an era of school reform.* London, England: Paul Chapman.

Gross, S. J., Shaw, K., & Shapiro, J. P. (2003). Deconstructing accountability through the lens of democratic philosophies: Toward a new analytic framework. *Journal of Research for Educational Leadership, 1*(3), 5–27.

Gumport, P. J. (1997). First words. Still words. In A. Neumann & P. L. Peterson (Eds.), *Learning from our lives* (pp. 183–193). New York, NY: Teachers College Press, Columbia University.

Gunter, H. (2001). *Leaders and leadership in education.* London, England: Paul Chapman.

Gutmann, A. (1999). *Democratic education.* Princeton, NJ: Princeton University Press.

Halpin, D. (1994). Practice and prospects in education policy research. In D. Halpin & B. Troyna (Eds.), *Researching education policy: Ethical and methodological issues* (pp. 198–206). London, England: Falmer Press.

Hamdan, A. (2009). *Muslim women speak: A tapestry of lives and dreams.* Toronto, Ontario: Women's Press.

Hankivsky, O. (2004). *Social policy and the ethic of care.* Vancouver and Toronto: UBC Press.

Hanrahan, M., Cooper, T., & Burroughs-Lange, S. (1999). The place of personal writing in a PhD thesis: Epistemological and methodological considerations. *Qualitative Studies in Education, 12*(4), 401–416.

Hargreaves, A. (1994). *Changing teachers, changing times.* New York, NY: Teachers College Press.

Hargreaves, A. (2003, March). Sustaining professional learning communities. Paper presented at the meeting of New Brunswick Educational Leaders, Saint John, New Brunswick.

Hatch, J. A., & Wisniewski, R. (1995). *Life history and narrative.* I. F. Goodson, (Ed.). Washington, D.C.: The Falmer Press.

Hatcher, C. (2008). Becoming a successful corporate character and the role of emotional management. In S. Fineman (Ed.), *The emotional organization: Passion and power* (pp. 153–166). Oxford: Blackwell.

Haughney, M. (2006). The impact of computers on the work of the principal: Changing discourses on talk, leadership and professionalism. *School Leadership and Management, 26*(1), 23–36.

Held, V. (1995). *Justice and care: Essential readings in feminist ethics.* Boulder, CO: Westview Press

Helgesen, S. (1995). *The female advantage: Women's ways of leadership.* New York, NY: Doubleday Currency.

Henry, J. D., & Henry, L. S. (2006). Caring for your employees: The bedrock of productivity, employee retention, and patient satisfaction. Retrieved from http://www.pugetsoundparishnurses.org

Herendeen, R. A. (1998). *Ecological numeracy: Quantitative analysis of environmental issues.* New York, NY: John Wiley and Sons Inc.

Higgins, J. (1998). Cod Moratorium. Newfoundland and Labrador Heritage Website, http://www.heritage.nf.ca/society/moratorium.html. Accessed February 16, 2014.

Hobbs, L. (2007). Frequently asked questions. *the bulletin, 10.*

Hochschild, A. R. (1983). *The managed heart: Commercialization of human feeling.* Berkley, California: University of California Press.

Hochschild, A. R. (1997). *The time bind: When work becomes home and home becomes work.* New York, NY: Henry Holt and Company.

hooks, b. (1989). *Talking back: Thinking feminist, thinking black.* Boston, MA: South End Press

Hoy, W. K., & Miskel, C. G. (2001). *Educational administration: Theory, research, practice.* Boston, MA: McGraw-Hill.

Imre, R. W. (1982). *Knowing and caring: Philosophical issues in social work.* New York, NY: University Press of America.

Jager, S. (2001). Discourse and knowledge: Theoretical and methodological aspects of a critical discourse and dispositive analysis. In R. Wodak & M. Meyer (Eds.), *Methods of critical discourse analysis* (pp. 33–62). London, England: Sage Publications.

Jagger, A. M. (1995). Caring as a feminist practice of moral reason. In V. Held (Ed.), *Justice and care: Essential readings in feminist ethics* (pp. 179–202). New York, NY: Westview Press.

Jeong, M. (2011, September 23). Imposter syndrome: The flip side of success. *The Globe and Mail,* p. B15.

Kamler, B. (2001). *Relocating the personal: A critical writing pedagogy.* Albany: State University of New York Press.

Kamler, R. M. (1996). Collective trust and collective action: The decision to trust as a social decision. In *Trust in organizations* (pp. 357–389). Thousand Oaks, CA: SAGE Publications.

Kathy Dunderdale and the PC Party of Newfoundland and Labrador: Call a new election. (2013, April 16). *Dunderdale Must Go.* petition. Retrieved June 20, 2013, from http://www.change.org/petitions/kathy-dunderdale-and-the-pc-party-of-newfoundland-and-labrador-call-a-new-election?utm_campaign=action_box&utm_medium=twitter&utm_source=share_petition

Katz, M. S., Noddings, N., & Strike, K. A. (1999). *Justice and caring: The search for common ground in education.* New York, NY: Teachers College Press.

Kincheloe, J. L. (2005). *Critical pedagogy: Primer.* New York, NY: Peter Lang.

Kincheloe, J. L., & McLaren, P. (2000). Rethinking critical theory and qualitative research. In N. Denzin & Y. Lincoln (Eds.), *Handbook of Qualitative Research* (pp. 279–313). Thousand Oaks, CA: SAGE Publications Inc.

Kochan, F. K., & Reed, C. J. (2005). Collaborative leadership, community building, and democracy in public education. In F. W. English (Ed.), *The SAGE handbook of educational leadership: Advances in theory, research, and practice* (pp. 71–72). Thousand Oaks, CA: SAGE Publications.

Kohn, A. (2003). Professors who profess: Making a difference as scholar activists. *Kappa Delta Pi Record, 39*(3), 108–113.

Lambert, L. (1998). *Building leadership capacity in schools.* Alexandria, VA: Association for Supervision and Curriculum Development.

Launt, P. (2006). How to be a top 10 employer. Retrieved from http://www.herald.ns.ca/Search/534225.html

Layton, J. (2011, August 20). Jack Layton's Last Letter to Canadians. Retrieved from http://www.cbc.ca/news/politics/story/2011/08/22/pol-layton-last-letter.html

Leader of the Opposition. (2013). *Government continues to risk student education with lack of planning and consultation* (News release). St. John's, Newfoundland and Labrador.

Leithwood, K., & Aiken, R. (1995). *Making schools smarter.* Thousand Oaks: Corwin Pubs.

Leithwood, K., & Jantzi, D. (2000). The effect of different sources of leadership on student engagement in school. In K. A. Riley (Ed.), *Leadership for change and school reform* (pp. 50–66). London, England: Routledge Falmer.

Levin, B., & Riffel, A. (1997). *Schools and the changing world: Struggling towards the future.* London, England: The Falmer Press.

Lingard, B., & Douglas, P. (1999). *Men engaging feminisms: Pro-feminism, backlashes and schooling.* Buckingham: Open University Press.

Little, J. W. (1994). Teachers' professional development in a climate of educational reform. Retrieved from www.ed.gov/pubs/EdReform Studies/SysReforms/little1.html

Lowe, G. S. (2000). *The quality of work: A people-centred agenda.* Oxford, England: University Press.

Lucas, J. R. (1999). *The passionate organization: Igniting the fire of employee commitment.* New York, NY: AMACOM.

MacLellan, D. (2009). School boards and educational leadership in Canada: The changing landscape. In *Canadian educational leadership* (pp. 117–148). Calgary, Alberta: Detselig Enterprises Ltd.

Martin, J. R. (2011). What school can and cannot do. In *Education reconfigured: Culture, encounter, and change* (pp. 183–202). New York, NY: Routledge.

May, H. (2013a, March 27). Education funding focused on the classroom, students: Minister. Government of Newfoundland and Labrador Queen's Printer. Retrieved from http://www.releases.gov.nl.ca/releases/2013/edu/0327n02.htm

May, H. (2013b, April 18). Regions will have strong educational presence under provincial school board: Minister. News Release, St. John's, Newfoundland and Labrador.

McCann, P. (1998). Newfoundland and Labrador heritage: Education. Memorial University of Newfoundland. Retrieved from http://www.heritage.nf.ca/society/education.html

McLaren, P. (2007). *Life in schools: An introduction to critical pedagogy in the foundations of education* (5th ed.). Boston, MA: Pearson Education Limited.

McLaren, P., & Farahmandpur, R. (2005). *Teaching against global capitalism and the new imperialism: A critical pedagogy.* New York, NY: Rowan & Littlefield Publishers, Inc.

McNeil, L. M. (2000). *Contradictions of school reform: Educational costs of standardized testing.* New York, NY: Routledge.

McNiff, J., & Whitehead, J. (2000). *Action research in organizations.* London, England: Routledge.

Mehan, H. (2004). The construction of an LD student: A case study in the politics of representation. In M. Wetherell, S. Taylor, & S. Yates (Eds.), *Discourse, theory and practice* (pp. 345–363). Thousand Oaks, CA: SAGE Publications.

Mills, S. (1997). *Discourse.* J. Drakakis, (Ed.). New York, NY: Routledge.

Mulhearn, G., & Rogers, T. (2004). *Value guided practice: What counts?* (pp. 1–37). Adelaide, Australia: University of South Australia.

Murphy, J., & Seashore Louis, K. (1999). *Handbook of research on educational administration* (2nd ed.). San Francisco, CA: Jossey-Bass.

Neumann, A. (1997). Ways without words: Learning from silence and story in post-Holocaust lives. In A. Neumann & P. L. Peterson (Eds.), *Learning from our lives* (pp. 91–123). New York, NY: Teachers College Press, Columbia University.

Neumann, A., & Peterson, P. L. (1997). *Learning from our lives: Women, research, and autobiography in education.* New York, NY: Teachers College Press, Columbia University.

Noddings, N. (1984). *Caring: A feminine approach to ethics and moral education.* Berkeley, Los Angeles: University of California Press.

Noddings, N. (1992). *The challenge to care in schools: An alternative approach to education.* J. F. Soltis, (Ed.) (Vol. 8). New York, NY: Teachers College Press, Columbia University.

Noddings, N. (1997). Accident, awareness, and actualization. In A. Neumann (Ed.), *Learning from our lives* (pp. 166–182). New York, NY: Teachers College Press, Columbia University.

Noddings, N. (1999a). Care, justice, and equity. In M. S. Katz, N. Noddings, & K. A. Strike (Eds.), *Justice and caring: The search for common ground in education* (pp. 7–20). New York, NY: Teachers College Press, Columbia University.

Noddings, N. (1999b). Caring and competence. In G. A. Griffin (Ed.), *The education of teachers* (pp. 205–220). Chicago, IL: University of Chicago Press.

Noddings, N. (1999c). Introduction. In M. S. Katz, N. Noddings, & K. A. Strike (Eds.), *Justice and caring: The search for common ground in education* (pp. 1–4). New York, NY: Teachers College Press, Columbia University.

Noddings, N. (2001). Care and coercion in school reform. *Journal of Educational Change, 2,* 35–43.

Noddings, N. (2002). *Starting at home: Caring and social policy.* Berkeley, Los Angeles: University of California Press.

Noddings, N. (2003). *Happiness and education.* New York, NY: Cambridge University Press.

Noddings, N. (2005). Identifying and responding to needs in education. *Cambridge Journal of Education, 35*(2), 147–159.

Noddings, N. (2007). *When school reform goes wrong.* New York, NY: Teachers' College Press.

Northouse, P. G. (2004). *Leadership theory and practice.* Thousand Oaks, CA: SAGE Publications.

O'Toole, J. (1996). *Leading change: The argument for values-based leadership.* New York, NY: Ballantine Books.

OECD. (1993). *Education at a glance.* Paris: OECD.

Pellicer, L. O. (2003). *Caring enough to lead: How reflective thought leads to moral leadership.* Thousand Oaks, CA: Corwin Press, Inc.

Peterson, P. L. (1997). Learning out of school and in: Self and experience at home, school and work. In A. Neumann & P. L. Peterson (Eds.), *Learning from our lives: Women, research and autobiography in education* (pp. 209–227). New York, NY: Teachers College Press, Columbia University.

Phillips, N., & Hardy, C. (2002). *Discourse analysis: Investigating processes of social construction* (Vol. 50). Thousand Oaks: SAGE Publications.

Pollock, K. (2008). *Occasional teachers' work engagement: Professional identity, work-related learning and access to the profession and to daily work.* (Unpublished doctoral dissertation). University of Toronto.

Popper, M., & Lipshitz, R. (2000). Organizational learning mechanisms, culture, and feasibility. *Management Learning, 31*(2), 181–196.

Purpel, D. E., & Shapiro, S. (1995). *Beyond liberation and excellence: Reconstructing the public discourse on education.* Westport, CT: Bergin & Garvey.

Rebbick, J. (2009). *Transforming power: From the personal to the political.* Toronto, Ontario: Penguin Canada. Retrieved from http://transformingpower.ca/en/chapter-eleven-indigenous-ideas-diversity-dignity

Reid, A. (2005). Rethinking the democratic purposes of public schooling in a globalizing world. In M. Apple, J. Kenway, & M. Singh (Eds.), *Globalizing education policies, pedagogies, and politics* (Vol. 280, pp. 281–296). New York, NY: Peter Lang.

Retired School Board CEO Action Group. (2013a, April 10). School board consolidation: Government delivers another blow to rural Newfoundland and Labrador. Save regional school boards in Newfoundland and Labrador. Facebook. Retrieved April 10, 2013, from https://www.facebook.com/SaveRegionalSchoolBoardsInNewfoundlandLabrador

Retired School Board CEO Action Group. (2013b, April 23). School board consolidation: One giant board to rule them all. News Release, Newfoundland and Labrador.

Rhoades, G. (1996). *Managed professionals: Unionised faculty and restructuring academic labour.* Albany, NY: State University of New York Press.

Rhodes, L. A. (1990). Beyond your beliefs: Quantum leaps toward quality schools. *School Administrator, 26.*

Richardson, L. (1990). *Writing strategies: Researching diverse audiences.* Newbury Park, CA: SAGE Publications.

Richardson, V. (1973). *The teacher, the school and the task of management.* London, England: Heinemann.

Roland Martin, J. (1992). *The schoolhome: Rethinking schools for changing families.* Cambridge, MA: Harvard University Press.

Rowe, F. W. (1952). *The history of education in Newfoundland.* Toronto, Ontario: Ryerson Press.

Ryan, J. (2006). *Inclusive leadership* (First Edition). San Francisco, CA: Jossey-Bass.

Ryan, T. G. (2009). *Canadian educational leadership.* Calgary, Alberta: Detselig Enterprises Ltd.

Sachs, J., & Blackmore, J. (1998). You never show you can't cope: Women in school leadership roles managing their emotions. *Gender and Education, 10*(3), 265–280.

Santora, J. C. (1992). Schools for the 21st century: Leadership imperatives for educational reform. *Contemporary Education, 63*(2), 163–164.

Schlechty, P. C. (1990). *Schools for the 21st century: Leadership imperatives for educational reform.* San Francisco, CA: Jossey-Bass.

Schlechty, P. C. (1997). *Inventing better schools: An action plan for educational reform.* San Francisco, CA: Jossey-Bass.

Senge, P. M. (1990). *The fifth discipline: The art & practice of the learning organization.* New York, NY: Doubleday Currency.

Senge, P. M. (2000). *Schools that learn.* New York, NY: Doubleday.

Senge, P. M. (2006). Systems citizenship: The leadership mandate for this millennium. *Leader to leader,* 21–26.

Senge, P. M., Scharmer, C. O., Jaworski, J., & Flowers, B. S. (2004). *Presence.* New York, NY: Doubleday.

Sennett, R. (1998). *The corrosion of character: The personal consequences of work in the new capitalism.* New York, NY: W.W. Norton & Company. Retrieved from www.wwnorton.com

Sennett, R. (2004). *Respect: The formation of character in the global era.* St. Ives: Penguin.

Sergiovanni, T. J. (1992). *Moral leadership: Getting to the heart of school improvement.* San Francisco, CA: Jossey-Bass.

Sergiovanni, T. J. (2000). *The lifeworld of leadership: Creating culture, community, and personal meaning in our schools.* San Francisco, CA: Jossey-Bass.

Sergiovanni, T. J. (2003). The lifeworld at the center: Values and action in educational leadership. In M. Bennett, M. Crawford, & M. Cartwright (Eds.), *Effective educational leadership* (pp. 14–24). London, England: Paul Chapman.

Sernak, K. (1998). *School leadership—Balancing power with caring.* New York, NY: Teachers College Press, Columbia University.

Seymour, M. (Ed.). (2004). *Educating for humanity: Rethinking the purposes of education.* Boulder, CO: Paradigm Publishers.

Shapiro, J. P., & Gross, S. J. (2008). *Ethical educational leadership in turbulent times: (Re)solving moral dilemmas.* New York, NY: Lawrence Erlbaum Associates Taylor and Francis Group.

Shaver, P., Schwartz, J., Kirson, D., & O'Connor, C. (2001). Emotion knowledge: Further exploration of a prototype approach. *Journal of Personality and Social Psychology, 52*(6), 1061.

Sheppard, B. (2000a). *Merchant of Venice, Act 1 Scene 2.* Avalon West School District, Spaniard's Bay, Newfoundland and Labrador. Unpublished manuscript.

Sheppard, B. (2000b). Message from the director of education. *Avalon West School District Newsletter, 4,* 1–2.

Sheppard, B., Galway, G., Brown, J., & Wiens, J. (2013, January 9). School boards matter: The report of the pan-Canadian study of school district governance. Canadian School Boards' Association. Retrieved from http://cdnsba.org/all/announcements/study-shows-that-school-boards-are-a-successful-and-effective-model-for-governance-of-the-public-school-system

Shields, C. (2003). *Good intentions are not enough: Transformative leadership for communities of difference.* Landam, MD: Scarecrow Press Inc.

Shields, C. (2004). Dialogic leadership for social justice: Overcoming pathologies of silence. *Educational Administration Quarterly, 40*(1), 109–132.

Silins, H., Zarins, S., & Mulford, B. (2002). What characteristics and processes define a school as a learning organization? Is this a useful concept to apply to schools? *International Education Journal, 3*(1), 24–32.

Sinclair, A. (1989). Public sector culture: Managerialism or multiculturalism? *Australian Journal of Public Administration, 48*(4), 382–397.

Smallwood, J. R. (1967). *Dr. William Carson: The great Newfoundland reformer: His life, letters and speeches.* St. John's, Newfoundland and Labrador: Newfoundland Book Publishers.

Smallwood, J. R. (Ed.). (1981a). Cocomalt. In *Encyclopedia of Newfoundland and Labrador* (Vol. 1, pp. 466–467). St. John's, Newfoundland and Labrador: Newfoundland Book Publishers.

Smallwood, J. R. (Ed.). (1981b). Effects of (the Great Depression) depression and destitution. In *Encyclopedia of Newfoundland and Labrador* (Vol. 1, pp. 612–613). St. John's, Newfoundland and Labrador: Newfoundland Book Publishers.

Solomon, R. (2011). *Brave new teachers: Doing social justice work in neoliberal times.* Toronto, Ontario: Canadian Scholars' Press.

Solomon, R. P., Singer, J., Campbell, A., Allen, A., & Portelli, J. P. (2011). *Brave new teachers doing social justice work in neo-liberal times.* Toronto, Ontario: Canadian Scholars' Press.

Spillane, J., Halverson, R., & Diamond, J. B. (2001). Investigating school leadership practice: A distributed perspective. *Educational Researcher, 30*(3), 23–28.

Starratt, R. J. (1991). Building an ethical school: A theory for practice in educational leadership. *Educational Administration Quarterly, 27*(2), 185–202.

Steinem, G. (1992). *Revolution from within.* Boston, MA: Little, Brown and Company.

Stewart, D. W., & Shamdasani, P. N. (1990). *Focus groups theory and practice.* L. Bickman & D. J. Rog, (Eds.) (Vol. 20). Newbury Park: SAGE Publications.

Stone, D. (2000). Caring by the book. In M. Harrington Meyer (Ed.), *Care work gender labor and the welfare state* (pp. 89–111). New York, NY: Routledge.

Strike, K. A. (1999). Justice, caring and universality: In defense of moral pluralism. In M. S. Katz, N. Noddings, & K. A. Strike (Eds.), *Justice and caring: The search for common ground in education* (pp. 21–36). New York, NY: Teachers College Press, Columbia University.

Taylor, S. (2001). Locating and conducting discourse: Analytic research. In M. Wetherell, S. Taylor, & S. Yates (Eds.), *Discourse as data: A guide for analysis* (pp. 5–48). Thousand Oaks, CA: Sage Publications.

Taylor, S., Rizvi, F., Lingard, B., & Henry, M. (1997). Educational politics and the politics of change. In *Educational politics and the politics of change* (p. 197). New York, NY: Routledge.

The Good News Bible. (1976) (Fourth Edition, Today's English Version.). Toronto, Ontario: Canadian Bible Society.

The Holy Bible. (1946) (Good Leader Edition, Authorized King James Version.). Chicago, IL: Consolidated Book Publishers.

Thomson, P. (2001). How principals lose "face": A disciplinary tale of educational administration and modern managerialism. *Discourse, 22* (1), 1–30.

Thomson, P. (2002). *Schooling of the rustbelt kids: Making the difference in changing times.* Sydney, Australia: Allen & Unwin.

Thomson, P. (2009). *School leadership: Heads on the block.* New York, NY: Routledge.

Tripp, D. (1998). Critical incidents in action inquiry. In J. Smyth & G. Shacklock (Eds.), *Being reflexive in critical educational and social research* (pp. 36–49). London, England: The Falmer Press.

Tronto, J. C. (1989). Women and caring: What can feminists learn about morality from caring. In V. Held (Ed.), *Justice and care: Essential readings in feminist ethics* (pp. 101–115). New York, NY: Westview Press.

Tronto, J. C. (1993). *Moral boundaries: A political argument for an ethic of care.* New York, NY: Routledge.

Tschannen-Moran, M. (2004). *Trust matters: Leadership for successful schools.* San Francisco, CA: Jossey-Bass.

Tucker, J. (2005). *Literacy policy in the province of Newfoundland and Labrador.* Bloomington, IN: University of Indiana

Tyack, D., & Cuban, L. (1995). *Tinkering toward utopia: A century of public school reform.* London, England: Harvard University Press.

Ungerleider, C. (1996). Globalisation, professionalisation and educational politics in British Columbia. *Canadian Journal of Education and Policy, 9,* 9.

Valentine, P. (1995). Women's working worlds: A case study of a female organization. In D. M. Dunlap (Ed.), *Women leading in education* (pp. 340–357). New York, NY: State University of New York Press.

Vanderberghe, R., & Huberman, A. M. (1999). *Understanding and preventing teacher burnout.* Cambridge, MA: Cambridge University Press.

VOCM. (2013, April 14). School board concerns in Central. VOCM. Retrieved from http://www.vocm.com/newsarticle.asp?mn=2&id=33081

Walkerdine, V. (1994). Subjectivity, gender and method. In *Annual meeting of the Australian Association for Research in Education.* Lismore, NSW. Unpublished manuscript.

Warren, P. (1967). *Report of the Royal Commission on education and youth, Vol. #1.* St. John's, Newfoundland and Labrador: Government of Newfoundland and Labrador.

Weiler, K. (2001). Reading Paulo Freire. In K. Weiler (Ed.), *Feminist engagements: Reading, resisting and revisioning male theorists in education and cultural studies* (pp. 67–88). New York, NY: Routledge.

Wells, M. (1999). *The imposter phenomenon.* University of Wiacato, New Zealand Editor.

Wheatley, M. J. (1999). *A simpler way.* San Francisco: Berrett-Koehler Publications, Inc.

Wheatley, M. J. (2002). *Turning to one another: Simple conversations to restore hope to the future.* San Francisco, CA: Berrett-Koehler Publishers, Inc.

Wheatley, M. J. (2005). *Finding our way: Leadership for an uncertain time.* San Francisco, CA: Berrett-Koehler Publishers, Inc.

Wheatley, M. J. (2010). *Leadership and the new science: Discovering order in a chaotic world.* ReadHowYouWant.com.

Wheatley, M. J., & Frieze, D. (2011). *Walk out walk on: A learning journey into communities daring to live the future now.* San Francisco, CA: Berrett-Koehler Publishers.

Whitaker, P. (1997). *Primary schools and the future.* Buckingham: Open University Press.

Williams, L., & Sparkes, R. (2000). *Supporting learning: Ministerial panel on educational delivery in the classroom.* St. John's, Newfoundland and Labrador: Government of Newfoundland and Labrador.

Williams, L., Warren, R., & Pound-Curtis, T. (1992). *Our children, our future: Royal Commission of inquiry into the delivery of programs and services in primary, elementary, secondary education.* St. John's, Newfoundland and Labrador: Government of Newfoundland and Labrador.

Willick, F. (2013, March 27). Frustrated board member leaves as 53 plead to save their schools. *The Chronicle Herald.* Retrieved from http://www.thechronicleherald.ca/metro/1117582

Witherell, M., Taylor, S., & Yates, S. (2001). *Discourse as data.* Thousand Oaks, CA: Sage Publications and The Open University.

Wodak, R., & Meyer, M. (2001). *Methods of critical discourse analysis.* D. Silverman, (Ed.). Thousand Oaks, CA: SAGE Publications.

Wolcott, H. F. (1990). On seeking—and rejecting—validity in qualitative research. In E. Eisner & A. Peshkin (Eds.), *Qualitative inquiry in education: The continuing debate* (pp. 122–152). New York, NY: Teachers College Press, Columbia University.

Wrigley, T., Thomson, P., & Lingard, B. (Eds.). (2012). *Changing schools: Alternative ways to make a world of difference.* New York, NY: Routledge Taylor and Francis Group.

Young, M. D., Skrla, L., & Skrla, L. (2003). *Reconsidering feminist research in educational leadership.* Albany: State University of New York.

Zimbalist, R. A. (2005). *The human factor in change.* Toronto: Scarecrow Education.

Zipin, L., & Brennan, M. (2003). The suppression of ethical dispositions through managerial governmentality: A habitus crisis in Australian higher education. *International Journal of Leadership in Education, 6*(4), 351–370.

About the Author

Mary G. Green, currently Adjunct Professor, School of Education, Acadia University, enjoys collaborative research projects and teaching graduate classes in equity and leadership, inclusive education, and curriculum studies.  She has served in a number of leadership roles throughout the Canadian education system over the past 30 years, including high school teacher, school district and provincial curriculum specialist, assistant superintendent, assistant director, and visiting professor at Memorial University. Dr. Green received degrees from Memorial University (BA, BEd, and MEd) and a Doctor of Education degree from the University of South Australia. She has presented her research at several national and international conferences and published peer-reviewed journal articles and book chapters related to the practice of care in organizations, education reform, and improvization in education. She is a proud Newfoundlander now enjoying life in Nova Scotia, Canada, with her husband Greg Foley and Border Collie Jewel. Ever appreciative of learning adventures beyond the realm of academia, she is enlightened by time spent travelling and with her adult children and new grandchild.

Caring Leadership in Turbulent Times, page 273
Copyright © 2014 by Information Age Publishing